3D STUDIO
MAX 3 MAGIC

By Jeffrey Abouaf, Neil Blevins, Sean Bonney, Brandon Davis, Sanford Kennedy, Douglas King, Eni Oken, Michael Todd Peterson, and Sung-wook Su

New Riders

201 West 103rd Street, Indianapolis, Indiana 46290

3D Studio MAX 3 Magic

International Standard Book Number: 0-7357-0867-3

Library of Congress Catalog Card Number: 00-102444

Printed in the United States of America

First Printing: May 2000

04 03 02 01 00   7 6 5 4 3 2 1

Interpretation of the printing code: The rightmost double-digit number is the year of the book's printing; the rightmost single-digit number is the number of the book's printing. For example, the printing code 00-1 shows that the first printing of the book occurred in 2000.

Trademarks

All terms mentioned in this book that are known to be trademarks or service marks have been appropriately capitalized. New Riders Publishing cannot attest to the accuracy of this information. Use of a term in this book should not be regarded as affecting the validity of any trademark or service mark.

Warning and Disclaimer

Every effort has been made to make this book as complete and as accurate as possible, but no warranty or fitness is implied. The information provided is on an "as is" basis. The authors and the publisher shall have neither liability nor responsibility to any person or entity with respect to any loss or damages arising from the information contained in this book or from the use of the CD or programs accompanying it.

Publisher
David Dwyer

Associate Publisher
Brad Koch

Executive Editor
Steve Weiss

Acquisitions Editor
Stacey Beheler

Development Editor
Christopher Morris

Managing Editor
Jennifer Eberhardt

Project Editor
Caroline Wise

Copy Editor
Linda Morris

Technical Editors
Larry Minton, Jeff Solenberg

Cover Design
Aren Howell

Interior Design
Steve Balle-Gifford

Cover and Project Opener Images
Wil Cruz

Compositor
Ron Wise

Proofreaders
Teresa Hendey, Bob LaRoche

Indexer
Lisa Stumpf

Software Development Specialist
Jay Payne

CONTENTS AT A GLANCE

ABOUT THE AUTHORS

Jeffrey Abouaf

Jeffrey Abouaf is a fine artist, designer, and instructor whose experience includes animation and design for television, print, and the Web. He is a contributing author to *Inside 3D Studio MAX Release 2.0*, Volumes I and III, *Inside 3D Studio MAX 3*, and *3D Studio 2 Effects Magic*. He follows industry developments in 3D graphics, animation, and virtual reality as a reporter and product reviewer for several publications, including Computer Graphics and Applications (IEEE), IEEE Multimedia, Game Developer Magazine, CGI, and CyberEdge Journal. He holds B.A., M.F.A., and J.D. degrees. He teaches 3D Studio MAX at San Francisco State's Multimedia Studies Program and the Academy of Art College in San Francisco. He has authored online tutorials for Kinetix for 3D Studio MAX R2 and spends substantial time exploring 3DS MAX as a fine-art tool. He can be reached at jabouaf@ogle.com or www.ogle.com.

Neil Blevins

It was a dark day in Canadian history back in '76 when Neil Blevins was born. Discovering early his love for art, he has attended numerous art classes and programs in the Montreal area, as well as several years of pure and applied science and computer programming. Graduating last year from Concordia University with a B.F.A. in design art, he now works full-time at Blur Studios in Venice, California, making special effects for film, video games, and broadcast media. His involvement with 3D Studio started back in the DOS days, when he was obsessed with making more complex and realistic images for video games. He's known in the 3D Studio community for many things, among them his involvement in the Kinetix Web board as a forum assistant, frequently answering questions and giving tips. He's also known for his distinct art style: dark, somber, and slightly disturbing images of alien and robotic life forms living in fantastic worlds, somewhere between Giger and the Top Cow comic books that he collects and loves. As quoted several years back, "All my life all I've ever really wanted to do was make cool monsters and get paid for it. And this is exactly what I'm doing." His Web page is located at www.soulburn3d.com.

Sean Bonney

Sean Bonney is a 3D animator, fine artist, and game designer who lives in historic Fredericksburg, Virginia. Sean graduated from Virginia Commonwealth University in Richmond, Virginia, in 1991, with a B.F.A. in Illustration and Design. He has been employed as graphic designer for the Central Rappahannock Regional Library system for eight years. He has worked for Rainbow Studios in Phoenix, Arizona, on a variety of game and broadcast projects. Sean is currently the principal of Anvil Studios and specializes in freelance animation and game design. For more information about Sean Bonney or Anvil Studios, visit their Web site at anvil-studio.com or email sbonney@anvil-studio.com.

Brandon Davis

Brandon Davis has a long and varied background in art and animation. While serving overseas in the 10th Special Forces Group (Airborne), he gained a reputation for his traditional artwork created in his spare time. However, at that time, the digital revolution in animation was beginning. In 1995, he left the service after six years and pursued a career in digital animation. He has since worked on projects ranging from architectural and engineering animation to games and visual effects for film and broadcast. Since 1998, he's been filling the role of effects animator at Computer Café, a visual effects studio on the central California coast. His credits include the films *Armageddon*, *Fever*, and *The Crow: Salvation*, as well as dozens of commercial spots. Currently he's creating several shots for the new film *Battlefield: Earth*. For more information about Brandon, check out his Web site at www.3dluvr.com/brandon/.

Sanford Kennedy

Sanford Kennedy is an animator, author, and teacher of 3D computer graphics in Los Angeles, California. He worked in the motion picture special effects industry for 20 years and then moved into computer graphics. He has his own studio and currently teaches 3DS MAX at four colleges.

Douglas King

Douglas King is a professional writer and animator for the film and entertainment industry. He is also a contributing editor for *Computer Graphics World* magazine. He has written the script for an animated feature film to be released in 2001 and will be working on the production of the film as well.

Eni Oken

Eni Oken is a freelance 3D artist based in Los Angeles. As an architect with 12 years of experience in computer graphics, she has participated in the creation of 3D art for numerous interactive projects, such as games, Web sites, virtual worlds, and multimedia for well known companies, including Activision, Sierra On-Line, L-Squared, and others. She has received several awards for her work, including two *3D Design* Big Kahunas and others. She is also the author of three books, various magazine articles, and some chapters covering topics related to computer graphics. She is a frequent lecturer at well known conferences such as the 3D Design Conference and GDC. Currently, Eni devotes her time to creating texture collections, tutorials, writing, and creating unique pieces of 3D art. To contact Eni, or to see samples of her work, go to www.oken3d.com.

Michael Todd Peterson

Michael Todd Peterson is the owner of MTP Grafx, a digital media company. MTP Grafx is located in New Orleans, Louisiana, and has a close working relationship with Digimation. In addition to writing, Todd still teaches, plays golf, and watches movies.

Sung-wook Su

Sung-wook Su is a 3D artist and writer. He is currently working for NueArt Pictures in Montrose, California, which is making a 3D feature film. He received a B.F.A. degree in sculpture at Hong-Ik University in Seoul, Korea and has been involved in computer graphics for the past 10 years. Previous projects include creating CG simulations of the artist Nam Joon Paik's video art. He has served as an instructor of sketching, drawing, and computer graphics at various arts academies in recent years. He has also written the books *3D Studio MAX* and *Hints for 3D Studio MAX*, versions 1.2 and 2.5. They are currently bestselling books in Korea and Japan. His Web page can be found at www.cyber.co.kr/~ssumax.

DEDICATION

Jeffrey Abouaf: To Annette, who understands it, always did, and still remains unflinching in her support and enthusiasm, keeping me honest and making sure I learn something from it all.

Sean Bonney: To my wife Sydney, whose love and support gets me through the day.

Brandon Davis: To my grandparents, Ralph and Rudelle Davis, and Michael and Marie Chaplinsky. Their unconditional love and support throughout my years has given me strength and wisdom.

ACKNOWLEDGMENTS

Jeffrey Abouaf

Many thanks to my editors, Steve Weiss, Stacey Beheler, and Chris Morris for their guidance and shepherding of this project. They made it fun. Special thanks to those individuals and companies who contributed product and support for this project, including Clive "Max" Maxwell of Intergraph Computer Systems and Elizabeth Riegel of 3Dlabs, Inc.. Thanks also to Blur Studios, Habware, Effectware, and the many other talents and developers for contributing free plug-ins and MAXScripts to the MAX community, some of which helped in the creation of this book.

Neil Blevins

I'd like to thank my family; Renate, my art teacher and all from her classes; my friends at Concordia University for being there; my non-Concordia friends for the support; Tim, David, Steve, and all the guys and gals at Blur for helpful hints and for putting up with me; and all the artists, visual and musical, that inspire me each day and give me the creative energy to make everything happen.

Sean Bonney

Thanks go to Earl Simpson and Chad Carter for researching appropriate quotes.

Douglas King

I'd like to thank God for the gifts and talents I have and my wife for her patience as I work long hours on these and many other projects.

Sung-wook Su

I would like to thank the following people for their assistance with this project: Jay, Brad, and the NueArt artists. Special thanks to Kevin for helping me finish this project. Most importantly, I appreciate the support of my wife, Jee yeon, who is my best friend.

A Message from New Riders

Ever been to one of those CG conferences where they set aside one evening for a catch-all session, in which various experts show off their fave tricks? That's kinda what we have going on here with *MAX 3 Magic*. Only you can take the evening home with you and use it for inspiration, for learning new spins on techniques you've already got down, for saving time when you need an effect in a pinch.

This is the successor to the bestselling title *3D Studio MAX 2 Effects Magic*. As proud as we've been of the continuing success of that book, we're even prouder of *3D Studio MAX 3 Magic*. We've updated the series look and design, making a bit more approachable (and appropriate) for the working professional and the truly serious student. We've also assembled a team of MAX f/x specialists who generally divide their time between development gigs and then occasionally writing about what they did in said development gigs. Hey, it's a living...

We've tried to include an array of effects that accurately reflects the ever-increasing power of MAX. And of course, there's no way that can truly be done in one book. But what we've got in here, we feel, is a pretty good start.

Thanks to the gang of nine-plus-two: Jeff, Neil, Sean, Brandon, Sanford, Douglas, Eni, Todd, Sung-wook, plus Jeff Solenberg and Larry Minton. Let's keep this going for next time, okay?

And to our readers: Let us know what type of material you'd like to see in the next book...the magicians are taking requests and the lines are open.

How to Contact Us

As the reader of this book, you are our most important critic and commentator. We value your opinion and want to know what we're doing right, what we could do better, in what areas you'd like to see us publish, and any other words of wisdom you're willing to pass our way.

As the Executive Editor for the Graphics team at New Riders, I welcome your comments. You can fax, email, or write me directly to let me know what you did or didn't like about this book—as well as what we can do to make our books better. When you write, please be sure to include this book's title, ISBN, and author, as well as your name and phone or fax number. I will carefully review your comments and share them with the authors and editors who worked on the book. For any issues directly related to this or other titles:

Email: steve.weiss@newriders.com

Mail: Steve Weiss
          Executive Editor
          Professional Graphics & Design Publishing
          New Riders Publishing
          201 West 103rd Street
          Indianapolis, IN 46290 USA

Visit Our Website: www.newriders.com

On our Web site, you'll find information about our other books, the authors we partner with, book updates and file downloads, promotions, discussion boards for online interaction with other users and with technology experts, and a calendar of trade shows and other professional events with which we'll be involved. We hope to see you around.

Email Us from Our Web site

Go to www.newriders.com and click on the Contact link if you

- Have comments or questions about this book

- Want to report errors that you have found in this book

- Have a book proposal or are otherwise interested in writing with New Riders

- Would like us to send you one of our author kits

- Are an expert in a computer topic or technology and are interested in being a reviewer or technical editor

- Want to find a distributor for our titles in your area

- Are an educator/instructor who wishes to preview New Riders books for classroom use. (Include your name, school, department, address, phone number, office days/hours, text currently in use, and enrollment in your department in the body/comments area, along with your request for desk/examination copies, or for additional information.)

Call Us or Fax Us

You can reach us toll-free at (800) 571-5840 + 9+ 3567. Ask for New Riders. If outside the USA, please call 1-317-581-3500 and ask for New Riders.

If you prefer, you can fax us at 1-317-581-4663, Attention: New Riders.

Technical Support/Customer Support Issues

Call 1-317-581-3833, from 10:00 a.m. to 3 p.m. US EST (CST from April through October of each year—unlike most of the rest of the United States, Indiana doesn't change to Daylight Savings Time each April).

You can also email our tech support team at userservices@ macmillanusa.com, and you can access our tech support Web site at http://www.mcp.com/support.

INTRODUCTION

3D Studio MAX is a powerful force in modern computer graphics. Since the early '90s, MAX has grown more popular and more powerful and is now a full-featured graphics medium with virtually limitless possibilities. 3D Studio MAX 3 Magic is about exploring some of these possibilities.

WHO WE ARE

The authors of this book are among the top 3D artists in the industry today. Some work as special effects artists, producing effects used in major Hollywood feature films. Others apply their skills to create effects for regular television and commercials. Still others make their living helping to create many of the most popular video games sold today.

None of the authors who contributed to this book make their living solely as writers, and that's a good thing. Although these folks do write and contribute to many of the top-selling books and magazines on 3D Studio MAX and CG in general, their focus and their time is spent is on their art. This book is not a rehash of the product manual or feature sets; it's a source of great inspiration and technical savvy brought to you by the people who actually live in and are connected to the CG industry.

WHO YOU ARE

This book is intended for intermediate to advanced users of 3D Studio MAX. We have striven to provide you all the instruction you will need to work through a project to achieve a spectacular effect, without spoon-feeding you every detail of every step. Every effort has been made to strike a balance between clarity and functionality.

We assume you are familiar with the fundamentals of 3D Studio MAX. We assume you either have, or have access to, 3D Studio MAX 3 and that you've read the documentation that comes with the program and worked through the tutorials. In other words, you have a basic understanding of features like the Modify Command panel, the Material Editor, Space Warps, NURBS, Particle Systems, Video post, and so on.

This doesn't mean that if you are a beginner you can't use this book. On the contrary, if you're the type of person who likes to learn by diving in head-first, you will find that this book will help accelerate your understanding of MAX 3 and quickly bring you up to speed.

If you are new to computer graphics in general and you are still concerned that this book may be a little beyond your level, you should consider starting with books like *CG 101: A Computer Graphics Industry Reference* by Terrence Masson. This is a comprehensive resource guide that will help you understand the fundamentals and terminology of computer graphics in general. It's an excellent resource for anyone involved in the computer graphics industry from beginner to professional. From there, you should consider *3D Studio MAX 3 Fundamentals* by Michael Todd Peterson. This book starts with the basics of computer graphics and how to get started with 3D Studio MAX 3. It will take you from subjects as basic as how to draw lines and simple primitives in MAX to creating complex effects using Space Warps, Particle systems, NURBS, Volume Lighting, Fog and Video Post techniques.

If you're experienced with MAX and are looking for more extensive resources on the program (this is an f/x how-to cookbook, after all), New Riders probably has a book that can help. *Inside 3D Studio MAX 3* covers the whole program feature set, *3D Studio MAX 3 Professional Animation* focuses on animation techniques, *Inside 3D Studio MAX 3 Modeling, Materials and Rendering* thoroughly covers the areas mentioned in the title, and *3D Studio MAX 3 Media Animation*, by Emmy-award-winning f/x specialist John Chismar, is an absolutely amazing book on this growing application of MAX.

WHAT'S IN THIS BOOK

Every chapter in *3D Studio MAX 3 Magic* is a step-by-step project explaining how to create eye-popping effects ranging from a Wet Paint look using a multi-layered material in the Material Editor to creating a realistic planet

complete with an atmosphere and signs of civilization. These effects are achieved using not only the standard tools that ship with MAX, but also several freeware plug-ins that greatly enhance the power and flexibility of MAX, many of which can be found on this book's accompanying CD. In addition to the plug-ins included for use with some of these projects, you will find information about where you can download dozens, if not hundreds of additional plug-ins to enhance the power of 3D Studio MAX 3 even further.

THE COMPANION CD

Included on the CD that comes with the book you will find all the necessary files and images needed to complete the exercises in each chapter. In addition to the working files necessary for some of the chapters, there is a finished version of each effect with which you can compare your result. You will also find any plug-ins necessary to complete some of the chapters. You'll also find four bonus chapters to help you continue learning and improving, even after you've finished this book. Be sure to check out Appendix A, "What's on the CD-ROM," at the back of this book for more information.

OUR ASSUMPTIONS AS WE WROTE THE BOOK

We had six assumptions when we wrote this book. These assumptions are based on our collective experience in learning and working with software.

You Don't Have Time to Spend Forever Learning One Effect

Don't you hate working through a tutorial that seems to go on and on forever? The steps in these chapters have been designed to help you quickly achieve the final effect without unnecessary fluff. You won't find any pointless humor or rambling. Each chapter begins with a short paragraph explaining what you will be doing, as well as a brief summary of what steps will be taken to achieve the effect.

You Don't Want to Sit Down and Read the Book from Start to Finish

This book wasn't intended to be read in a linear fashion. Each chapter is unique unto itself. Everything you will need for any chapter is contained within those pages. Find the effect that most fascinates you and start with that chapter.

You Want to Be Able to Reproduce the Effects Demonstrated in This Book

One of the common complaints about tutorial-style books is that often after setting this parameter and tweaking that transform according to the instruction, you may have a nice effect, but not understand exactly how you accomplished it or why you ended up with the result you did. One of the goals of this book is to not only take you through the necessary steps toward the end result, but to make sure you understand why it's necessary to set a given parameter to a certain value. You will find that most steps and parameters include a brief explanation about why you're changing it to this value. Sometimes, for example, you may see a note to let you know that you will change it later on when it's animated.

You Want Additional Ideas to Enable Variations on the Effect

The best way to solidify your knowledge when learning new effects is repetition. At the end of each chapter, you will find suggestions for variations on each of the effects. One characteristic top computer graphic experts share is that when they learn something new, they will they will

work with many different variations until they have thoroughly mastered it. Try the variations suggested with these effects and then come up with some of your own. This is the best way to really gain an understanding of how all of these different parameters work.

You Want to Take Your Learning Beyond the Scope of This Book

Possibly the most powerful feature of 3D Studio MAX is its open architecture. The source code is available to anyone who wants to write plug-ins to add features and increase usability. Consequently, hundreds of plug-ins have been written and are available for you to buy or download. The last section of each chapter includes a list of plug-ins that the author feels can enhance that particular effect or make it easier to do. Many of the plug-ins listed are freely available on the Web.

You Like to Learn Visually

A picture is worth a thousand words. It's doubly true when speaking of computer tutorials. There's nothing more frustrating than working through step after step in a tutorial, unsure if you're following the instruction correctly because you have no visual cue. We've added a figure adjacent to as many steps as necessary to make sure it's easy to stay on track.

CONVENTIONS USED IN THIS BOOK

Every computer book has its own style of presenting information. In this book, you'll notice that we have an unusual layout. Because we know that most of our readers wouldn't be reading this book if they weren't into graphics, the project openers are cool-looking eye candy. The real meat of the project starts on the next page.

In the left column, you'll find step-by-step instructions for completing the project, as well as succinct but extremely valuable explanations. In the corresponding column to the right, you'll find screen captures illustrating these steps.

We want to say it one more time: If you get lost at any time in the completion of a project, just refer to the completed project file on the CD and you'll find the answer to your quandary.

JOIN THE REVOLUTION

The world of computer graphics and animation is an exciting, rapidly expanding field. Every day it becomes more pervasive in the world around us. Computer graphics are used for education and entertainment in movies, television shows, documentaries, commercials, games, and more. Graphics also exist outside the world of entertainment in architectural renderings and walkthroughs, courtroom forensic animations, technical training programs, and prototype product visualization. As Internet bandwidth increases, it is even becoming a way to make World Wide Web sites more exiting and appealing. There doesn't seem to be any end to the possible uses of computer enhanced effects.

3D Studio MAX is rapidly becoming one of the most dominant forces in this computer graphics revolution. From its humble beginning as 3D Studio for DOS in the early 1990s, it sought to fill a need in the market as an affordable alternative to the high-end and outrageously expensive 3D graphics packages of the time. In fewer than 10 years it has become arguably the most versatile and powerful professional modeling and animation program available. The introduction of 3D Studio MAX release 3 in mid-1999 removed any doubt that this program is capable of producing effects just as eye-catching and spectacular—if not more so—than even the most powerful and expensive of the 3D programs available.

3D Studio MAX 3 Magic is a valuable tool that will help further your understanding of 3D Studio MAX 3 and the potential it offers you as an artist. This book was designed to help you take your skills to the next level by demonstrating the techniques used by the top innovative professionals in the industry.

S U P E R N O V A

"Supernovae are stars that divest themselves of material not in the orderly demeanor of a 'planetary' nebula but with explosive violence. The name 'nova,' meaning new star, is an index to the spectacle they create."

—TIMOTHY FERRIS, WRITER, EDITOR, TEACHER, AND AUTHOR OF *GALAXIES*

CREATING AN EXPLODING STAR

In this project, we will create a scene where

a star explodes into a blinding brilliant light,

sending matter shooting into space. This effect

can also be used for other deep-space

explosions.

In creating this effect, we will use multiple

Video Post effects including glows, lens flares,

and a starfield. We will use different glows

within the same scene to achieve different

effects. A particle system will provide the

pieces of debris sent out into all corners of

space. A RingWave object will add some final

detail to the scene.

PROJECT 1

SUPERNOVA

BY DOUGLAS KING

GETTING STARTED

We have created a somewhat simple scene so you can focus on the effect itself.

1   Load the 01mem01.max file from the project's preload subdirectory
    on the accompanying CD–ROM. You will find a sphere and a camera
    in the scene.

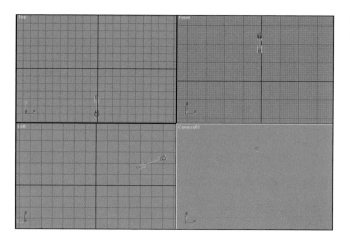

Open the scene provided to create the effect.

4

SET UP THE SCENE

The first object we will create is the shockwave after the explosion. This will be the main object in the scene, so it's important to create an object with a level of detail with which you are happy.

1   In the Objects tab, select RingWave object. In the top viewport, place a RingWave object around the sphere. From the Main Toolbar tab, click the Align Tool button and select the Star object. Check X, Y, and Z Position to align the RingWave perfectly to the star. Click OK. In the Modify Command panel (with the RingWave still selected), set the parameters as follows:

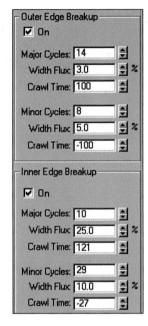

Create a RingWave and set its parameters as shown. Set the Edge Breakup parameters as shown.

RingWave Size

Radius:	1100.0
Radial Segs:	1
Ring Width:	150
Sides:	250
Height:	2.5
Height Segs:	1

RingWave Timing

Check Grow and Stay

Start Time:	90
Grow Time:	60
End Time:	160

Inner Edge Breakup

ON

Major Cycles:	10
Width Flux:	25
Crawl Time:	121
Minor Cycles:	29
Width Flux:	10
Crawl Time:	−27

Outer Edge Breakup

ON

Major Cycles:	14
Width Flux:	3.0
Crawl Time:	100
Minor Cycles:	8
Width Flux:	5.0
Crawl Time:	−100

2   You can't see the RingWave now because you are at frame 0 and it hasn't started to grow yet. Scrub the Time slider to frame 100 so you can easily see the RingWave object. Right-click the RingWave and select Properties. In the Motion Blur section, select Object and make sure Enabled is checked. Click OK and set the Time slider back to 0.

3   Add a Ripple Modifier to the RingWave object. Set the parameters as follows:

Amplitude 1:   1.0
Amplitude 2:   2.0
Wave Length: 10
Phase: 0.0
Decay: 0.0

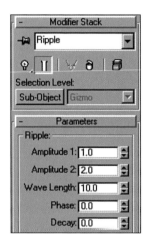

Create a Ripple modifier and set the parameters as shown.

SET UP THE PARTICLE SYSTEM

The particles represent the debris created from the exploding star. By using a particle array, we shoot the particles in every direction.

1   Create a particle array in the top viewport. Center it in the scene with the star and RingWave centered in it. Pick the Star object as the emitter. Under Particle Formation, check Over Entire Surface.

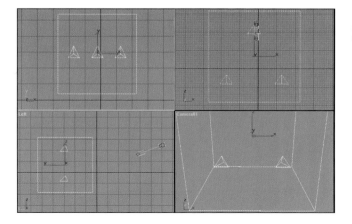

Create a particle array in the scene with the Star object in the center.

2   Set the Particle Generation parameters as follows:

Particle Quantity

Use Rate: 14

Particle Motion

Speed: 20

Variation: 10

Divergence: 10

Particle Timing

Emit Start: 90

Emit Stop: 120

Display Until: 160

Life: 45

Variation: 20

Check Creation Time

Check Emitter Translation

Particle Size

Size: 4.0

Variation: 65.0

Grow for: 2

Fade for: 10

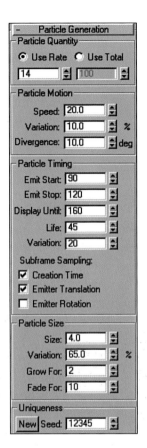

Set the Particle Generation
parameters as shown.

3   Set the Particle Type parameters to Standard particles.
     Select Sphere from the Standard Particle Types.

4   Right-click the Particle Array object and select
     Properties. In the Motion Blur section, select Object,
     make sure Enabled is checked, and click OK.

5   Enter the Render Scene dialog box. Scroll down to
     the Object Motion Blur panel and set the parameters
     as follows:

Duration: 1.0

Samples: 16

Duration Subdivisions: 16

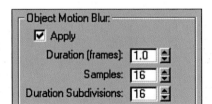

Change the default motion
blur settings in the Render
dialog box.

CREATE MATERIALS

The next step is to create materials for each of the objects.

1 Open the Material Editor. Select one of the material slots and name it Shockwave. Set the parameters as follows:

Self-Illumination: Color

Color: (R=83, G=0, B=208)

Change the Material Effects channel to 1.

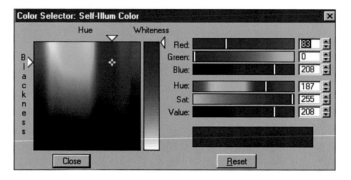

Change the parameters to get a nice purple color.

2 Under Maps, click Diffuse Color Map channel and select Noise. Set the Noise parameters as follows:

Noise Type: Fractal

Noise Threshold

High: 1.0

Size: 45

Levels: 4.0

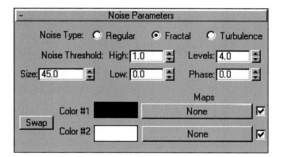

Set the Noise parameters as shown for the Shockwave.

3 Click Go to Parent. Drag the Noise map from the Diffuse Color channel to the Opacity channel as an instance. Apply this material to the RingWave object.

4 Select the next material slot. Name it Star. In the Blinn Basic Parameters rollout under Self-Illumination, check Color. Click the Diffuse Color Map channel and Select Noise. Leave the settings at the default. Change the Color #1 and #2 settings as follows:

Color #1: (R=255, G=90, B=0)

Color #2: (R=255, G=192, B=0)

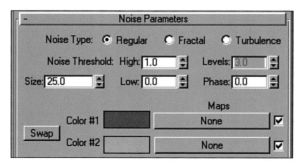

Set the Noise parameters as shown for the star.

5 Click Go to Parent. Drag the Noise map from the Diffuse Color channel to the Self-Illumination channel as an instance. Set the Self-Illumination amount to 80. Change the Material Effect channel to 2. Apply the material to the Star object.

6 Copy the star material to a new material slot and rename the material Particles. In the Diffuse Color Map channel, click the Noise map. Change the Color #1 and #2 settings as follows:

Color #1:   (R=42, G=0, B=255)

Color #2:   (R=129, G=194, B=255)

7 Apply the material to the Particle Array.

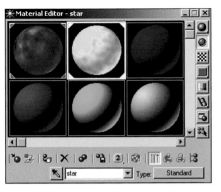
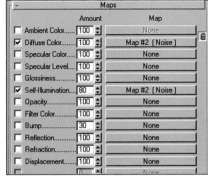

Apply the material to the Star object.

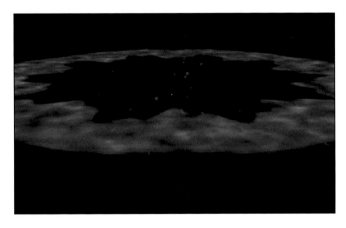

The rendered explosion.

SET UP LIGHTING

Because we will be setting up a Lens Flare effect, we will need a light with which to work.

Create an Omni light in the scene. Place it behind the Star object. Make sure that the light is partially hidden in the camera view. Leave the settings at the defaults.

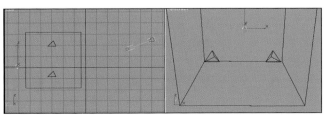

Add an Omni light to the scene.

Set Up the Video Post

This is where this effect will really come to life. We will use a series of glow filters, each with unique settings to achieve a number of looks for our scene. We will also add a flare filter for some detail and then a starfield filter for the background. If you prefer, you can start here using 01mem02.max from the CD.

1   Open the Video Post dialog box. Add a Scene event and select the Camera01 view.

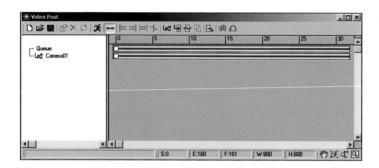

Open the Video Post dialog box.

The first Image Filter we will create will be used for the initial explosion of the star. We will use a glow that intensifies enough to completely illuminate the screen.

2   Select the camera and add an Image Filter event. Select Lens Effects Glow. Set the Video Post parameters to:

VP Start Time: 0
VP End Time: 101
Click OK.

3   Double-click the Lens Effect Glow event to access the Edit Filter Event dialog box. Click the Setup button. Set the parameters as follows:

Properties
Source: Whole
Filter: All
Preferences
Effect Size: 2.0
Color: Pixel
Intensity: 35.0

4   Scrub to frame 92, turn Animate on, and set the
Intensity: 75.

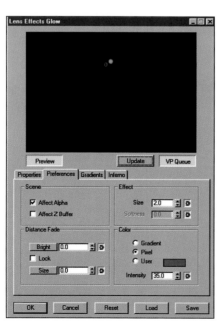

Set the Lens Effect Glow parameters as shown.

10

5 Scrub to frame 99. Set the parameters as follows:

Preferences

Effect Size: 2.0

Intensity: 100

Turn off the Animate button.

6 Click OK to return to the Video Post dialog box. Select the camera event and add another Image Filter event. Select Lens Effects Glow. Set the Video Post parameters to:

VP Start Time: 102

VP End Time: 160

Click OK.

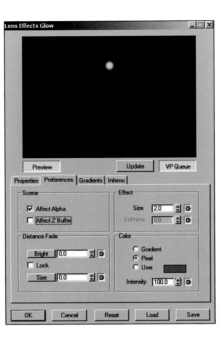

Scrub to frame 99. Set the basic parameters.

7 Double-click the new Lens Effect Glow just above the camera event. Click the Setup button and set the parameters as follows:

Source

Object ID Off

Effects ID On

Effects ID: 1

Filter: Edge

Preferences

Effect Size: 2.0

Color: Pixel

Intensity: 100

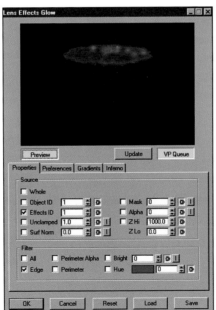

Add a glow to the RingWave.

8 Click OK to return to the Video Post dialog box. Select the camera event, and add a third Image Filter event. Again, select Lens Effects Glow. Set the Video Post parameters to:

VP Start Time: 102
VP End Time: 160
Click OK.

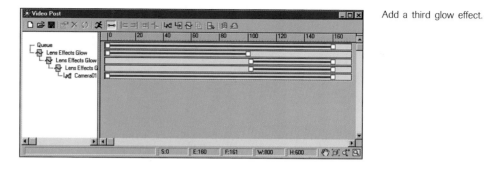

Add a third glow effect.

9 Double-click the new Lens Effect Glow, click Setup, and set the parameters as follows:

Source
Object ID Off
Effects ID On
Effects ID: 2
Filter: All

Preferences
Effect Size: 7.0
Color: Pixel
Intensity: 95.0

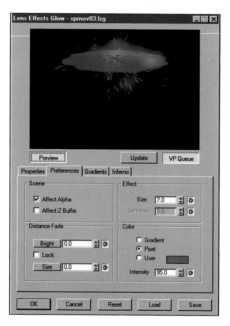

Set the glow parameters.

10 Click OK to return to the Video Post dialog box. Select the camera event and add another Image Filter event. This time, select Lens Effect Flare from the drop-down menu. Set the Video Post parameters to:

VP Start Time: 60
VP End Time: 160
Click OK.

Double-click the new Lens Effect Flare event. Click the Setup button. Scrub to frame 60 and set the parameters as follows:

Lens Flare Properties

Seed: 2001
Size: 5.0
Hue: 0.0
Angle: 0.0
Intensity: 10
Squeeze: 10
Node Sources: Omni01

Lens Flare Effects

Brighten: 100

11 In the Prefs tab, make sure the following options are the only ones checked under Render: Glow, Ring, Rays, Star, and Streak.

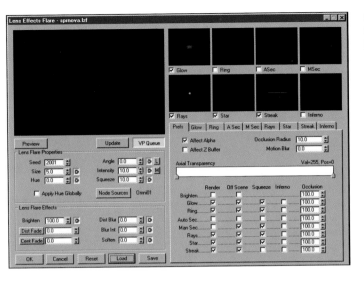

Add a Lens Flare to the scene and animate the parameters.

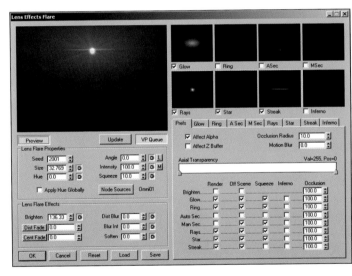

Click the Preview and VP Queue buttons to see the effect of changing the Lens Effect Flare parameters.

12 Under the Glow tab, set the parameters as follows:

Size: 246.0

You can add new flags to the Gradients by left-clicking the gradient bar. You can edit these flags by right-clicking them. On the Radial Transparency Gradient Set, the parameters should be as follows:

Flag #3

R, G & B Value=102, Position=60

Flag #4

R, G & B Value=197, Position=36

Flag #5

R, G & B Value=217, Position=50

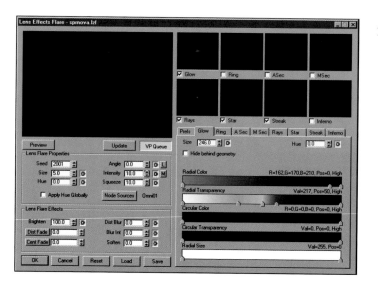

Adjust the Radial Transparency Gradient set.

13 Under the Ring tab, set the Size: 96

Under the Rays tab, set the Size: 150

Under the Streak tab, set the Size: 25

Width: 6.0

14 On the Section Transparency Gradient Set, the parameters should be:

Flag #3

R, G & B Value=255, Position=50

Flag #5

R, G & B Value=213, Position=70

15 Scrub to frame 99. Turn Animate on and set the Lens Flare properties as follows:

Size: 138

Intensity: 100

16 Set the Lens Flare Effects parameters as follows:

Brighten: 274

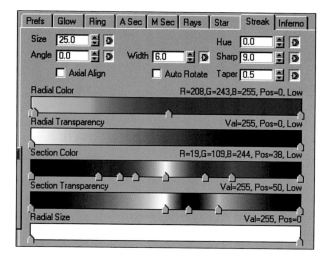

Adjust the Streak parameters.

17 Under the Glow tab, set the Size: 500.

On the Radial Transparency Gradient set, the parameters should be:

Flag #3 Position: 94

Flag #4 Position: 90

Flag #5 Position: 75

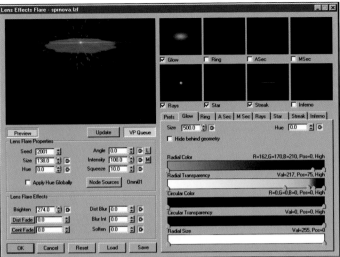

Animate the parameters.

18 Under the Ring tab, set the Size: 167. Under the Rays tab, set the Size: 481. Under the Streak tab, set the Size: 100.

On the Section Transparency set, the parameters should be as follows:

Flag #3 Position: 52

Flag #5 Position: 64

Turn off the Animate button.

19 Click OK to exit the Lens Effects Flare dialog box.

20 Open the TrackView and open the Video Post Lens Flare Track. Move all of the keys at frame 0 to frame 60. Copy all of the keys that are now at frame 60 to frame 120.

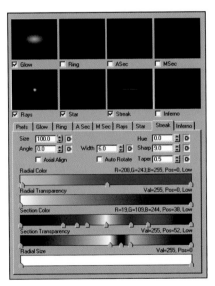

Animate the Streak parameters.

21 Select the camera input and add one last Image Event filter. Select Starfield and click OK. Double-click the Starfield event and set the parameters as follows:

Dimmest Star: 1
Brightest: 255
Linear
Star Size: 1.5

Click OK, close any open dialog boxes, and return to Video Post.

22 Finally, add an Image Output event. Name the file Supernova.avi.

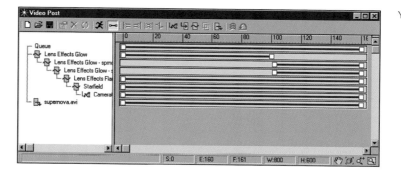

Your final Video Post settings.

Return to the Video Post dialog box to execute the rendering of the scene. You can view a finished version of this file by opening Supernova.max from the CD-ROM.

Plug-Ins

Because the majority of this effect is accomplished in Video Post, you could easily enhance and differentiate their Supernova effect by using ProOptic Suite by Trinity.

You can modify this effect by adjusting your particle settings, the settings for the RingWave, and, of course, adjusting the Lens effects.

- Adjust particle settings including size and speed.
- Experiment with different Lens Flare effects.
- Experiment with different glow settings.
- Use ProOptic Suite (Trinity) for lens effects.

Variations

Creating a Supernova effect is certainly subjective because not many of us have actually experienced a supernova firsthand. Some ways you might use to create a unique look for your supernova are to add additional particle systems with varying degrees of motion blur and glow. Also, adjust the Lens Flare in the Video Post to add more flares, streaks, and stars. Finally, adjust the glow settings for many different looks.

WATER SURFACE

"We find ourselves in a bewildering world."

—STEPHEN HAWKING

Using Falloff Maps to Create Realistic Water Surfaces

Making realistic water surfaces can be
deceptively difficult. When creating a body of
water there are a few basic factors to consider:
opacity, shininess, and reflectivity. To accurately
mimic a water surface, you must pay careful
attention to how light reacts with the environment. In this project, you'll use the new Falloff
map to control the amount of opacity and
reflectivity in the water surface to simulate
this effect.

WATER SURFACE

BY BRANDON DAVIS

GETTING STARTED

To accurately portray a water surface, you must pay careful attention to how light reacts with the environment. Most reflective surfaces vary the amount of reflection based on the angle of viewing. For example, a body of water or a glass table appears to be more reflective and opaque when observing it "edge on" or parallel to your line of sight. On the other hand, look at the water or glass table from directly overhead or perpendicular to your line of sight and it appears less reflective and more transparent. This is an optical effect called the *Fresnel effect* and is the direct result of a changing angle of incidence as light passes from one medium (water or glass) to another (air).

In this chapter, you'll use a Plane primitive to create a calm water surface with realistic reflection and transparency. You'll use a similar Plane primitive with a Noise modifier to create a sandy ground floor. Next, you'll create some stones with Sphere primitives and Noise modifiers and distribute them along the ground floor with a Scatter Compound object. Lastly, you'll create a sky Environment map from a Gradient Ramp and light the scene accordingly.

In this section, you'll create the water surface.

1 Create a Plane primitive in the top viewport so it is aligned to the Z-Axis, using the following parameters:

Length: 500

Width: 500

Length Segs: 4

Width Segs: 4

Scale: 5

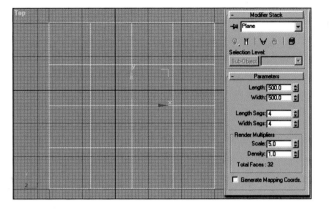

Create the water surface with a Plane primitive.

2 Right-click the plane and select Properties from the popup menu. In the Display Properties group, turn See-Through on. The object will remain transparent in a shaded viewport, regardless of material settings.

3 Name the plane Water.

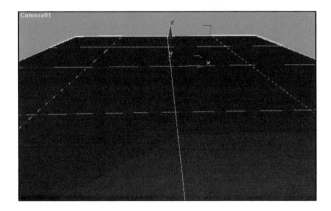

Assign the See-Through property to the Water object.

Note: Scale allows your object to scale uniformly by a given amount at render time. In this example, the Plane primitive will scale to five times its size at render time, allowing you to work with a smaller model in the viewport without having to worry about being able to fill the viewport or camera's field of view.

CREATING THE GROUND FLOOR

In this section, you'll clone the existing Water object and modify it to create the ground floor object.

1   Click the Select and Move icon, hold down Shift,
    and click the Water object. Don't drag the mouse
    during this process or it will cause the cloned object
    to move.

2   In the new popup dialog box, name the object
    Ground Floor and click OK.

3   In the Ground Floor's parameters, change the
    following parameters:

    Length Segs: 50
    Width Segs: 50
    Scale: 1

4   With the Ground Floor selected, go to the Modify
    panel and add a Noise modifier. Use the default
    parameters for the Noise modifier with one
    exception:

    Strength Z: 20

    This will cause the surface to bump up a bit, creating
    "dunes" on the ground floor.

5   Select the Move tool, right-click the icon, and, in the
    Move Transform Type-In dialog box, set the Z-Axis
    value to −20.

    The Ground Floor moves below the water.

Assign a Noise modifier to
the Ground Floor object.

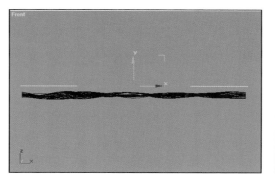
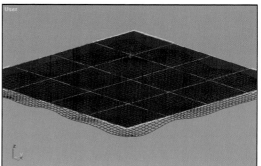

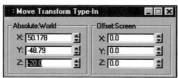

Use the Move Transform
Type-In dialog box to move
the Ground Floor object to
−20 on the Z-Axis. Clone the
Water object to create the
Ground Floor object.

CREATING STONES IN THE WATER

You should lay some stones on the ground surface so you'll be able to see the Fresnel effect on the water surface better. This effect is more obvious when you have objects behind a Fresnel-shaded surface. In this case, the sand dunes of the ground floor object may not provide enough contrast.

1   Create a Sphere primitive with the following settings:

Radius: 10

Segments: 16

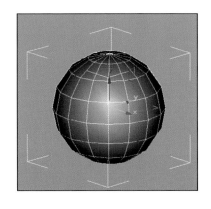

Create a Sphere.

2   In the Modify panel, add a Noise modifier to the Sphere. Set the Noise parameters to:

Scale: 15

Strength X,Y, and Z: 25

3   Name the Sphere Stones.

4   Now you need to copy the stone into several variations and scatter them on the Ground Floor. Select the Stones object, go to Compound Objects in the Create panel, and click Scatter. Set the Scatter parameters to:

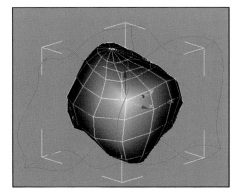

Add a Noise modifier to the Sphere to distort it into a stone shape.

Pick Distribution Object:	Ground Floor
Duplicates:	10
Use Selected Faces Only:	Checked
Distribute Using:	Random Faces
Transforms Scaling X,Y,Z:	50%
Hide Distribution Object:	Checked

Because you're using Selected Faces Only, you won't see the Stones scatter properly. You have to select a set of faces on the Ground Floor for the Scatter object to reference.

5   Select the Ground Floor object. In the Modify panel, add a Mesh Select modifier. This will allow you to select a patch of faces on the object not for editing, but for passing on to the Scatter object. Click the Polygon button and drag a square box around the front center of the Ground Floor object.

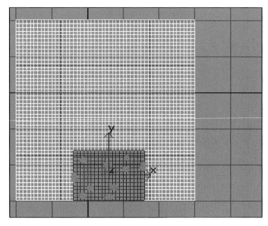

Use a Mesh Select modifier to select an area of faces on the Ground Floor object.

GROUND FLOOR MATERIAL

Now you will set up the Ground Floor material.

1   In the Material Editor, set Slot 1 to active and the material type to Standard.

2   Assign a Bitmap map to the Diffuse Color slot. Use Sandshor.jpg, which is located in MAX's maps\ground directory.

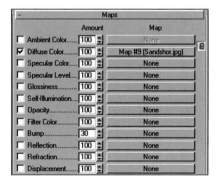

Assign Sandshor.jpg to the Diffuse Color slot.

3 In the bitmap rollout, set the following parameters:

U Tiling: 8

V Tiling: 8

The Bitmap parameters.

4 Name the material Ground Floor and assign it to the Ground Floor object.

STONES MATERIAL

Now you will set up the Stones material.

1 In the Material Editor, set Slot 2 to Active and the material type to Standard.

2 Set the Basic parameters to

Diffuse: (R=176, G=171, B=157)

3 Assign a Cellular map to the Bump slot with these settings:

Cell Characteristics: Chips

Size: 2.0

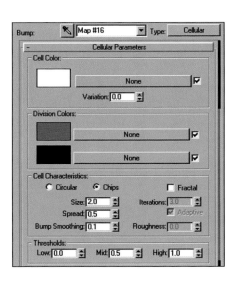

Assign a Cellular map to the Bump slot of the Stones material.

4 Adjust the Bump amount to 25.

5 Name the material Stones and assign it to the Stones object.

CREATING A SKY ENVIRONMENT

Next, you will create a sky environment for the water to reflect properly. Instead of creating geometry for a skydome, you'll use a simple spherical Environment map.

1 Open the Environment dialog box.

2 Click Environment map and choose Gradient Ramp from the Material Map Browser. This automatically assigns the map to the environment; however, it doesn't automatically show up in the Material Editor.

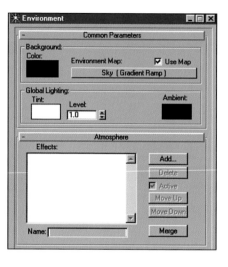

Assign a Gradient Ramp in the Environment dialog box.

3 In the Environment dialog box, click and drag the Gradient Ramp into an open slot in the Material Editor. In the resulting dialog box, choose Instance. This allows you to edit the Gradient Ramp in the Material Editor and have the changes affect the recently assigned Environment map.

4 In the Material Editor, go to the slot to which you dragged the Gradient Ramp. Set the parameters to the following:

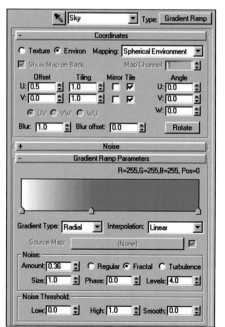

The Gradient Ramp parameters.

Coordinates:	Environment
Mapping:	Spherical Environment
U Offset:	0.5
Gradient Type:	Radial
Flag #1:	RGB (255,255,255)
Position:	0
Flag #2:	RGB (29,128,183)
Position:	100
Flag #3:	RGB (29,128,183)
Position:	39
Noise Amount:	0.36
Noise Type:	Fractal

This will create a radial gradient that goes from white to blue with fractal noise to simulate clouds.

5 Name the map Sky.

CREATING THE WATER SURFACE MATERIAL

Now you need to create the material for the surface of the water. This is a bit more complex than the previous materials you've created. You'll be creating a very shiny surface material with a Bump map to simulate small waves. More importantly you'll use the new Falloff map to control raytraced reflections and opacity with the Fresnel shader.

1 In the Material Editor, select an unused slot. Set the Basic parameters as follows:

Ambient: (R=23, G=16, B=46)

Diffuse: (R=49, G=126, B=133)

Specular: (R=255, G=255, B=255)

Specular Level: 100

Glossiness: 90

This will create a very shiny blue–green material with very crisp highlights.

2 In the Maps rollout, assign a Noise map to the Bump channel. This automatically takes you to the Noise map's parameters. You only have to make one change from the default settings:

Size: 5

3 Use the Go to Parent button or the Material/Map Browser to return to the Maps rollout. By default, the Bump amount is 30. Adjust this to 15 to lessen the amount of distortion on the water surface.

4 Assign a Falloff map to the Opacity channel with the following settings:

Falloff Type: Fresnel

Set the Mix Curve similar to that of the figure on the right by adding a Bézier control point. This will cause the Opacity channel to look at two colors: black and white and how you mix them. In this case,

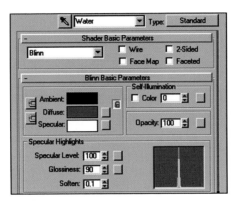

The water surface material's basic parameters.

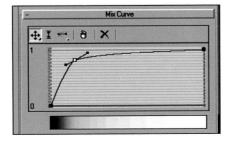

Adjust the Mix Curve slightly to alter the effects of the Falloff map.

you're mixing them with the Fresnel shader, which applies more of the white color (opaque) as the viewing angle to the surface lessens. Inversely, black (transparent) is applied as the viewing angle increases, such as looking straight down at the water. By adjusting the Mix Curve, you slightly tweak the results of the Fresnel shader to suit the scene. The result is water that is almost completely transparent when looking directly down on it, but totally opaque when looking more perpendicular to the surface.

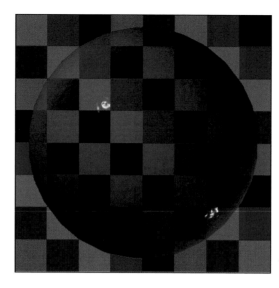

Change the material slot background to checkerboard to see the effect of the Falloff map.

5　Return to the Maps Rollout and adjust the Opacity amount to 50.

6　Click and drag the newly created Falloff map from the Opacity channel to the Reflection channel. In the resulting dialog box, choose "Copy." You will use most of the same settings as before, but with some slight modifications.

7　Click the new Falloff map in the Reflection channel to view its parameters. Click the white color channel (not the color swatch) and assign a Raytrace map. Use the default settings for this map.

8　Return to the Maps rollout and set the Reflection amount to 75. Your water material should look like the figure on the right.

9　Name the material Water and assign it to the Water object.

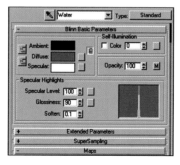
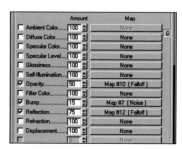

The completed water surface material.

LIGHTING THE SCENE

Now that you've created all of the necessary elements, you must light the scene accordingly. There are several different ways to approach this, but a proven method for creating outdoor lighting is to use a single Omni light as a fill light and a directional light to cast the sun's parallel rays as a key light.

1   Start by creating an Omni light and place it high above your scene. You only need to change two parameters:

Multiplier: 0.5

Specular: Unchecked

A low multiplier won't over–light the scene, but will wash out shadows realistically. Making the light exclude specularity in its illumination is important because you don't want it to appear that multiple light sources are present in your outdoor scene.

Create an Omni light.

2   Click and drag a target direct light and line it up according to the figure on the right. This should cause a nice set of visible highlights on the surface.

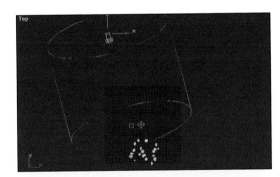

Line up the target direct light

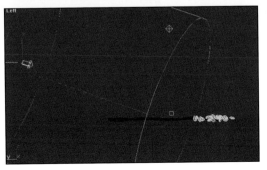

3 Set the target directional light's parameters as follows:

Cast Shadows:	Checked
Multiplier:	1.33
Hotspot:	407
Falloff:	409
Overshoot:	Checked
Object Shadows:	Raytraced Shadows

The higher multiplier is important so the directional light is the dominant light source, just like the sun. The Hotspot and Falloff need to be large enough to encompass your scene; however, the geometry will scale outwards at render time via the Plane primitive's Render Scale parameter. This normally would facilitate a much larger hotspot; however, you're concerned with casting shadows only within the area of view. By checking Overshoot, you're telling the directional light to act much like an Omni light by casting light in all directions, but shadow casting will remain within the Falloff parameter. Another important thing you did was set the shadow type to Raytraced. This is important because Shadow maps don't handle Opacity maps well. Raytraced shadows are slower than Shadow maps, but return accurate results. In this case, the directional light will cast light through the water surface and properly shadow the stones below.

The complete target direct light rollout.

Plug-Ins

A few water and ocean simulation plug-ins have been released for 3D Studio MAX 3 that could possibly increase the realism of a scene such as this.

■ Arete Image Software, famous for its Digital Nature Tools, has ported to MAX via Sisyphus Software. This package includes several tools for generating ocean meshes that move and interact realistically with the environment. It includes air and cloud environment tools, as well as special procedural maps for shading the water realistically.

■ Seascape from Australia's Driftwood Thinktank, distributed by Digimation, is similar to Digital Nature Tools with the exception that it focuses primarily on creating realistic oceans and wave motion.

■ Splash!MAX from Rubicon Beach Software, also distributed by Digimation, is a fluid mechanics tool that creates a procedural Water object. This object can interact with objects by creating wakes or impact ripples with reflecting "walls" or "edges."

■ RealWave from Spain's Next Limit Software is a standalone water surface simulator that plugs into 3D Studio MAX. It's similar to Splash!MAX in that it's primarily a procedural water surface generator. Its strength lies in its ability to accurately simulate water ripples and wakes as well as secondary motion caused by these disturbances. For example, you could have a boat sailing by a number of stationary objects in the water with the resulting wake causing these objects to bob about as it disturbs their position.

Variations

When using the Fresnel shader within the Falloff map, you are given the option of adjusting both the Mix Curve and the Index or Refraction (IOR). This allows you to tweak the effect in limitless ways. The Index of Refraction value is important for the Fresnel effect because essentially it's simulating the bending of light rays as they move from one medium (water) to another (air). By adjusting this value you can more accurately simulate different mediums, such as ice, crystal, jelly, and so on.

GLOWING TRAIL

"The pen is mightier than the sword, until it runs out of ink."

—ANONYMOUS

Deforming an Object to Create a Glowing Trail

These days many 3D real-time fighting games, such as Soul Blade and Final Fantasy VIII, use a glowing trail effect to emphasize the effect of a swinging sword. First noticed in the light saber battles of the movie Star Wars, this visual is commonly created by programmers for use in video games.

However, an identical effect can be achieved manually by utilizing the Path Deformation feature of 3D Studio MAX 3, as this tutorial will demonstrate.

PROJECT 3

GLOWING TRAIL

BY SUNG-WOOK SU

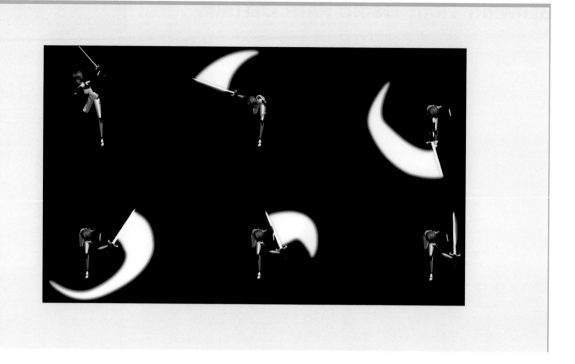

GETTING STARTED

Before we start this tutorial, we must configure the location of the mapping file to open the MAX scene file.

1　Launch 3D Studio MAX 3.0.

2　At Customize, Configure Paths, Bitmaps, press the Add button and select the Chapter 3 folder on the CD-ROM. Another way to access the Chapter 3 folder is to copy it onto your hard drive and assign this path as demonstrated above.

GLOWING TRAIL USING PATH DEFORM

First, open 03mem01.max from the CD-ROM. A picture as shown on the right should appear. Usually, character animations are made with the Character Studio plug-in, but because everyone might not have this plug-in, the character in this sample has been made to swing a sword with MAX's built-in forward kinematics (FK).

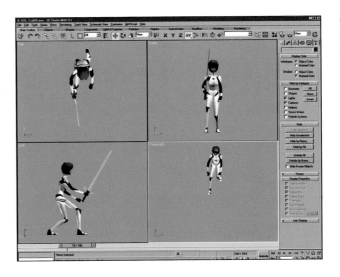

Open the 03mem01.max file from the CD.

MAKING THE PATH

The path of the glowing trail follows the sword's pivot, so it is necessary to move the pivot to the middle of the sword and away from the hand.

1   Select the sword.

2   Go to Hierarchy and select the Pivot button.

3   Click the Affect Pivot Only button.

4   Click the Select and Move icon and move the pivot to the middle of the sword as shown.

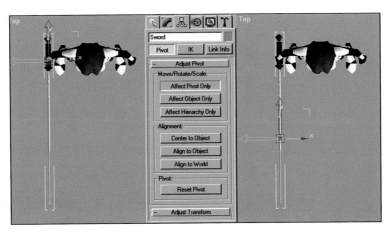

Click the Affect Pivot Only button and adjust the pivot as shown.

5 Go to Motion and click the Trajectories button. The path should appear as shown on the right.

Now we must designate the time the trail starts appearing within the path. If you play the animation, you will see that the sword has a big movement between frames 90 and 100.

6 Change the Trajectory menu:

Sample Range

Start Time: 90

End Time: 100

Sample: 11

7 Now click the Convert To button in Spline Conversion.

There should now be a spline as shown on the right.

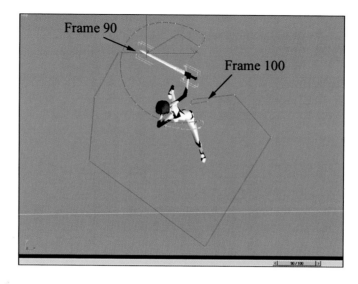

Note the distance the sword travels from frame 90 to frame 100.

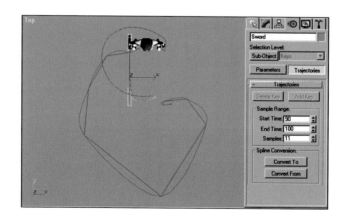

Convert sword's trajectory to a spline.

MODIFY THE PATH

Now we must refine the curve to smooth the animation because the trail object will move along the curve.

1 Click the spline(Shape01) and go to Modify.

2 Click the Vertex button and click and drag over the entire area to select all vertexes on the spline.

3　Move the mouse over a selected vertex and right-click to bring up a menu.

4　Select the Bézier option on the menu.

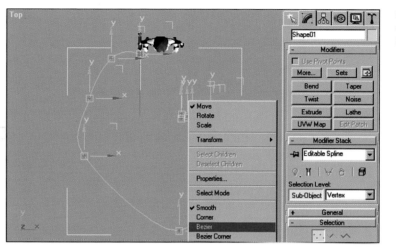

Select all vertexes on the spline and change type Smooth to Bézier.

5　Click the Select and Move icon and click and adjust the green control handles to shape the spline as shown on the right.

Delete as many vertices as possible to achieve approximately this shape.

6　Drag the time slider from frame 90 to frame 100. Make sure that the sword's path corresponds to the spline. Check all windows to make sure that the middle of the sword cuts through the spline path. Adjust if necessary.

These steps are an important part in the creation of the glowing trail effect. If you find it necessary to change the shape of the path, do so at any time.

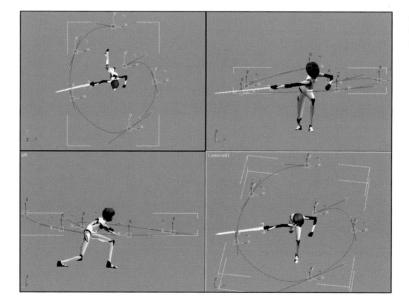

Adjust the green control handles to shape the spline as shown.

CREATE THE DEFORMING OBJECT

This section shows how to make the shape of the glowing trail.

If you want to start from here, open 03mem02.max from the CD-ROM.

1   Go to Create, Geometry and click the Plane button.

 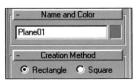

Go to Create and click Plane.

2   Go to the top viewport and click and drag to make the plane.

Change the parameters:

Length: 15
Width: 2
Length Segs: 1
Width Segs: 20

3   Go to Modify and click the Taper button.

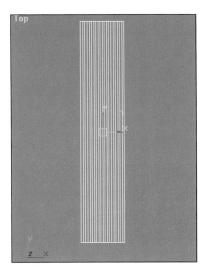

Drag on top viewport to create a plane.

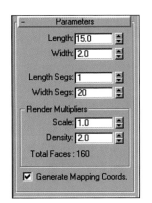

Change the parameters.

4 Change the parameters:

Amount: 2

Curve: 0

Primary: X

Effect: ZY

Apply Taper and change the parameters. The Plane object changes its shape.

After applying Taper.

MATERIAL

Now we must select the material of the glowing object. This color will be the base of the glowing color. This tutorial uses green, but you may select any color desired.

Another important step is assigning the 2-Sided material option. So far, the Plane object is made up of polygons. It is important to remember that polygons are rendered only on one side by default. Here, we set it up to render both sides of the polygon.

1 Open the Material Editor.

2 Click any sample sphere on the menu.

3 Check the 2-Sided option as shown.

4 Change the color to green.

5 Click the Plane01 object on the viewport.

6   Click the Assign Material to Selection icon on the
    Material Editor to assign the material to the object.

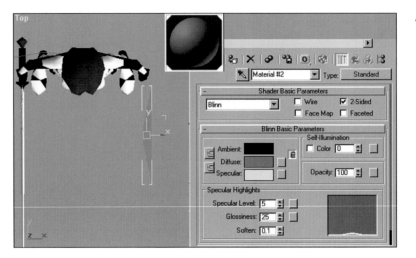

Assign the material as shown.

ANIMATION OF THE OBJECT

Now we will add animation to the trail, the process of making the animation.
Depending on the exact layout of the spline path, the PathDeform parameters will
differ. At this point in the tutorial, check the parameters as shown, but make sure to
adjust them depending on the path you have created. If you want to follow the steps
on this tutorial exactly, open the 03mem03.max file on the CD-ROM.

1   Select the Plane object, go to Modify, and click the
    More button.

2   On the menu, select *PathDeform.

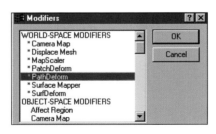

Click More and select
*PathDeform in Modify.

3   Click the Pick Path button on the control panel and
    pick the spline path.

4   Click the Move to Path button to move the object
    onto the path.

5   Select X on the Path Deform Axis to change the direction of the object.

6   Click the Animate button on the bottom of the window to animate the object.

7   Move the Time Slider to frame 91.

Click the Pick Path button and pick the spline path.

Move the Plane object on to the spline.

8   Change the parameters:

Percent: 6.5

Stretch: 17

Rotation: 125

Twist: 0

9   Move the Time Slider to frame 92.

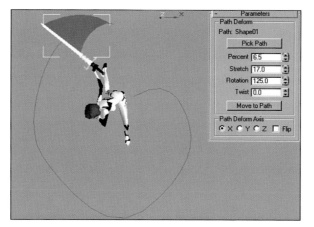

Go to frame 91 and change the parameters.

10 Change the parameters:

Percent:	12
Stretch:	28
Rotation:	120.5
Twist:	0

11 Move the Time Slider to frame 93.

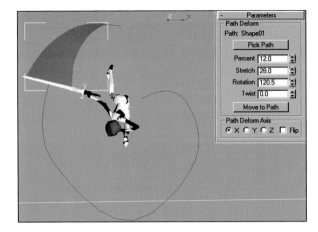

Go to frame 92 and change the parameters.

12 Change the parameters:

Percent:	19.5
Stretch:	40
Rotation:	126
Twist:	0

13 Move the Time Slider to frame 94.

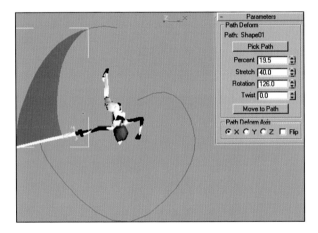

Go to frame 93 and change the parameters.

14 Change the parameters:

Percent:	40
Stretch:	64
Rotation:	124.5
Twist:	0

15 Move the Time Slider to frame 95.

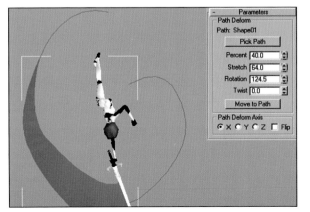

Go to frame 94 and change the parameters.

16 Change the parameters:

Percent: 54
Stretch: 94.349
Rotation: 124.3
Twist: 0

17 Move the Time Slider to frame 96.

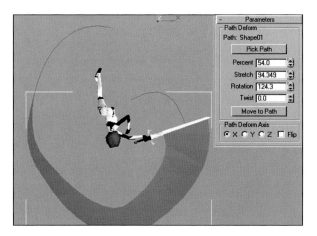

Go to frame 95 and change the parameters.

18 Change the parameters:

Percent: 71
Stretch: 70
Rotation: 114.602
Twist: 0

19 Move the Time Slider to frame 97.

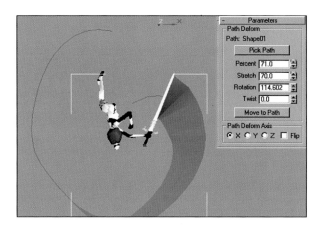

Go to frame 96 and change the parameters.

20 Change the parameters:

Percent: 80.5
Stretch: 60
Rotation: 102.5
Twist: 0

21 Move the Time Slider to frame 98.

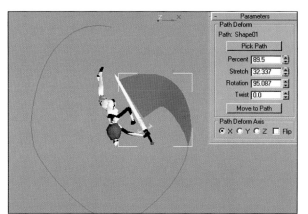

Go to frame 97 and change the parameters.

22 Change the parameters:

Percent:	89.5
Stretch:	32.337
Rotation:	95.087
Twist:	0

23 Move the Time Slider to frame 99.

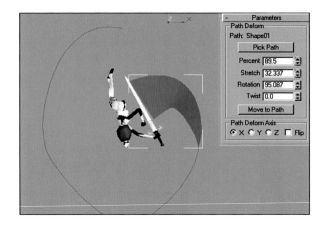

Go to frame 98 and change the parameters.

24 Change the parameters:

Percent:	97
Stretch:	6.5
Rotation:	95
Twist:	0

25 Move the Time Slider to frame 100.

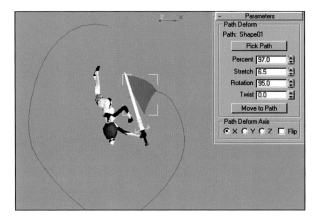

Go to frame 99 and change the parameters.

26 Change the parameters:

Percent:	98.5
Stretch:	1
Rotation:	95
Twist:	0

27 Now click the Play button to play the animation. Following the path of the sword, a trail should appear.

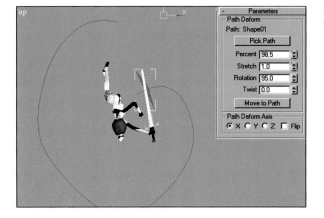

Go to frame 100 and change the parameters.

HIDE THE ANIMATION

At this point, the glowing trail exists before frame 91, which is unnecessary.

In this section, we use Hide Animation to hide the unnecessary trail object on the earlier frames.

If you want to start from here, open 03mem04.max from the CD-ROM.

1 Select the Plane01 object and right-click on it to bring up a menu.

2 Select the TrackView Selected option to bring up the TrackView window.

3 Click the Plane01 on the left list to highlight it.

   The Add Visibility icon should now be activated.

4 Click the Add Visibility Track icon on the TrackView toolbar.

5 Click Visibility on the left list to highlight it.

   The Assign Float Controller icon should be activated.

6 Click the Assign Float Controller icon on the TrackView toolbar.

7 Select On/Off on the menu. Click OK.

   There should be a blue bar on the visibility track.

8 Click the Add Keys icon on the TrackView toolbar.

Open TrackView and highlight Plane01.

Click the Assign Float Controller icon and Select On/Off.

9   Add the keys by clicking on frames 0 and 91 on the blue bar as shown.

10 Click the Play button to play the animation. The trail should appear only between frames 91 and 100.

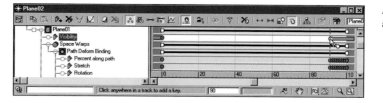

Add the keys on frame 0 and 91.

GLOWING EFFECT

Finally, we will add a glow to our trail by adding the glowing effect on the trail animation. In this section, it is very important to follow the sequence exactly. If the steps are done out of order, unexpected results may occur.

If you want to start from here, open 03mem05.max From the CD-ROM.

1   Go to Display.

2   Uncheck the camera option to unhide Camera01.

3   Use the Select and Move icon to move the camera to the position desired.

    Now we must select the object to which the glow effect will be added.

4   Select Plane01 and right-click.

5   Select the Properties option.

6   On the Object Properties menu, type 2 for Object Channel in the G-Buffer section.

7   Click the Image option in Motion Blur to add this motion blur effect.

8   Close the menu.

9   Go to Rendering in the main menu and select Video Post.

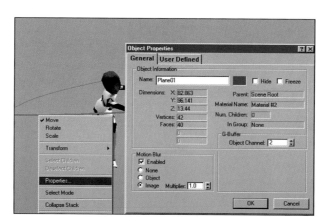

Open the Object Properties menu; type 2 for Object Channel in the G-Buffer section.

10 Click the Add Scene Event icon on the Video Post toolbar.

11 Select Camera01 on the menu and then click the OK button.

Open Video Post and click the Add Scene Event icon to add Camera01.

12 Click the Camera01 label on the left list.

13 Click the Add Image Filter Event icon. Select the Lens Effect Glow option on the menu.

Note: You must highlight by clicking the Camera01 label because the glow effect is a filter effect that is inserted after rendering.

14 Don't select the Setup button; just click OK to close the menu.

15 Double-click the Lens Effect Glow label on the left list to bring up the menu again.

Add the Lens Effect Glow event.

16 Now click the Setup button.

17 On the menu, click the Preview and VP Queue button.

18 Type 2 for the Object ID option as shown.

19 Click Preferences tab on the menu.

20 Type 2 for the Size on Effect.

21 Type 80 for the Intensity on Color. Adjust this option as much as desired.

22 Click OK.

23 Click a blank area on the left side list to unhighlight everything.

24 Select Add Image Output Event and type the name (Gtrail.avi).

25 Change the file format to AVI.

26 Click the Setup button and select Microsoft Video1.

27 Click the OK button.

28 Click the Execute Sequence icon.

29 Set the Range from 0 to 100.

30 Click 320×240 button.

31 Click the Render button.

After rendering, play the animation with Media Player. If you want to see the rendered animation, open the file GTrail.avi from the CD-ROM.

Add the Add Image Output event.

Add the Add Image Output event.

PLUG-INS

There are no plug-ins for this effect.

VARIATIONS

You can try this effect with other types of animations—flying an airship, fighting, or shooting.

Keep in mind that although you can use the Flex modifier in MAX 3, you will not be able to control the shape as shown in this tutorial.

"All the power in the world resides in the eyes…"

—TOP DOLLAR, The Crow

MIXING MAPS TO CREATE COMPLEX MATERIALS

USING MIX MAPS, MULTIPLE MAPPING COORDINATES, AND PROCEDURAL TEXTURES TO MAKE CONVINCING, REALISTIC MATERIALS

Mapping and making materials for simple

shapes, such as a sphere, is reasonably easy.

But what happens when you need to make a

convincing material for a complex creature

with arms and legs? In this chapter, we will

take the provided model of an eyeball crea-

ture and apply a complex texture by using mix

maps, multiple mapping coordinates, and pro-

cedural textures. A good paint program such

as Photoshop is also needed for this tutorial.

MIXING MAPS TO CREATE COMPLEX MATERIALS

BY NEIL BLEVINS

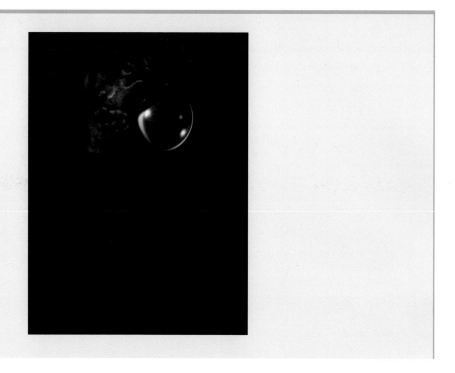

GETTING STARTED

Making a complex material involves making layers of separate materials that, when combined, form the whole material. Using layers is the best way to do this because layers can interact with each other to make two simple textures more complex. It's also easier and faster to edit a single layer than it is to edit a whole material, and lastly, in nature, that's how things work. An animal, for example, has a base texture (the appearance it is born with), which is then put through years of wear and tear, being splashed by mud, walking through grime, and so on, resulting in the final texture.

Before we start with the material, let's quickly go over our scene, 04mem01.max.

In this file, we have a few different objects. We have our main body, which is currently naked. The body was created by pulling and pushing the vertices of an editable mesh, and then applying MeshSmooth to the object. We have an eyeball that I have already textured. We have several lights in the scene and one camera, but you don't need to worry about those. Open the Material Editor. You will see the eyeball texture, and the texture currently applied to the body, which is just a standard material with no maps and a brownish diffuse color.

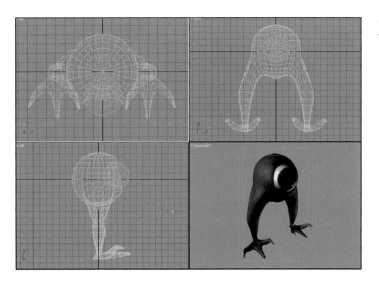

Open and examine our scene with the eyeball character.

THE PROBLEMS WE FACE

If you've tried mapping and applying a material to a complex character before, you know the problem. It starts off with mapping. Mapping is the process of telling your texture what part of the bitmap you want applied to what part of your object. The problem is that on complex models, there is no good mapping icon to handle them. A sphere can use spherical mapping, a cylinder can use cylindrical mapping, but what about a two-legged monster eyeball? If we apply the wrong type of mapping to the object, we'll get streaking, which occurs when the mapping gizmo is parallel to a face, or perpendicular to that face's normal. Ideally, to have perfect mapping, your mapping icon must always be perpendicular to the face and parallel to its normal. Then there's no streaking. But how can you achieve this on an object with face normals going in all kinds of different directions? The answer is to use layers, and this is how we will proceed.

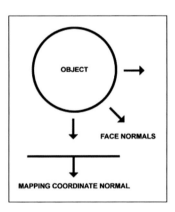

The desired condition: The mapping icon is always parallel to the face normal of the face to which it's applying mapping. If this is not the case, we get...

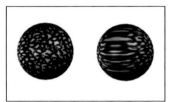

...streaking! Oh no!

PROCEDURALS VERSUS BITMAPS

A procedural map is a map that is created mathematically in 3D space. Examples in MAX are Noise, Speckle, Cellular, Wood, and so on. They are useful because they require no mapping coordinates and so will not streak when applied to an object. Their disadvantage is they're mathematically based, so it's tough to get a lot of artistic control over how they are placed on your object.

A bitmap is a 2D image that is applied to your object via mapping coordinates. The advantage of maps is that you have complete control over what colors and textures go where when making the map. The disadvantage is that if your mapping isn't right, the colors and textures will streak. What we want to do is use the strengths of both methods.

LET'S GET STARTED: CREATING THE BASE LAYER

Our base layer will be made up of several layers of noise. This will teach you a thing or two about procedurals, and the most basic way to mix materials, aptly called the Mix map.

1 First, quickly render out your camera view by selecting the view. Go to the rendering menu and click Render. Now you see your model in more detail. From now on, when you want to see how your model looks, you can click the Render Last button, bypassing all these steps.

Render our naked model to see more detail.

2   Now we need to set up our base layer. The base layer of color will cover the entire surface of the body. Think of this as the first coat on your canvas. You don't need to worry about adding much detail—you can add that afterwards on top. Anywhere you do not add detail to later will still look visually interesting thanks to the base layer. Because we want to apply this base to the whole object, let's use a procedural noise texture because we won't have to worry about mapping coordinates. Go to the Body texture, select Diffuse Color map, and choose Noise. Change its type to fractal, size 5; color 1 to 100, 87, 54; and color 2 to 210, 200, 175 (all colors RGB). Now Render Last. There's our first layer.

Add the first layer of noise.

3   We now have a base layer, but I think our base layer should be more complex than this. Let's apply a second layer of procedural noise, this time using the Smoke Procedural map. Click on the Noise button, choose Mix, and Keep Old Map as Submap. Now we have a Mix map. Mix will mix between two different maps using either a percentage (0% being totally map1, 100% being totally map2, 50% a combination of the two) or the values from a third map. We'll start off with the percentage method. Click on slot 2 and select Smoke. Change its size to 20; color 1 to 94, 84, 77; and color 2 to 165, 118, 100. Now hit the Go to Parent button and change the Mix amount to 50. Now Render Last. Notice, you have a mix of two different types of noise. Already, things are looking more complex.

Add the second layer of noise to the first layer using a Mix map.

4 We've applied a layer of noise whose pattern is of a medium size, and then combined it with a smoke whose pattern is considerably larger. Mixing different sizes of noise is much more visually appealing than if all the noise is the same size. Let's now mix in some very small noise. We'll do this using the Map method of mixing. Click the Mix button, choose Mix again, and select Keep Map as Submap. Now we have a mix whose first slot is your original mix and whose second slot is currently blank. If you start getting confused, click the Material/Map Navigator button to see a tree diagram of what you're doing.

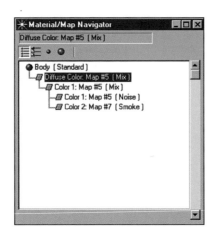

If you get confused, use this tree diagram of what we're doing.

5 Now instead of placing a third noise in slot 2, just leave it empty. Change the color swatch beside slot 2 to 110, 98, 84. Instead of changing the %, let's click in the third slot, the Mix Amount slot, and choose Noise again. Change to fractal, Size 2; High to 0.7; low to 0.5; Levels to 4; and phase to 5. We've shown our original mix of two noises and then applied the color in slot 2 anywhere where our third noise map is white, and not applied the color where the third noise is black.

Add the third layer of smaller noise.

6 Now how about some *really* small noise? Click on
the Noise button and click Mix again. Choose Keep
Map as Submap. Now we have a mix that is affecting
the mix of our original mix. Yes, I know the mental
gymnastics are starting to get to you, but practice
will make this process much easier to understand.
Basically, we originally had a noise that was dictating
where our brown color is being applied on top of
your original base layer. Now instead of just one
noise, we'll have a mix of two. Slot 2 should be
empty, and the color swatch should be white. In Slot
3, choose Speckle. Color 1 should be white, color 2
black, and size 10. Now Render Last.

Add the fourth layer.

7 If you're still confused about what's going on, right-
click your sphere and select Render Map. Choose a
larger size, such as 600×600, and click Render. This
shows you in 2D all the layers of your map up to the
level at which you currently are. The monster has its
original white-on-black noise and then smaller
speckle noise applied on top of that noise (because
white [the color is swatch 2] is being applied everywhere the speckle's white color is, and nothing is
being applied to the slot1 map where the slot3
speckle map is black).

The combination of two noise
maps is used as a mix map
between a brown color and
your original mix of two
different noises.

ANIMATION

Before we start adding details, consider one last thing. When we try to animate this character using a skeletal deformation system (such as Character Studio or Bones Pro), the procedural textures will not work properly. Why? It's because the procedural textures are locked to world space, and not to the object or a specific mapping icon. The texture will remain still in 3D space while your object moves through it, creating a "swimming" effect.

What we want is to lock the procedural texture to our mesh. We do that by adding a UVW mapping icon to our mesh, changing it to Map Channel 1, and choosing XYZ to UVW. Now go back to your two noises, speckle and smoke (this is easiest done using the Material/Map Navigator). Change the source to Explicit Map channel and choose Map Channel 1. You will notice the texture in your Material Editor sphere seems to be gone, but it's actually just so large that it's only covering the sphere with a single solid color. If you Render Last, everything will look just the way it was, except now future animations will have the procedural textures locked to your deformed mesh.

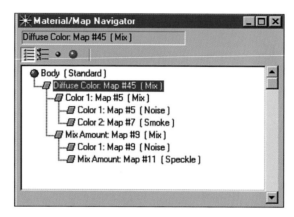

Use the Map Navigator to quickly move between different layers of procedural textures.

ADDING DETAILS

Now that we have our base layer, let's start adding details. Details are treated differently than the base layer because you want more control over the position of the detail. With the base layer, you were less concerned over its overall position on your object. To start, let's assume this creature we're texturing has been running through the dirt a bit. On his lower body, he'd probably have a darker color than on his upper body, with a smooth gradation in between.

1 First, choose your body mesh and apply a second UVW map to it. Choose Planar and Map Channel 2 (in MAX 3, we now have a virtually unlimited number of mapping channels, which means we can

apply several kinds of mapping to your object at the same time). Choose alignment y, and then press Fit. This will align your icon so it's projecting on your character from the front view.

2   Now back to your material: Go back up the tree to the top of your material and click the Diffuse Color slot so you're at the highest level mix. Click Mix and choose another mix. Select Keep Subobject. Now change color 2 to black. Change slot 3 to a gradient. Choose Map Channel 2 (so it uses your UVW mapping from the planar view) and change color 2 to 100,100,100 and color 3 to 170,170,170. Now Render Last. This applies the color black to the bottom of your character, but because the gradient goes from black to gray instead of black to white, the lower body that has black applied to it is still slightly transparent—the original base layer shows through.

3   Now let's heighten this effect by working on his feet a little more. We have to assume that if this character is running around a lot with no shoes, his feet will have a slightly different texture of skin than the rest of his body. The skin may be tougher and possibly cracked from all the wear and tear. Go to your highest level mix and change it to another mix (always keeping subobject materials). Change color 2 to black and, in slot 3, place a Cellular noise. Change the source to Explicit Map channel and choose map channel 1 (do this with all other procedural maps you apply). Change size to 6. Click and drag the white color under Cell Color and drop it into the second division color (black). Choose Swap. This makes the white parts of cellular black, and vice versa.

Add a layer of black to the lower half of your model.

Add some cellular noise on the monster's feet.

4   Now click the Cellular button and choose Mask and
     Keep Subobject. A mask covers certain areas (as
     dictated by the black-and-white values of the map in
     your mask), allowing the map to be placed only in
     the uncovered areas. Click the Mask slot, select
     Browse from Scene, and grab that gradient you
     already made. Choose a copy, not an instance of that
     gradient. Now Render Last.

5   We still haven't really given the impression that the
     legs are a different substance. What we need is some
     actual cracks. That's one thing Bump maps are good
     for. All these layering techniques, of course, work
     perfectly in all map slots, even Bumps. We've
     neglected them for too long, so let's change that
     now. Go to the Bump slot of your material, change
     amount to 100, and place a noise. Choose Explicit
     Map Channel 1. Reduce size to 3, change type to
     fractal, and, in the output area, change Bump
     Amount to 0.5. This is a quick way to change the
     overall bump strength of any particular map. Now
     we have our base bump. Now let's add the cracks
     that need to match up with our black cellular noise.
     The noise slot should be changed to a mix. Click
     slot 2, choose Browse from Scene, pick your mask
     that includes your cellular and your gradient, and
     choose Instance. Now change the mix amount to
     70. Now Render Last.

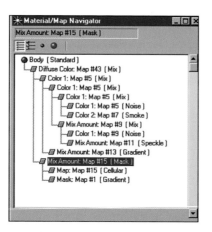

Pick the mask that includes
your cellular and your gradient, which, in this case, is
Mix Amount: Map #15
(Mask).

Now we have our base noise
Bump map and a Cellular
map whose bump matches
up perfectly with the black
cellular Diffuse map.

6   Let's add some veins near our creature's eye. We can do this by placing painted maps instead of procedural textures into the Mix slot of the mix maps. To do this, open a copy of Photoshop (or another good paint program). We will paint a map that will place the veins on only the area of the monster that we choose. Go to your mesh in MAX, apply a third UVW Mapping icon, change it to Map Channel 3, change type to Cylindrical, and click the Fit button. Now, for the next step, be sure you have installed the plug-in Texporter by Cuneyt Ozdas (http://www.cuneytozdas.com). This plug-in can be run as a utility (simply choose More from the Utilities panel and choose Texporter from the scene). Change the Image size to whatever you prefer, uncheck Polygon Fill, choose Colorize by Constant, change the color swatch to pure white, map channel 3, and then pick your body mesh object. This now shows you the unwrapped version of your mesh, as seen from mapping icon 3. Save this image as EyeMap3.tga. Now open this file in Photoshop.

7   In Photoshop, choose New Layer in the Layers palette. Click OK. On this layer, paint a white, circular area that covers the area of your mesh where the eye sits. Then select your background layer and fill it with the color black. Now flatten your image and save as EyeMap3_complete.tga.

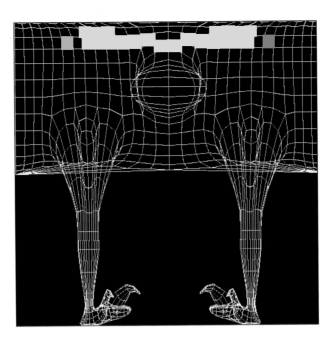

Using Pick and picking your object will show you your unwrapped mesh as seen by mapping icon 3.

Paint a white, circular area that covers the area of the eye.

8 Go back into MAX. Go to your first Diffuse mix, choose Mix again and Keep Submap. In slot 3, choose Bitmap and place your EyeMap3_complete. tga as your bitmap. Choose Map Channel 3 as the mapping channel to which your bitmap is applied. Now click Show Map in Viewport.

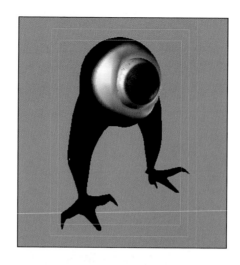

Notice how the area you painted now shows up on your mesh.

9 Turn Show Map in Viewport off. Click Type Bitmap and choose Mask. Keep Submap. Drag your bitmap from Map slot to Mask slot and choose Swap. Under Map, choose Noise and Explicit Map Channel 1, type Turbulence. Size should be 8.0, High 0.15, Levels 2, and Phase 2. Click the Swap button to exchange the black-and-white colors. Double-click Go to Parent and change slot 2 to Noise. Choose the Explicit Map Channel 1. The size should be set to 10; color 1: 80, 71, 49; color 2: 220, 217, 163. Click Render Last.

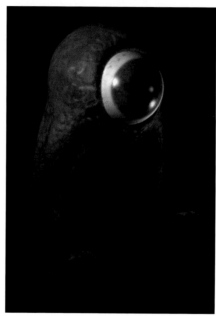

After rendering: A monster with veins and highly textured skin.

FINISHING UP

That's the end of our step-by-step tutorial. The end result can be seen in the file 04mem02.max. Now it's your turn to take the final steps in any direction you choose. I continued with the model for a few more iterations, adding a few more layers of texture, as well as shininess maps and a little extra mesh editing. Check out 03mem03.max to see the result. Hopefully, this tutorial has now given you some tools to help finish off this model or to texture any other model you choose.

PLUG-INS

Just about anything that creates or manipulates materials can be used. Tons of procedural textures are out there to be tried. Many are from Blur (http://www.blur.com/BlurBeta). The Essential Textures by Worley (http://www.worley.com/) and DarkTree from Darkling Simulations (http://www.darksim.com/) are also good sources to use. Also, Instant UV (distributed by Digimation) is a useful plug-in that provides a new mapping type that works in many situations to remove stretching from maps. It's probably most useful for making base layers with maps instead of procedural textures, on which you'd want to layer bitmaps using the methods shown earlier in this chapter.

VARIATIONS

Variations are as plentiful as the number of monsters you wish to create. We have learned how to mix maps using percentages, and using another map. We covered how to mask out parts of maps and how to apply multiple mapping coordinates, using them to place texture on different parts of your mesh. We have used procedurals and painted maps to place detail at specific areas. And of course, you can go the full map route, and forget about procedurals altogether. You would do this by applying a base texture, and then applying several mapping icons to specific parts of the body, giving them unique mapping channels. On your texture, you would paint the sort of texture you want at that area, and then paint a mask to blend between the detail on your map and your base material. (Both the map and mask, of course, would use the appropriate map

The finished monster.

channel.) You can also use a blend material instead of mix maps. That enables you to have many material layers, each with its own material properties. And lastly, for this tutorial, I did not spend much time optimizing. Remember, each layer you make means more memory needed and more time to render. If you layer your creature too deeply, it could be slow to render. You can get around this by using maps when you can (maps tend to render faster than procedurals), by collapsing several layers of maps in Photoshop to form one new layer, and by limiting the number of layers to just what you need to make it look good while still rendering quickly.

"The last of the V8 Interceptors! Would have been a shame to blow it up."

—MECHANIC, The Road Warrior

CAR PAINT

MATERIAL

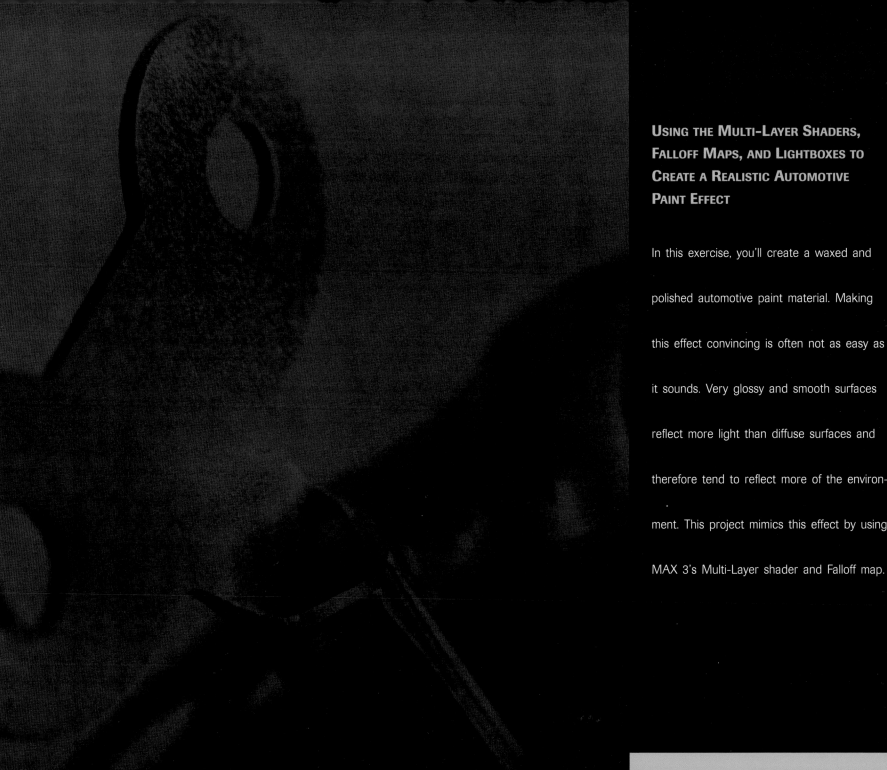

USING THE MULTI-LAYER SHADERS, FALLOFF MAPS, AND LIGHTBOXES TO CREATE A REALISTIC AUTOMOTIVE PAINT EFFECT

In this exercise, you'll create a waxed and polished automotive paint material. Making this effect convincing is often not as easy as it sounds. Very glossy and smooth surfaces reflect more light than diffuse surfaces and therefore tend to reflect more of the environment. This project mimics this effect by using MAX 3's Multi-Layer shader and Falloff map.

CAR PAINT MATERIAL

BY BRANDON DAVIS

GETTING STARTED

A car's surface actually has two layers of reflective material: the paint itself and the wax layer on top of it. 3D Studio MAX 3 has two new tools that make simulating car paint easier. The Multi-Layer shader allows you to have two specular settings on the same surface, and the Falloff map allows you to control reflections based on viewing angles.

In this exercise, you'll take an existing scene of an organic curved surface and create a car paint material for it. You'll use this stand-in object instead of an actual car mesh to help simplify and speed up the task. You can take what you learn from this exercise and apply it to any automotive mesh. The goal of this exercise is to create the car paint material with the new Multi-Layer shader to control multiple specularity settings. Because the car paint surface is smooth and polished, you'll use a Raytrace map to generate reflections. You'll use the Falloff map to realistically control these reflections based on viewing angle and surface curvature. Finally, you'll create lightboxes from Plane primitives to help simulate the box lighting and reflections often seen in automotive imagery.

Load the 05mem01.max file from the project's folder on the accompanying CD-ROM.

It should contain an automotive-looking object, perhaps a motorcycle gas tank, with rounded contours. There is also a ground plane and default lighting.

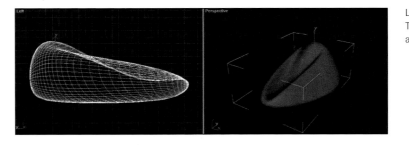

Load the 05mem01.max file. This scene file contains an automotive-looking object.

CREATING THE CAR PAINT MATERIAL

In this section, you'll create the basic car paint material.

1   In the Material Editor, select the Paint material in slot 2.

2   Using the existing settings, change the Paint material parameters as follows:

Shader Type: Multi-Layer

First Specular Layer

Color: (R=255, G=255, B=255)

Level: 200

Glossiness: 90

Second Specular Layer

Color: (R=229, G=229, B=229)

Level: 10

Glossiness: 40

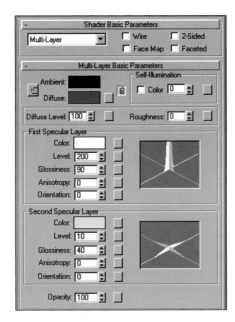

Create a Standard material using the Multi-Layer shader.

The first specular layer will create a very solid, sharp highlight consistent with a buffed and polished surface. This is what is used to fill in the microscopic pits and depressions in a diffused surface such as metal. By smoothing out and polishing the surface, you make it highly reflective. The second specular layer adds a very soft, almost diffused surface consistent with metal. This layer is much less pronounced, but subtly noticeable when overlaid with the previous layer.

3   Go to the Maps rollout and set the Reflection slot
    to 50%.

4   Assign a Falloff map to the Reflection slot. Use the
    default settings for now.

5   In the Falloff map parameters, assign a Raytrace map
    to the Side slot (the lower of the two slots at the top
    of the rollout). This directs the material to reflect
    more as the surface normals approach perpendicular
    angles.

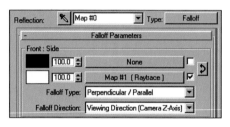

Assign a Falloff map to limit
the Raytrace map's influence
in the Reflection channel.

6   Use the default settings for the Raytrace map.

CREATING LIGHTBOXES FOR ILLUMINATION AND REFLECTION

In this section, you'll create lightboxes—rectangular light arrays that are often used to
shoot indoor settings. Not only will you be using these for illumination (via linked
spotlights), but you can also use them to add reflections in the paint's surface. To
accurately gauge reflections, you must have some kind of environment to reflect.
Lightboxes are often used to properly light automotive products for commercial
imagery, but they also have the added benefit of filling the reflections. This really
helps make the polished paint stand out and look more appealing.

1   In the top viewport, create a Plane primitive by
    click-dragging. Set the Plane's dimensions as follows:

    Length: 200
    Width: 200

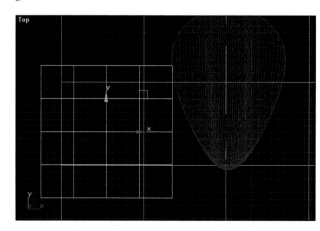

Create a Plane primitive by
click-dragging.

2 Also in the top viewport, create a Free spotlight in the center of the recently created Plane. Set the Free spotlight's parameters as follows:

Cast Shadows: Checked (on)
Multiplier: 3
Hotspot: 43
Falloff: 75
Decay: Inverse
Shadow Type: Shadow Map
Sample Range: 8

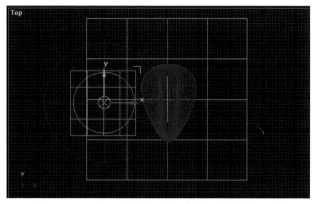

Create a Free spotlight in the center of the recently created Plane.

3 Select the Plane and link it to the spotlight.

4 Name the Plane Lightbox.

5 Select the spotlight and move it upwards along the Z-Axis so it is above the scene.

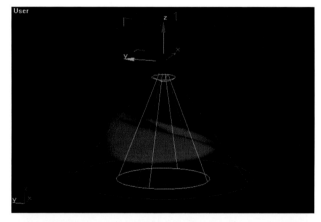

Move the spotlight so it is above the scene.

6 With the spotlight still selected, go to the Motion panel. In the Assign Controller group, select the Transform: Position/Rotation/Scale track.

7 Click the Assign Controller button and assign a Look At controller.

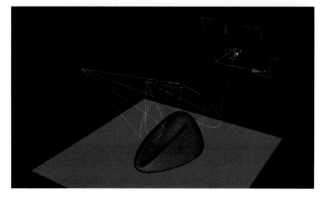

Rotate the spotlight in the Motion panel.

8 In the Look At parameters, click the Pick Target button and select the Sphere object in the center of your scene. This makes the Free spotlight act much like a target spotlight. Notice that no matter how you move the spotlight, the lightbox stays oriented to the target object.

Assign a Look At Controller.

9 Because you created the Plane primitive in the top viewport, its normals are facing the wrong way for the lightbox to appear in reflections. To remedy this, select the Lightbox object and assign a Normal modifier (you may have to use the More button to access more modifiers). Set the following parameter:

Flip Normals: Checked (on)

There is an added advantage to flipping the normals on the lightbox. In most cases, you might be tempted to just use a Box primitive instead of a Plane. However, having a single-sided lightbox allows you to "look through" it. Because the normals are always facing the target object, the rear of the lightbox will not render because, theoretically, it doesn't have any polygons facing in that direction. This prevents lightboxes from obscuring your view.

Assign a Normal modifier to the Plane and set it to Flip Normals.

10 In the Material Editor, assign the lightbox material to the Lightbox object. This is a self-illuminated white surface.

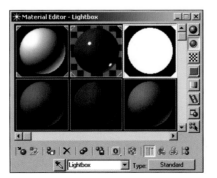

Assign the lightbox material to the Lightbox object.

Arranging the Lightboxes and Rendering

In this section, you'll take the lightbox you just created and instance it across three more objects. When arranged properly, these lightboxes will properly illuminate the scene and add to the reflections in the paint.

1 Select the Spotlight and Lightbox object.

2 Click the Move tool and shift-drag the objects. This brings up the Clone Options dialog box. Choose Instance from the list. This will allow you to make changes to multiple spotlights and lightboxes globally.

3 Repeat step 2 until you have four spotlights and lightboxes.

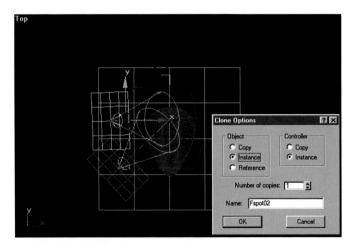

Choose Instance in the Clone Options dialog box to allow for global changes to multiple spotlights and lightboxes.

4 Arrange them so they are angled approximately 45 degrees towards the ground object.

The scene is now complete. If you render, you should have a deep red, shiny car paint material that catches the lightbox in the reflections. The reflections are also controlled with the Falloff map, limiting their intensity to perpendicular angles. At this point, you should rearrange the lightboxes to test different lighting and reflections. You can also find a file of the completed scene called 05mem02.max on the CD-ROM that accompanies this book.

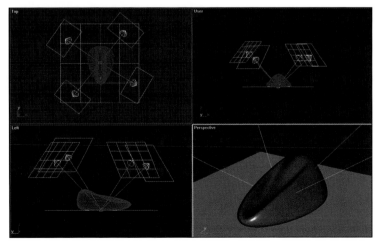

Arrange the lightboxes in the scene as shown.

Something to keep in mind while using the Raytrace map is antialiasing. By default, raytraced reflections are not antialiased. This is primarily because antialiasing is computationally very expensive. The RayFX engine includes two different methods for antialiasing reflections, both of which are satisfactory. When experimenting with raytraced surfaces, it's a good idea to keep antialiased reflections turned off. This is accessed through the global parameters of the Raytrace map. A fast way to smooth out aliased reflections is to use supersampling. The reflections are not antialiased, but supersampling with any one of the many supersamplers built into MAX 3 will smooth out the reflections at a very low cost in terms of speed.

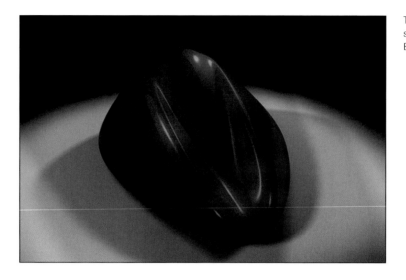

The completed scene with specular bloom added via the Blur Render effect.

Plug-Ins

There aren't any "Car Paint" plug-ins, but there are a couple of freeware plug-ins from the generous folks at Blur Studio that could help make a scene like this more realistic.

- RayFX Area Shadows adds to MAX's shadow options, allowing your lights to access the RayFX raytrace engine to calculate area shadows. Area shadows are much more realistic than both Shadow maps or standard raytraced shadows. They realistically simulate shadow detail falloff by causing a shadow to spread and blur more as it stretches away from the object.

- MultiBlender Material allows you to blend several materials together with varying degrees of control. This tool allows you to create a much more advanced multi-layer material.

Variations

Obviously, it makes more sense to experiment on simple geometry such as this organic object, but at some point, you'll want to try it on a car mesh. One simple modification that comes to mind is to use the Blur Render effect included with MAX 3. This render effect can be used to blur an image based on several different options. Most relevant to this project is blur based on Luminance. These controls will allow you to add specular bloom or softness to the reflections and highlights, much as some photo processes do.

"There are fields, Neo, endless fields, where human beings are no longer born, we are grown. For the longest time I would not believe it, till I saw the fields with my own eyes."

—MORPHEUS (LAURENCE FISHBURNE),
THE MATRIX

LIGHTING EFFECTS: RIM LIGHTING AND DIFFUSE GLOW

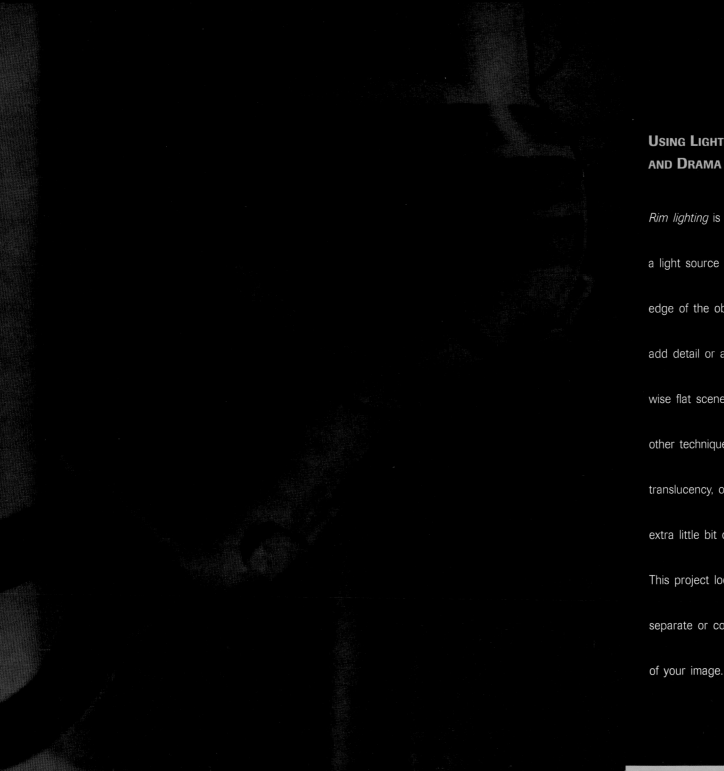

USING LIGHTING TO ADD DETAIL AND DRAMA

Rim lighting is a technique achieved by placing a light source behind an object so only the edge of the object is lit. This technique can add detail or a dramatic element to an otherwise flat scene and, when combined with other techniques such as fill lights, backlighting, translucency, or diffuse glows, can add that extra little bit of frosting to any plain cake. This project looks at how these effects, separate or combined, can affect the look of your image.

LIGHTING EFFECTS: RIM LIGHTING AND DIFFUSE GLOW

BY NEIL BLEVINS

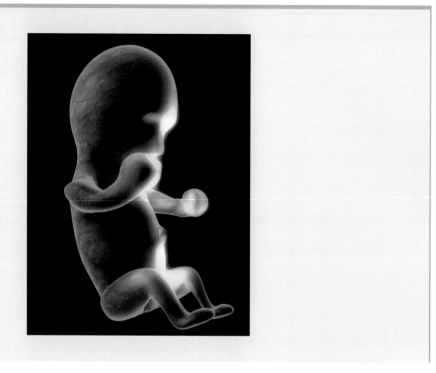

GETTING STARTED

Before you start messing with lighting and materials, take a moment to get acquainted with the sample file I have provided.

The first sample file is called 06mem01.max and can be loaded with the File, Open command. Inside this file, you'll find a model of a fetus that is a simple editable mesh you'll use as the model for these experiments. You'll find a camera and a single spotlight illuminating the object from the left side. (You can see both of these objects by going to the Display tab panel and deselecting the Camera and Lights checkboxes in the Hide By Category rollout.)

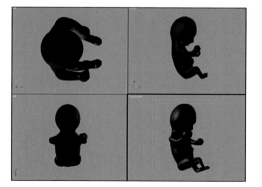

Use the fetus as the base model for this project.

If you look in the Materials Editor, you'll find a material called "Baby Temp" that is already assigned to the model. The material is a raytraced material with mostly default settings, with a few exceptions. It has been altered to make the model look more flesh-colored, the highlight has been made slightly larger and a yellow color, and I have turned off the raytraced reflections and refractions (which can be turned off by unchecking the boxes under Raytracer Controls).

Open the Material Editor to see your base material for the baby.

Note: "Why did you use the raytraced material if you don't want reflections or refractions?" you may ask. The answer is simple: Most people think the raytraced material should be used only for reflections and refractions and don't realize there are many other useful map types such as translucency and fluorescence in this material. Therefore, for many more complex materials, I use the raytraced material, and you'll do the same for this example.

KEY AND FILL LIGHT

Start out by adding another light to the scene. You can either follow along or look at 06mem02.max to see the final effect.

1 First, render the camera viewport using the defaults I have provided. You will see the model, but it looks rather uninteresting because you can really see only one side of it.

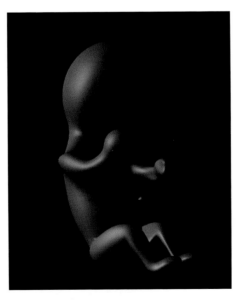

Render the camera viewport using the defaults. The baby model with default lighting is uninteresting.

2　Some people compensate for this by moving their main light (known as the *key* light) so they can see everything. Move the light already in the scene to a position of [110, −245, 0] so the light is now shining directly at your model from approximately the same direction as the camera. (You can move your light to this position by opening the Transform type-in dialog box and placing your three positions in the first three slots.) Now render. You have created a second problem by solving the first—the model looks flat and uninteresting again, this time because the model no longer has any darkness to it. Interesting images are images with a good combination of dark and light areas, so the real answer is to add some more lights to your scene to accentuate the darkened parts of your model without washing those areas out with light.

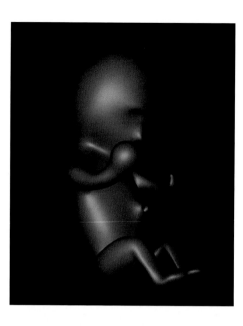

Moving the key light so you can see more of the model causes too much illumination, flattening out the image.

3　Before going to rim lighting, try adding a fill light. A *fill light* is similar to a rim light, but the effect isn't as harsh. A fill light is usually a colored light at a low intensity placed opposite the key light. Because the key light in the original scene is to the upper left from the front, the fill light should be in the lower right. You will also place the light towards the back, behind the subject, which makes the fill light now a *back* light. Reopen the original 06mem01.max and place an omni light at [65,25,−45]. Turn its multiplier to 0.35 and change the color to RGB 255, 255, 255. (For this example, don't worry about coloring the light.) Now, rerender your camera view and see that you still have your main lit area, you still have dark areas, and you also can now see all the detail on the edge of your model that used to be totally black.

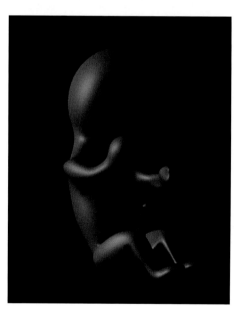

Adding a fill light helps us see the detail without getting rid of the dark shadowy areas.

RIM LIGHTING USING LIGHTS

But now, maybe the effect just isn't dramatic enough for what you're trying to do. Maybe you don't want a low-intensity light in the corner; you want a high-intensity light. Try it. You can either follow along or check out 06mem03.max to see the final effect.

1   Change the multiplier of your light to 1.0. Rerender. Oops—you're back to the washed-out image.

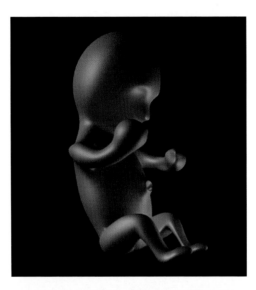

Beware: Too much fill lighting can wash out your image again.

2   How can you fix it? By moving the position of the light to 37,96,–45 and increasing the multiplier to 2.0. Now render. You have a much more pronounced light from the back, and the light just affects the very edge of your model, or the rim of the model. Congratulations! You now have rim lighting.

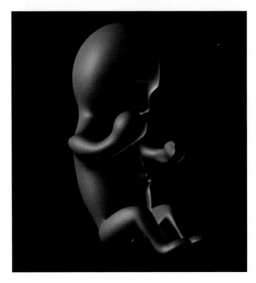

By moving the light more directly behind the object, you achieve rim lighting.

RIM LIGHTING USING MATERIALS

A similar effect can be achieved using materials. You can either follow along or examine 06mem04.max to see the final effect.

1 First, turn off the omni light by deselecting the On checkbox in the Modify panel. Now open the Materials Editor and select the raytrace material you already have applied. Go to the color swatch called Luminosity and change the color to RGB 100, 100, 100. Notice the entire model now glows white when rendered. This is a problem similar to washing out the scene with too much lighting. You see, luminosity as well as self-illumination and extra lighting are all variations on the same thing (all properties of a raytraced material). It takes the material and washes out the dark areas, making the material look as if it's glowing.

So, now that you know what you don't want, how do you achieve what you're looking for? Think about it logically: We first want strong light, which you can achieve by bumping up the luminosity. You then want that light to show up only in the parts of the model that are dark (so you can see the details), and then you want the effect to show up only at the edge of this dark space, so you don't wash out the image. The answer is to use the Falloff map, a new map type in MAX 3 that lets you place a map or color based on a falloff type.

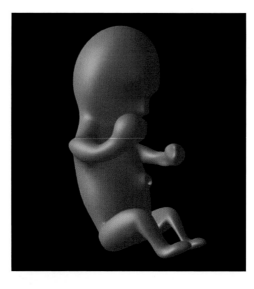

Applying a luminosity color to your material can also wash out your image.

Next, we'll use the new Falloff map type on the Luminosity Map channel.

2	Turn your luminosity color back to black. Then, go down to the Maps area and add a Falloff map to the Luminosity channel. Note how your material has changed. Now the edges are glowing, and the inside is the same color as it always was. That's what the Falloff map does. It applies two maps or colors to your object based on a falloff type. The default type is Perpendicular/Parallel, which means the parts of your model that are on the edge get one color (white, in this example) and the parts of your model that are facing you get black. When this is applied to the Luminosity channel, it makes the object glow white at the edge, and not glow at all in the parts facing you.

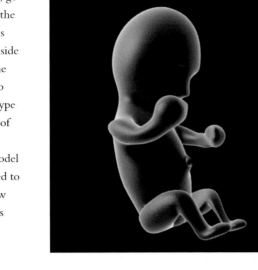

Add a falloff map to your luminosity and use the Perpendicular/Parallel Falloff type.

3	You control the intensity of this effect with two things: the color of the swatches and the mix curve. Try changing the color of your white swatch to gray to see how it affects the material. The effect is not as strong. Bring the color back to white and go to the mix curve. Add a point somewhere in the middle and drag it around. See how the edge is affected by the glow as you move the point. Also, if you right-click any point on your mix curve, you can turn that point into a Bézier point, which lets you further adjust the effect by moving the Bézier handles on the point.

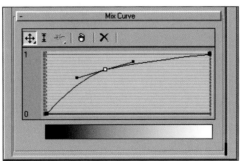

Experiment with the Mix Curve settings to see how it affects the material.

4 Now you're halfway there, but the glow is illuminating everything at the edge, not just the dark areas. The answer is to turn your falloff material into a second falloff material. Click the Type button at the top of your Falloff dialog box and select Falloff from the list again. Select Keep Old Map as Submap. Now you have a Falloff map, and the map in the first map slot is your original Falloff map. Now go to Falloff Type, and change it to Shadow/Light from Perpendicular/Parallel. What this does is apply your maps or colors to your model in such a way that the dark areas of your model get your first map and the light areas get the second map. The dark areas are getting an edge glow, and the light areas are getting white. Wait, that's not right! You want light areas to have no luminosity. Change the second slot color to black. Now rerender and see how it has affected the scene.

This kind of rim lighting is different from using a light because it affects the whole object and cannot be positioned as quickly or precisely as a light. However, it can be used to achieve an eerie unearthly glow, which is perfect for a fetus because there's something about the miracle of creating life that's sort of unearthly.

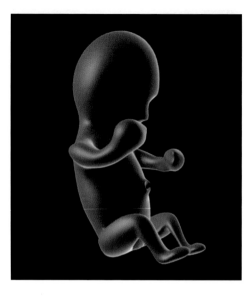

Adding a second Falloff map using the Shadow/Light falloff type lets you illuminate the edges of only the lit areas of your model.

Adjust the Falloff parameters to achieve the proper lighting effect on the material.

5   Now combine the two effects. You can either follow
    along or check out 06mem05.max to see the final
    effect. Turn your omni light back on. Go to your
    material and change the overall amount of your
    luminosity to, for example, 75%. Go down to your
    Falloff map that affects the Perpendicular/Parallel
    values and change the white color swatch to RGB
    255, 190, 115. Now rerender. You have a slight
    orange glow around the whole edge of your object,
    and a strong white glow at certain points on your
    edge from your rim light.

You can also change the
color of your luminosity, for
example, to orange.

DIFFUSE GLOW

Anyone who's watched a lot of Japanese animé knows this effect. The parts of your
scene that are brightly lit are so intense, they actually glow in the scene. This happens
in real life and can give your image a soft quality that's usually not associated with CG
art. Several methods of applying such an effect exist, but the easiest is through the
Effects dialog box. You can either follow along or view 06mem06.max to see the
final effect.

1   Deselect the checkbox beside your luminosity and
    change the multiplier of your omni light to some-
    thing really high like 5.0. Go to Rendering, Effects
    and then click the Add button. Add a Blur. (That's
    right, add a *Blur*, not a Lens Effect.) Technically, a
    glow is just a blur that is added to your original
    image. Go to the Blur Type tab and change the Pixel
    Radius to 5%. Go to the Pixel Selections tab,
    uncheck Whole Image, check Luminance, change
    Brighten to 250%, Blend to 75%, Min to 80%, and
    Feather Radius to 15%.

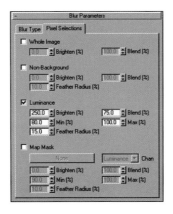

To create the diffuse glow,
create a blur with these
parameters in the effects
channel.

2 Now render. It renders your scene and then applies the glow. The figures below show the scene with and without glow.

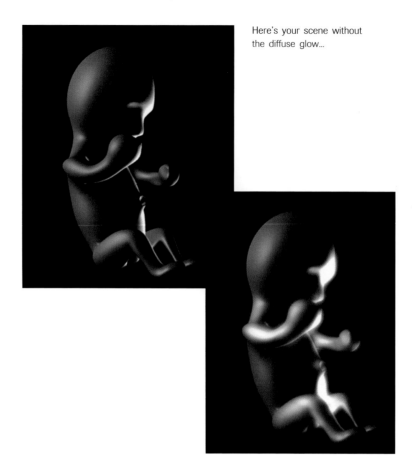

Here's your scene without the diffuse glow...

...and this is your scene *with* the diffuse glow.

Now, Combine Everything

The final step, of course, is to combine all of these effects, or variations of them, to form a single, complex, and visually interesting effect. Like a master chef, you have seen the recipe, you have seen the steps to make your basic dish. Now it's your turn to throw caution to the wind and throw in a pinch of this and a teaspoon of that, taking what you've learned and following or disregarding the rules until it looks just right. Start off with the scene you began with, 06mem01.max, or see the finished effect in the file 06mem026.max.

1. **The Spotlight:** Take the current spotlight and place it at −150, −250, 90. Change its multiplier to 0.45.

2. **The Omni:** Create an omni at 30, 96, −45. Change its multiplier to 1.1. Change its color to RGB 255, 255, 255. Increase its contrast to 25. Increasing the contrast of your light basically makes the effect more localized. The lit area will be smaller but more intense, with a harsher change between the light and dark areas. You can help make this change less harsh by increasing the Soften Diffuse Edge value, but for this example, leave it at 50.

3. **Material:** Go into the Materials Editor. Use the "Baby Temp" material you currently have assigned.

4. **Bump Map:** In the Bump channel, place a Falloff map. Change its Type to Shadow/Light. Slot 1 should be black. Slot 2 should be a Cellular map. Make sure the Cellular map's size is five.

5. **Diffuse Map:** In the Diffuse channel, place a Noise map. To color the fetus, you're first going to place a base Noise map and then layer on top of that two layers of veins. (For more information on layering materials, see the Texture Layering tutorial also in this book.) The noise should be of type Regular with Size=10, Color 1=RGB 60, 48, 49, and Color 2=RGB 255, 187, 176. Now click the Type Noise button. Choose Mix and select Keep Old Map as Submap. Slot 1 should have your Noise map. Slot 2 should be empty. Change the color 2 to RBG 71, 57, 97. Change slot 3 to a Noise map. This noise should be of type Turbulence with High=0.2, Size=20, Phase=4, Color 1 pure white, and Color 2 pure

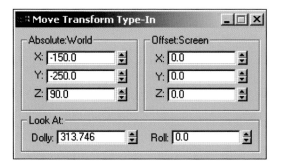

Use the Transform Type-In to place the spotlight at the proper location.

Your final diffuse map is a combination of three layers: a base Noise map, some blue veins, and some red veins.

black. Go up one level back to your Mix map. Click the Type button again, choose Mix again, and select Keep Old Map as Submap. Now you have a Mix map with slot 1 containing your original Mix. Slot 2 is empty. Change Color 2 to RGB 170, 77, 88. Change slot 3 to a Noise map. This noise should be of type Turbulence with High=0.2, Size=20, Color 1 pure white, and Color 2 pure black.

6　**Luminosity Map:** Place a Falloff map in Luminosity. Change its amount to 60. Change the second color swatch to RGB 255, 139, 26. Change its Mix Curve to look like this.

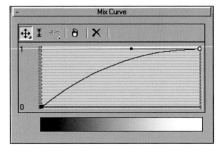

Change your Luminosity's Falloff map Mix Curve as shown here.

7　**Extra Lighting Map:** Place a Falloff map in Extra Lighting. Change the Falloff Type to Shadow/Light. The first slot is black. Change the second slot to a Noise map. This Noise map should be of type Regular with Size=30, High=0.85, and Low=0.3. The Mix Curve on your Falloff map should look like this.

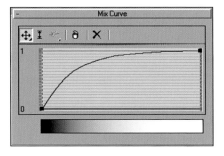

Change your Extra Lighting's Falloff map Mix Curve as shown here.

8　**Translucency Map:** Place a Falloff map in Translucency. Choose Perpendicular/Parallel. Color 1 is black. Color 2 is RGB 255, 152, 81. Change its Mix Curve to look like this.

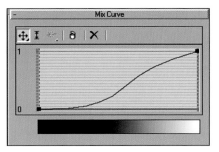

Change your Translucency's Falloff map Mix Curve as shown here.

9 **Fluorescence Map:** In the Fluorescence channel, place a Mix map. In Slot 1 of the Mix map, place a Falloff map. Make it Perpendicular/Parallel with black in Color 1 and white in Color 2. Change its Mix Curve to look like this figure.

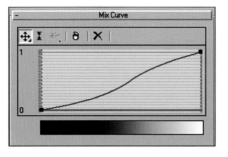

Change your Fluorescence's First Falloff map Mix Curve as shown here.

10 The second slot in your Mix map should be another Falloff map. Make it Perpendicular/Parallel with Color 1=RGB 255, 115, 0 and Color 2=black. Change its Mix Curve to look like this.

11 Back in your Mix map, set Mix Amount to 70%.

12 **The Diffuse Glow:** Go to Rendering, Effects. Click the Add button and add a Blur. Go to the Blur Type tab and change the Pixel Radius to 5%. Go to the Pixel Selections tab, uncheck Whole Image, check Luminance, change Brighten to 250%, Blend to 70%, Min to 78%, and Feather Radius to 15%.

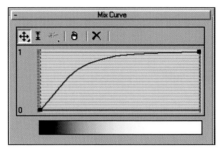

Change your Fluorescence's Second Falloff map Mix Curve as shown here.

13 **Here you go:** Render the camera view. Voilà! You have just performed a variety of lighting effects to help turn a regular mesh into something vibrant with color, contrast, and illumination values.

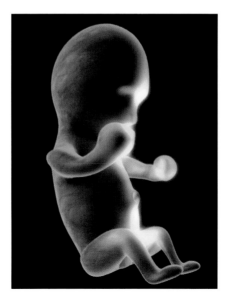

Render the camera view for the final effect.

Plug-Ins

Here are some plug-ins that can help you achieve different rim lighting effects:

- Instead of the maps listed here, you could substitute Blur's Side Fade and Shadow/Light maps for the Falloff map. These maps are available from http://www.blur.com/blurbeta. They do exactly the same thing as the falloffs, but with a slightly different interface. See which you like the most.

- Also, to create a diffuse glow, you could try the glow built into Real Lens Flare, part of the ProOpticSuite (POS) from Cebas (http://www.cebas.com). It has finer controls to help you achieve some really nice diffuse glows.

- If you do have POS, try using its built-in Fury maps—change their type to Electric and use that instead of the Turbulence Noise to make veins on your baby.

- You could also try running the Spectral Bloom script that ships with MAX 3.0. This script is written by Frank Delise, and it does the same thing as Blur, except with a different interface that makes the effect easier to achieve.

- Lastly, a post-process program such as Digital Fusion can be very useful in adding secondary effects like diffuse glows, and it provides a multitude of other image-tweaking features as well.

Variations

There are thousands of variations on this effect, depending on your scene. I use a diffuse glow in almost all my scenes. Rim lighting is used everywhere. Remember to play with the color of your rim lighting; white may not be the color you're looking for. The same goes for fill lighting; in fact, your fill light or lights should almost never be pure white.

- Contrasting colors and contrasting light and dark values are good things to do to create visual interest.

- Try combining fill lights and rim lights—just remember not to wash out your image with too much lighting.

- Also experiment with the Falloff map. It has many uses depending on which map you place it in. Try placing it in the Reflection slot, or try using some of the other falloff types such as Fresnel.

- Remember that good lighting is probably one of the most important elements in achieving a good image, certainly when trying to create a photoreal image. Dynamic lighting tricks like rim lighting should not be thrown aside as a special effect. To some degree, backlighting and rim lighting can and should be considered for most lighting situations.

EXPLOSION

"Should the whole frame of nature round him break,
In ruin and confusion hurled,
He, unconcerned, would hear the mighty crack,
And stand secure amidst a falling world."

—ADDISON

USING PARTICLE SYSTEMS, SPACE WARPS, AND PLUG-INS TO CREATE A REALISTIC EXPLOSION

One of the most common uses for computer graphics is the simulation of pyrotechnics, explosions, and destructive effects. The capability animation offers to fine-tune the pace of an explosion, the path of flying shrapnel, and the scorching aftereffects has obvious advantages over real-life pyrotechnics. In this tutorial, you will create an explosion with a glowing fireball, expanding fragments, and appropriate camera shake. You will also look at visually anticipating the explosion, as well as appreciating the atmosphere left in its wake.

PROJECT 7

EXPLOSION

BY SEAN BONNEY

GETTING STARTED

Although MAX has some great tools for simulating destruction, in this chapter
you will augment the default MAX toolset with several plug-ins:

- Particle Displace, from Peter Watje/Spectral Imaging. This modifier applies
  displacement mapping based on the proximity of particles.

- Particle Paint, from Peter Watje/Spectral Imaging. This material blends an
  object's texture based on the proximity of particles. Similar to the way you
  might use a can of spray paint, this plug-in allows you to color objects using
  particles.

- Solidify, from Andrey Zmievski/Terralux. This handy modifier adds thickness to geometry along face normals, essentially turning nonsolid faces into solid geometry.

In order to use these plug-ins, you must install them into your MAX Plug-ins subdirectory.

1   Before installing plug-ins, please exit MAX.

2   Copy the ppaint.dlt, pmod.dlm, and solidify.dlm plug-in files from the accompanying CD-ROM to the MAX Plug-ins subdirectory.

3   Copy the Explosion project map files from the accompanying CD-ROM to the MAX Maps subdirectory.

4   Start MAX and open the file 07mem01.max from this project's preload directory on the accompanying CD-ROM.

A simple indoor scene has been set up for you. A capsule sits in a sturdy bracket, ready to be blown up. The timeline for the explosion is as follows:

0–100	Anticipation
101–110	Explosion
111–200	Flying debris
201–300	Aftereffects

Note: For more information on these plug-ins, read the text files that accompany them or visit the authors' Web sites:

Peter Watje/Spectral Imaging: max3dstuff.com

Andrey Zmievski/Terralux: www.max3d.com/~terralux

Note: The Particle Displace modifier uses the same filename as another plug-in by the same author; specifically, the Deform Paint modifier. If you have already installed Deform Paint, simply place the new plug-in in another folder. To ensure that additional plug-in folders are recognized, open the text file "plugin.ini" in your MAX root directory and add a line to the [Directories] section, pointing to the appropriate folder.

PREPARING THE CAPSULE

Rather than blow up the entire object, you will carve out a section to destroy. Using two Boolean operations, you will divide the capsule into two halves.

1 In the top viewport, create a sphere at X=0, Y=0,
   Z=130, with the following parameters:

   Radius: 60
   Segments: 30

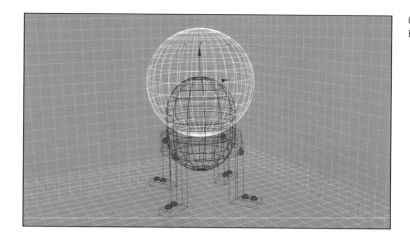

Create a sphere to use as a
Boolean operand.

2 To randomize this object, apply a Noise modifier
   with the following values:

   Noise
   Scale: 5

   Strength
   X: 25
   Y: 25
   Z: 25

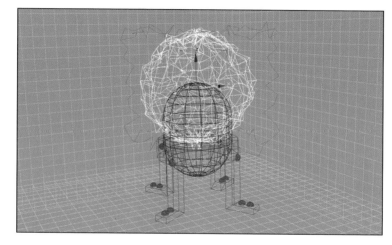

Apply Noise so the Boolean
operations will produce a
chaotic edge.

3 You will need this object for two Boolean operations,
   so Clone it using Copy as the method.

4 Leave the cloned sphere selected and create a
   Boolean compound object. Set the following values:

   Pick Boolean Mode: Copy

   Operation: Intersection

5 Click the Pick Operand B button and select the Capsule object. When the Inherit Material from New Operand? dialog box appears, click Yes. The resulting object represents the portion of the capsule that will be destroyed. Name this object capsule_top.

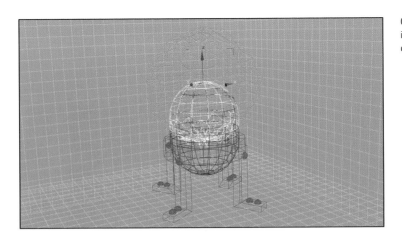

Create a Boolean object to intersect the top half of the capsule.

6 Apply an Edit Mesh modifier and go to Sub-Object, Polygon mode. By default, the faces of Operand B, the capsule, are selected. Invert the selection so only the faces representing the break are selected.

7 Delete these faces. When the Delete Isolated Vertices? dialog box appears, click Yes. Exit Sub-Object mode to continue.

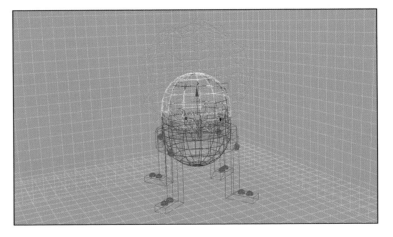

Invert the default face selection to the polygons along the break.

8 This will leave you with a non–solid object, which may cause problems later. Exit Sub-Object mode and apply a Solidify modifier with the following values:

Set Amount: −1

9 Select the Capsule object. Create a Boolean object using the following values:

Pick Boolean Mode: Move
Operation: Subtraction (A–B)

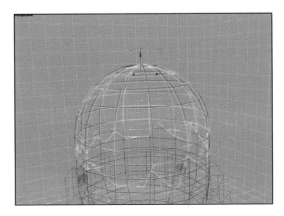

Use the Solidify modifier to convert to solid geometry (zoomed in for detail).

10 Click the Pick Operand B button and select the remaining sphere.

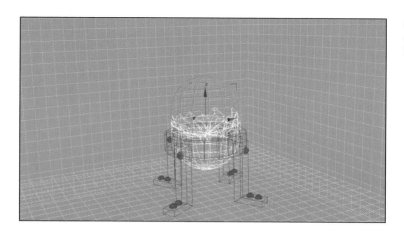

Create another Boolean object to produce the lower half of the capsule.

ANTICIPATING THE EXPLOSION

As you know from movies, before objects blow up, they strain and groan, quiver and crack. Not only do these effects serve to build tension, but they direct the viewer's gaze to the appropriate spot before the fireworks begin.

In this section, you will cause the gap between the top and bottom halves of the capsule to widen and quiver as the moment of detonation approaches.

1 Select the capsule_top object and apply a Skew modifier with the following values:

Skew Axis: X

Limit

Limit affection

Upper Limit: 0

Lower Limit: −40

Drag the Skew Amount slider to see how this modifier will cause a crack to appear where the two halves of the capsule join.

2 To create the base movement, set Amount=0 and turn on the Animate button.

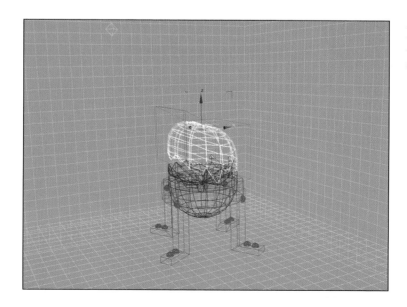

Apply a limited Skew modifier to create a gap between the two halves (shown here with Skew Amount=20).

3 Go to frame 100 and set Amount=10.

4 Go to frame 101 and set Amount=0. Turn the Animate button off.

5 The default controller applied to the Amount track will actually cause the crack to distort wildly. To correct this, right-click the capsule_top object and select TrackView selected. Expand Objects, capsule_top, Modified Object, Skew.

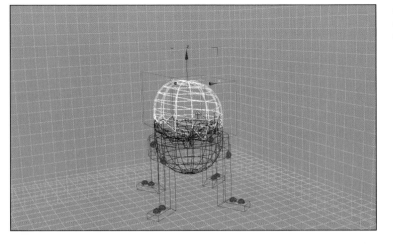

At frame 100, expand the crack to the maximum it will reach.

6 Select the Amount track and apply a Linear Float controller. This will result in the crack widening gradually over frames 0–100 and then disappearing at the moment of detonation.

7 Now you will add noise to this motion. Apply a Float List controller to the Amount track.

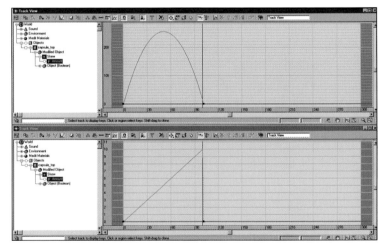

The Skew Amount track, before and after having a linear controller applied (shown in Function Curve mode).

8　Expand Amount and select the Available track. Note that the new track will not appear if you have checked Animated Tracks Only in the Filter dialog box. Apply a Noise Float controller. Right-click the Noise controller to open the properties dialog box and enter the following values:

Strength:　　5

Frequency:　　2

Ramp in:　　10

9　Close the Noise Controller properties dialog box and go to Edit Ranges mode.

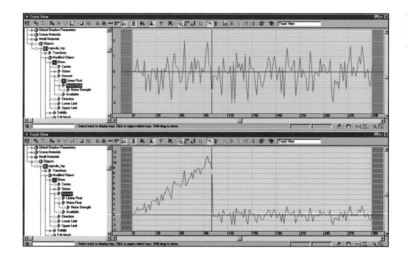

The Noise track as seen in Function Curve mode and its effect on the Amount track.

10　Select the node at the right end of the Noise Float track's range bar and drag it to frame 100 so noise will only be applied through frame 100.

Resize the track bar for the Noise controller to limit its effect to frames 0–100.

THE BLAST BUILDS

Now you will add a flickering light within the capsule. This light will be the source of a flickering volume light effect to simulate building energies escaping through the crack.

1　In the top viewport, create a Free Spotlight at X=12, Y=3, Z=90. Turn on Angle Snap and rotate the light −35 degrees on the View Y-Axis and 85 degrees on the View Y-Axis. Name this light spot_flicker. Set the following values for this light:

Color:　　(R=245, G=220, B=35)

Cast Shadows: On

Multiplier:　0

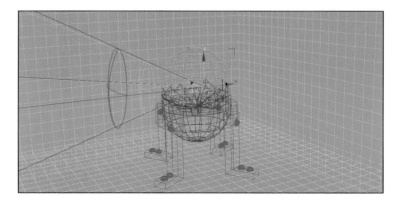

Create a spotlight to serve as a flickering source of escaping energy.

Attenuation Parameters		Shadow Parameters	
Far Attenuation		Type:	Shadow Map
Start:	75	**Shadow Map Params**	
End:	110	Bias:	0.1
Use:	On		

2 To make this light become brighter as the crack widens, turn the Animate button on, go to frame 100, and set Multiplier=1.5. Turn the Animate button off to continue.

3 Before adding volume to this light, scale it so its effect will only extend along the area of the crack. Select Non-Uniform Scale and scale the light 300% on the View Y-Axis and 60% on the View Z-Axis.

4 Go to the Atmospheres & Effects rollout, click the Add button, choose Volume Light, and click OK.

5 Select the Volume Light in the list and click Setup to open the Environment dialog box. Name this effect Volume Light Flicker. Go the Volume Light parameters and enter the following values:

Volume		Noise Threshold	
Density:	10	High:	0.8
Noise		Low:	0.1
Noise:	On	Levels:	4
Amount:	0.5	Size:	10
Link to Light:	On	Wind Strength:	100
Type:	Turbulence	Wind from the:	Back

6 The Wind portion of this effect will not be active unless the Phase is animated. Turn the Animate button on, go to frame 300, and set Phase=30. Turn the Animate button off to continue.

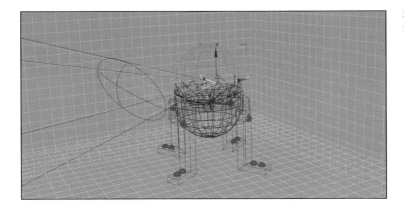

Scaling the light also scales the attenuated cone of effect.

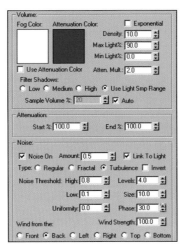

Set the Volume Light parameters.

7   To provide a general increase in scene lighting from this buildup of energies, create an Omni light at X=0, Y=0, Z=92. Name this light omni_heat. Set the following values for this light:

Color: (R=250, G=225, B=75)
Cast Shadows: Off
Multiplier: 0

Attenuation Parameters
Far Attenuation
Start: 112
End: 330
Use: On

8   Go to frame 100, turn the Animate button on, and set Multiplier=2. Turn the Animate button off to continue.

9   Before this light parameter will ramp smoothly, the controller must be changed. Go to TrackView, expand objects, omni_heat, Object.

10 Assign a Linear Float controller to the Multiplier track.

Create an Omni light to control scene lighting from the energy buildup and explosion.

DETONATION: EXPLODING DEBRIS

In the next few sections, you will create the actual explosion—both the flying debris and the pyrotechnics.

Two MAX features, the PArray particle system and the PBomb Space Warp, work very well together for exploding object geometry. PArray can be linked to an object to emit fragments of that object's geometry as particles. PBomb handles the timing, force, and direction of the explosion.

1   Create a PArray particle system. The position and orientation of the PArray gizmo have no bearing on its function.

2   Click the Pick Object button and choose the capsule_top object.

3   Set the following values for this particle system:

Basic Parameters

Viewport Display: Mesh

Particle Generation

Particle Timing

Emit Start: 100

Display Until: 300

Life: 300

Particle Type

Particle Types: Object Fragments

Object Fragment Controls

Thickness: 3

Number of Chunks: On

Minimum: 60

Get Material From: Picked Emitter

4   Click Get Material From to activate the material selection.

5   Go to the Rotation and Collision rollout. This section controls the spinning of the fragments. Turn the Animate button on, go to frame 100, and set Spin Time: 20

6   Go to frame 140 and set Spin Time=100.

7   Go to frame 150 and set Spin Time=999, effectively bringing the rotation to an end. Turn the Animate button off to continue.

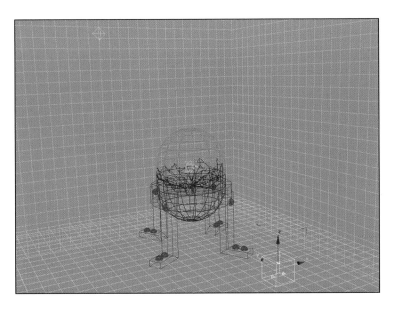

Create a PArray particle system to break the capsule_top object into fragments.

The PArray emitter converts the distribution object into object fragments (shown at frame 103).

101

8 Create a PBomb Space Warp at X=−42, Y=−7, Z=60. The position of the Space Warp determines the origin of the exploding force. In this case, placing the gizmo near the center of the crack will imply that the explosion is initiated in that area.

9 Set the following values for this Space Warp:

Explosion Parameters

Start Time: 100

Strength: 2

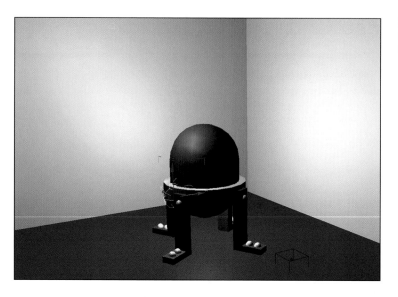

Create a PBomb Space Warp to provide a source for the exploding force.

10 Select the Bind to Space Warp tool and drag from the PBomb Space Warp to the PArray particle system. Scrub the Time Slider around frame 100 to see the capsule_top object explode away from the PBomb Space Warp.

The left figure shows the exploding fragments at frame 105 before they are bound to the PBomb Space Warp. The right figure shows how the PBomb Warp explodes the fragments away from the PBomb gizmo.

HIDING THE ORIGINAL

Note that the original object remains after the explosion. The PArray particle system is using the object to determine the shape of emitted objects, but is not actually replacing the original.

The visibility of the capsule_top object must be animated so it will not appear in the scene after the moment of detonation.

1 Select and right-click capsule_top and choose TrackView Selected. Expand Objects, capsule_top.

2 Select the capsule_top object and click the Add Visibility Track button. Note you must be in Edit Keys mode to do this.

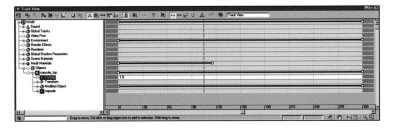

Add a Visibility track to make the original capsule top disappear when the explosion begins.

3 Select the new Visibility track and click the Add Keys button. Click at frames 0 and 100 to add keys. Right-click in the TrackView window to exit Add Keys mode. If you cannot precisely place the key, its timing can be corrected in the next step.

Add a Visibility track and create keys at frames 0 and 100 to control when the object becomes invisible.

4 Right-click the key near frame 0 to open its properties dialog box. Set the following values for this key:

Time: 0
Value: 1
Out Tangent Type: Step

5 Right-click the key near frame 100 and set the following values for this key:

Time: 100
Value: 0

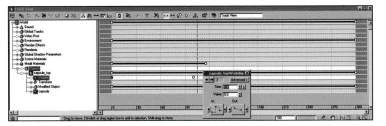

Edit the Visibility keys to make the capsule top disappear beginning with frame 100.

103

Explosion Pyrotechnics: Fireball

In this section, you will create a visible fireball, flaring light, and shower of sparks to accompany the geometric explosion.

1　Create a spherical atmospheric apparatus at X=–4, Y=2, Z=100, with Radius=60.

2　Add a Combustion effect to this apparatus using the controls in the Atmospheres rollout.

3　Go to the Environment dialog box and set the following values for this Combustion effect:

Colors

Inner Color:　(R=255, G=235, B=105)

Outer Color:　(R=235, G=135, B=30)

Shape

Regularity:　0.5

Characteristics

Flame Size:　20

Samples:　10

Explosion

Explosion:　On

Fury:　3

The progression of the explosion is controlled by the Phase value. The Setup Explosion dialog box will set keyframes to achieve the timing you desire.

4　Click the Setup Explosion button and enter the following values:

Start Time:　95

End Time:　150

5　Click OK to continue.

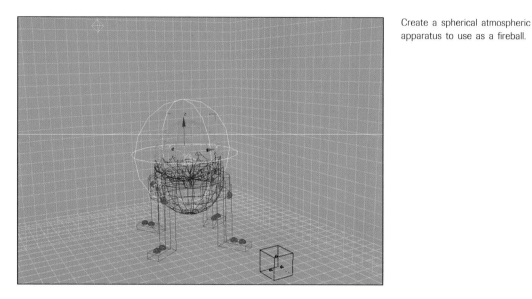

Create a spherical atmospheric apparatus to use as a fireball.

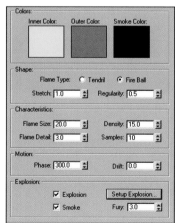

Set the Combustion parameters for the sphere gizmo.

6 Name this effect Combustion Explosion.

Use the Setup Explosion dialog box to time this fireball (shown at frame 105).

EXPLOSION PYROTECHNICS: FLARING LIGHT

Now you will animate the spot_flicker light to flare and expand as the explosion occurs.

1 Select the spot_flicker light. Turn on the Animate button.

2 Go to frame 100 and set rotation and scale keys, either by right-clicking the Time Slider and checking only Rotation and Scale, or by clicking the Create Key=Rotation and Scale buttons in the Motion panel.

3 Set the following values for this light:

Spotlight Parameters

Hot Spot: 50
Falloff: 65

Attenuation Parameters

Far Attenuation

Start: 80
End: 120

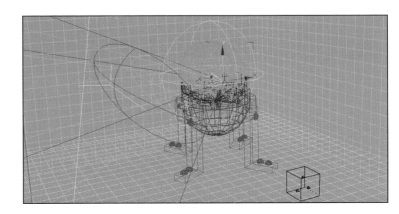

Increase the Hot Spot, Falloff, and Far Attenuation values to make this light expand with the explosion.

105

4　Go to frame 103 and scale the light 300% on the View Z-Axis.

5　Rotate the light 65 degrees on the Local Y-Axis.

6　Set the following values for this light:

Spotlight Parameters

Hot Spot:　　80
Falloff:　　　170

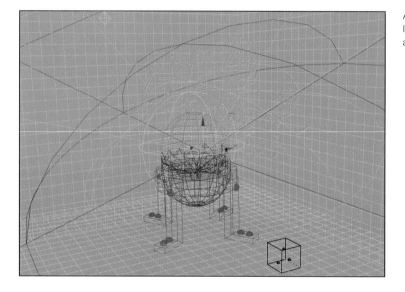

At frame 103, expand the light so it becomes more like an area effect.

7　Go to frame 108 and set the following values:

Multiplier:　　0

Attenuation Parameters

Far Attenuation
Start:　　　35
End:　　　　50

8　Before these light parameters will ramp smoothly, their controllers must be changed. Go to TrackView, expand Objects, spot_flicker, Object.

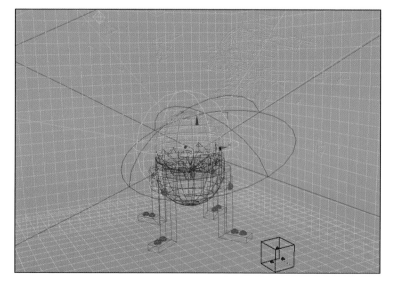

At frame 108, shrink the light and reduce its Multiplier to deactivate the effect.

9 Assign Linear Float controllers to the following tracks:

Multiplier

Hot Spot

Falloff

Attenuation Far Start

Attenuation Far End

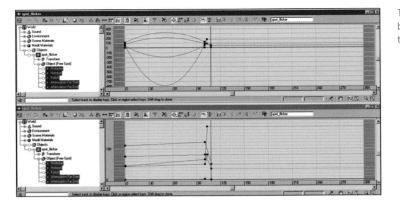

The spot_flicker light's tracks, before and after converting to linear controllers.

EXPLOSION PYROTECHNICS: EXPANDING LIGHT

1 To ramp up the general light level emanating from the blast, select the omni_heat light. Go to frame 104 and set Multiplier=4.

Increase the omni_heat light's Multiplier to reflect the intense energy of the blast.

2 Go to frame 114 and set Multiplier = 1.25. Turn the Animate button off to continue.

Reduce the light's intensity as the explosion fades.

EXPLOSION PYROTECHNICS: SPARKS

The shower of sparks produced by this explosion will be the result of a SuperSpray particle system, keyed to swing with the light flare at the moment of detonation.

1 In the top viewport, create a SuperSpray particle system at X=0, Y=0, Z=75. Set the following values for this emitter:

Basic Parameters		Particle Timing	
Particle Formation		Emit Start:	100
Off Axis		Emit Stop:	115
Spread:	40	Display Until:	300
		Life:	30
Off Plane		Variation:	20
Spread:	70		
Viewport Display:	Mesh	**Particle Size**	
Percentage of Particles:	100	Size:	5
		Variation:	20
Particle Generation			
Particle Motion			
Variation:	30		

Create a SuperSpray emitter to throw off sparks (shown at frame 115).

Particle Type

Standard Particles: Tetra

Rotation and Collision

Spin Speed Controls

Spin Time: 5

Variation: 30

Spin Axis Controls: Direction of Travel/Mblur

Stretch: 7

2 Open the Material Editor and assign the Sparks material to this particle system.

3 Turn the Animate button on, go to frame 100, and rotate the emitter −30 degrees on the View Y-Axis.

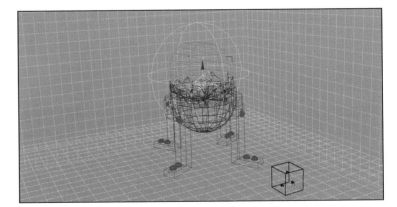

Rotate the emitter towards the crack at the start of the detonation.

4 Go to frame 115 and rotate the emitter 60 degrees on the View Y-Axis. Turn off the Animate button.

Rotate the emitter to follow the path of the explosion. Note how the particles trail behind.

DEBRIS COLLISION

Up to this point, particles have been allowed to pass through the walls and floor in this scene. Now you will set up some deflectors and a Gravity Space Warp to force the particles to behave more realistically.

1 First, you will create a deflector for the floor. In the top viewport, create a POmniFlect Space Warp at X=−130, Y=−130, Z=0. Set the following values for this object:

Timing

Time On: 0

Time Off: 300

Reflection

Bounce: 0.25

Variation: 15

Chaos: 15

Display Icon

Width: 600

Height: 600

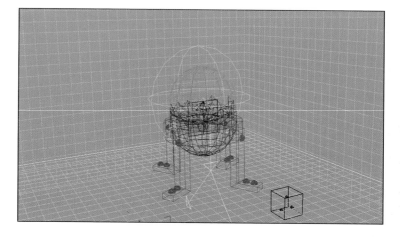

Create a deflector to keep particles from passing through the floor.

2 Clone this Space Warp, using Copy as the method. Go to a top viewport. Turn on Angle Snap and rotate the new deflector 90 degrees on the View Y-Axis. Move this object to X=170, Y=−130, Z=280. Set Bounce=0.7.

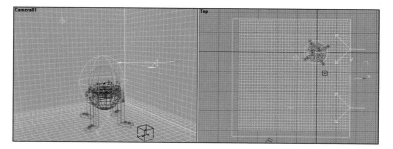

Clone this deflector to place behind one wall.

3 Clone this Space Warp. Rotate the new deflector 90 degrees on the View Z-Axis. Move this object to X=−130, Y=170, Z=280.

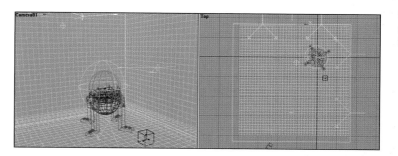

Create another cloned deflector to place behind the remaining wall.

4 In the top viewport, create a Gravity Space Warp. Set Strength=0.25.

5 Go to the camera viewport. Select the PArray particle system.

6 Select the Bind to Space Warp tool. Open the Select Objects dialog box (now labeled Select Space Warp).

7 Select the Gravity Space Warp and click Bind.

8 Select the first POmniFlect Space Warp and click Bind.

9 Select the second POmniFlect Space Warp and click Bind.

10 Select the third POmniFlect Space Warp and click Bind. Take care *not* to bind to the PBomb Space Warp.

11 Select the Pick tool and choose the SuperSpray particle system.

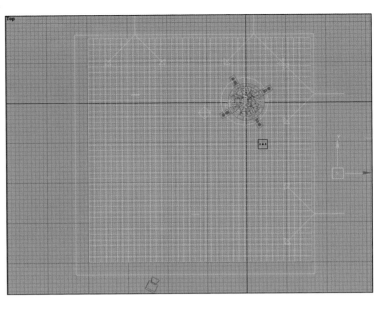

Create a Gravity Space Warp to pull shrapnel and sparks to the floor.

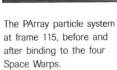

The PArray particle system at frame 115, before and after binding to the four Space Warps.

12 Repeat steps 6–10 for the SuperSpray particle system. Now both particle systems will be affected by the three deflectors and the gravity field.

The SuperSpray particle system at frame 115, before and after being bound to the four Space Warps. Note that the Gravity Space Warp is having the primary effect at this point.

AFTEREFFECTS

The aftereffects of an explosion like this might include dents and scorch marks on the walls and floor, fading light, and rising steam or smoke from the exploded object.

In this section, you will displace the wall geometry and add scorch marks to the walls and floor, using two of the plug-ins you installed earlier.

1 Select the Wall object and apply a Particle Displace modifier. This modifier displaces geometry in real time using the proximity of particles emitted from a chosen emitter. Set the following values for this modifier:

Parameters

Strength:	65
Effect Rad:	20
Remember Effect:	On
Effect Along Velocity:	On
Falloff:	Linear

Note that the Wall object is a medium–density mesh. The higher the mesh density, the more accurate the displacement will be.

2   Click the button labeled –None– and choose the PArray particle system from the dialog box that appears.

3   When using the Particle Displace modifier for impact marks, keep in mind that the plug-in makes no distinction between particles impacting the modified mesh at an acute angle and those moving parallel to its surface. This can cause some strange result as falling particles "drag" the displaced surface behind them. To avoid this, animate the Strength parameter.

Apply the Particle Displace modifier to displace the wall mesh using particles.

4   Turn on the Animate button, go to frame 115, and set another Strength=65 key. The easiest way to do this is to change the Strength value and then change it back.

Note: You must be aware of an important consideration: Viewport display can be erratic with this plug-in. The only reliable way to achieve accurate viewport displays of this effect is to begin at frame 0 and step through the animation.

Likewise, before rendering a still or animation, it is recommended that you return to frame 0.

5   Go to frame 116 and set Strength=0. Turn the Animate button off to continue.

6   For this parameter to ramp smoothly, the controller must be changed. Go to TrackView, expand Objects, Walls, Modified Object, Particle Displace, Falloff.

7   Assign a Linear Float controller to the Falloff track.

Reduce the strength of the Particle Displace modifier to 0 at frame 116 to end the displacing effect.

113

8 To account for the distortion caused by the Particle
Displace modifier, apply a Smooth modifier to the
Walls object, using the following settings:

AutoSmooth: On
Threshold: 20

Note that the purpose of this modifier is to remove excess
smoothing from the surface. Recalculating the smoothing
groups after the mesh has been displaced will enhance the
effect by creating sharp edges around the impacted areas.

Apply a Smooth modifier to
recalculate smoothing after
Particle Displacement.

IMPACT BY MAPPING

1 Open the Material Editor and create a new material.
In the New section of the Material/Map Browser,
select Particle Paint Material. Name this material
walls_impact.

2 Apply this material to the Walls object. Set the
following values for this material:

Mixing Curve

Persistence: 300
Effect Size: 25
Localize Paint Material: On
Y: On
Hose Paint: On

3 Click the Base Material button, choose Browse
From: Mtl Editor, and select the Walls material.
Choose Instance as the method. Go back to the
walls_impact material.

Create a new material of the
type Particle Paint.

4   Click the Paint Material button and select the Scorch material. Choose Instance as the method. Go back to the walls_impact material.

5   Click the button under the two material slots and choose the PArray particle system.

6   Create another Particle Paint material. Name it floor_impact. Apply this material to the Floor object. Set the following values for this material:

Mixing Curve

Persistance:	300
Effect Size:	15
Localize Paint Material:	On
Y:	On
Hose Paint:	On

7   Click the Base Material button, choose Browse From: Mtl Editor, and select the Floor material. Choose Instance as the method.

8   Click the Paint Material button and select the Scorch material. Choose Instance as the method.

9   Click the button under the two material slots and choose the PArray particle system.

Similar to the functioning of the Particle Displace modifier, the Particle Paint material is activated by proximity, not impact, so falling particles will "paint" impact marks as they fall. To work around this, you will animate the Effect Size value and "scorch" material Opacity maps.

10 Turn the Animate button on and go to frame 100. Set Effect Size=14. Note that the Effect value will *not* be highlighted in red at keyframes, as with other keyframed variables, but the key has been set.

The two materials that will be blended by the Particle Paint material for the walls, Walls and Scorch.

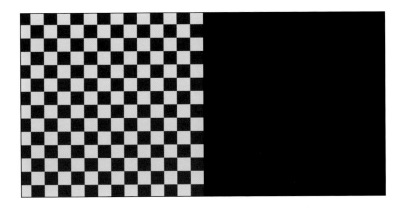

The two materials that will be blended by the Particle Paint material for the floor, Floor and Scorch.

11 Go down to the Scorch Opacity map in any instanced map (either Particle Paint material or the original material). Go to the Output rollout and set Output Amount=0.35.

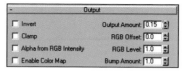

Animate the Output Amount in the Output rollout.

12 Go to frame 115 and set Output Amount=0.15.

13 Go up to the floor_impact material and set Effect Size=4. Turn the Animate button off.

FADING ENERGY

In this section, you will cause the heat energy being given off by the blast to fade away and provide visual evidence of this energy with a volume light effect.

1 Select the omni_heat light. Add a volume light effect to this light with the following values:

Volume		Noise Threshold	
Density:	0	High:	0.55
Attenuation		Low:	0.4
End%:	5	Uniformity:	0.5
Noise		Size:	25
Noise:	On		
Amount:	0.5		
Type:	Turbulence		

2 Name this effect Volume Light Heat.

3 Turn the Animate button on, go to frame 100, and set End%=17, Density=2.

4 Go to frame 125, set End%=20, Density=1.75.

5 Go to frame 250, set End%=10, Density=1.5, and the light's Multiplier=1.0.

6 Go to frame 300, set End%=7.5, and Phase=50. Turn the Animate button off.

Create a volume light effect to simulate an expanding shell of fading energy (shown at frame 100).

7   Go to TrackView, expand Environment, Volume Light Heat, and assign a Linear Float controller to the Density and Atten. End% tracks.

8   To add some random flicker to this light, remain in TrackView, expand Objects, omni_heat, Object, and select the Multiplier track.

9   Apply a Float List controller. Expand Multiplier and select the Available track. Note that this track will not be visible if you have checked Animated Tracks Only in the Filters dialog box.

10 Apply a Noise Float controller. Right-click the Noise Float controller to open the properties dialog box and enter the following values:

Frequency: 3
Strength: 0.7

11 Turn the Animate button on and go to frame 105. Set Strength=2.

12 Go to frame 300 and set Strength=0.2. Turn the Animate button off to continue.

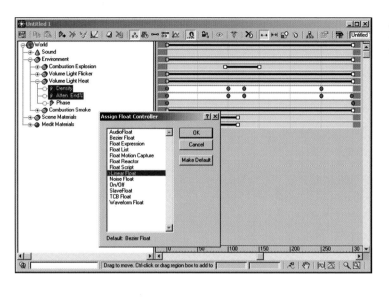

Assign a Linear Float controller to the Density and Atten. End% tracks.

RISING SMOKE

The final atmosphere to add to this scene is a column of rising smoke.

1   In the top viewport, create a spherical atmospheric apparatus at X=0, Y=0, Z=70. Set the following parameters for this gizmo:

Radius: 20
Hemisphere: On

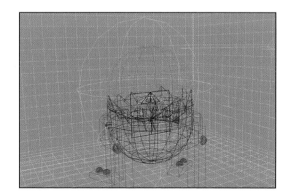

Create a hemispherical atmospheric apparatus to produce a column of smoke (zoomed in for detail).

2 Add a combustion effect, go to the setup for it, and name this effect Combustion Smoke. Set the following values for this effect:

Colors

Inner Color: (R=200, G=215, B=230)

Outer Color: (R=60, G=65, B=85)

Shape		**Characteristics**	
Flame Type:	Tendril	Flame Size:	5
Stretch:	5	Density:	0
Regularity:	0	Samples:	8

Motion

Drift: 1

3 Turn the Animate button on, go to frame 120, and set Regularity=0.3.

4 Set another Density=0 key to maintain this value.

5 Set a Scale key for the atmospheric apparatus.

6 Set another Radius=20 key for the apparatus.

7 Go to frame 250, set Regularity=0.8 and Density=10.

8 Scale the apparatus to 650% on the View Z-Axis.

9 Set Radius=35 for the apparatus.

10 Go to frame 300 and set Phase=1750.

11 Scale the apparatus 150% on the View Z-Axis.

12 Set Radius=38 for the apparatus.

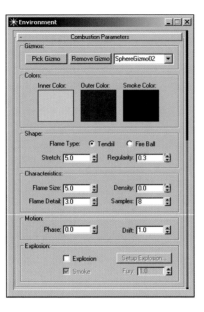

Set up the animation and parameters for the smoke.

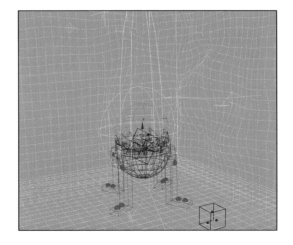

Key the apparatus to grow as the smoke rises.

CAMERA SHAKE

Now you will "shake" the camera to show reaction to the explosion.

1   Select the camera (this can be done from the camera
     viewport by right-clicking the Viewport label and
     choosing Select Camera).

2   Set Position keys at frames 98 and 105.

3   To add the main jolt caused by the explosion, go to
     frame 101, go to a left viewport, and move the
     camera approximately 20 units on the View Y-Axis.

4   Go to TrackView and expand Objects, Camera01,
     Transform. Select the Position track and apply a
     Position List controller.

5   Expand Position List and select the Available track.
     Apply a Noise Position controller.

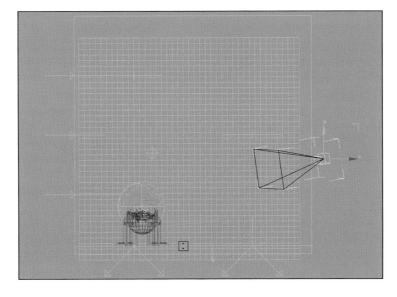

Add a manual camera move
at the moment of detonation.

6   Go to Edit Ranges mode and move the beginning
     node for this range to frame 80 and the ending node
     to frame 225.

7   Go to Edit Keys mode and right-click the Noise
     Position track to open its properties dialog box. Go
     to frame 0 and enter the following values:

     X Strength: 5
     Y Strength: 5
     Z Strength: 5

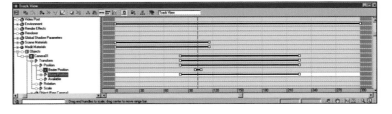

Scale the position range for
the Noise track so it will only
be in effect around the time
of the explosion.

8 Go to frame 100 and set the following values:

X Strength: 8
Y Strength: 8
Z Strength: 8

9 Go to frame 110 and set the following values:

X Strength: 3
Y Strength: 3
Z Strength: 3

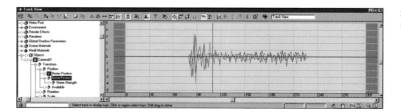

Set Strength keys to control the degree of noise applied.

10 Close the Noise Position properties dialog box.

11 Expand Noise Position and select the Noise Strength track. Apply a Point3 XYZ controller.

12 Expand Point3 XYZ, select all three tracks (X, Y, and Z), and apply Linear Float controllers.

The camera's position track. Note how small amounts of Noise are being applied up to and following the moment of detonation.

PLUG-INS

Many quality plug-ins for creating and enhancing pyrotechnic effects in MAX exist.

Some commercial plug-ins are:

- Atomizer ($95), from Digimation. Allows any 3D Studio MAX particle system to use any 3D Studio MAX object as a particle object.

- Fractal Flow MAX ($395), from Digimation. Uses fractal-based technology to distort an image or specific parts of an image. Create fire, heat waves, smoke, and more.

- Lightning ($95), from Digimation. Creates procedural lightning and electrical effects.

- Pandora ($150), from Digimation. Particles can change properties over time and be emitted from spheres and splines. Included are several new Space Warps.

- Particle Studio ($595), from Digimation. Control particles with unique particle events. Also includes solid assembly and disassembly of objects, realistic flocking and swarming, particles targets, particle spawning, and dynamic materials.

- Spray Master ($95), from Digimation. Allows the user to spray geometry, both 2D and 3D, as particles on or around other objects with an easy-to-use freehand brush.

- UltraShock ($295), from Digimation. Gives particles volumetric effects to simulate realistic clouds, sparks, fire, plasma, and more.

For more information on Digimation plug-ins, see their site: http://digimation.com/.

Several great free or shareware plug-ins can assist with this effect as well. Note that free or shareware plug-ins often represent side-projects or hobbies for their developers, and as such, are not always entirely stable.

- BlurFire, from Blur Studios. Enhanced fire combustion effects.

- BlurDeflector, from Blur Studios. A deflector with variable speeds.

- BlurPartForce, from Blur Studios. Includes two particle warps—BlurWind and RandomWalk.

- Chase Gravity, from Peter Watje/Spectral Imaging. A Space Warp that causes particles to chase the Space Warp or chase the vertices of another object.

- Deflector +, from Peter Watje/Spectral Imaging. Supports friction, energy transfer, and affects stationary particles.

- Firestorm, from Blur Studios. Atmospheric effect that supports multiple apparatus types, texture mapping, backlight scattering, particles, and volume scattering.

- Free Pyro, from Cebas. Enhanced volumetrics.

- Maelstrom, from Blur Studios. Space Warp that creates a whirlpool effect.

- Object Combustion, from Peter Watje/Spectral Imaging. Use any MAX object as a combustion apparatus.

- Particle Combustion, from Peter Watje/Spectral Imaging. Use particles as combustion apparatuses.

- Particle Gravity, from Peter Watje/Spectral Imaging. A Space Warp that allows for interparticle attraction and repulsion.

- Particle Spline, from Peter Watje/Spectral Imaging. Connects all particles with splines.

- Particles + 2.0, from Peter Watje/Spectral Imaging. Adds new particle types, emitter shapes, a particle position dump, and stream velocity and motion.

- Vertex Combustion, from Peter Watje/Spectral Imaging. Uses the vertices of mesh geometry as combustion apparatuses.

A nearly complete list of free and shareware MAX plug-ins is available at the Virtual Republic Boboland site at http://gfxcentral.com/bobo/. For more information on Blur Studios plug-ins, visit the Blur Beta R&D Project site at http://www.blur.com/blurbeta/.

VARIATIONS

The explosion techniques explored in this chapter could be elaborated on in a variety of ways:

- Shadow-casting atmospheres are new to MAX 3 and would allow for some very dramatic shadows if a strong light source were placed in front of an explosion.

- Use Dynamics, instead of deflectors and Space Warps, to direct the path of flying shrapnel. This is a more time-consuming process, but sure to enhance the bouncing motion of high-velocity fragments.

- More realistic fracturing effects (used in the anticipation sequence) could be achieved using the Morpher modifier to model cracks.

- Try customizing the Combustion explosion by setting Phase keys. The duration of the burn and smoke cycles can be as long or as energetic as you like.

The PArray particle system has several options not explored in this chapter that could prove useful:

- Any particle type can be emitted from a PArray system. Use this feature to emit particles such as escaping energy or steam from the surface of an object.

- Multi/Subobject materials can be used to apply up to three materials to the different sides of object fragments.

- Enable Interparticle Collisions to keep object fragments from intersecting one another. This could be a valuable feature for slow-motion explosions, where object penetration would be especially noticeable. Note that this form of collision detection does not take the dimensions of instanced or fragment geometry into account, so it is only recommended for Standard particle types.

Using complex objects with PArray can result in slow screen refreshes. Consider using a low-polygon version of the distribution object until you are ready to render.

These techniques could be put to use with moving objects such as spaceships or other vehicles. Simply parent the various components to a master dummy, animate its position, and use particle emitters to trail smoke or vapor.

If you need to create an explosion in a scene already populated with figures or props, consider simulating a shockwave effect. The new RingWave object would make a good visual effect, whereas a short duration Push Space Warp could provide the burst of momentum to impact objects. If other particles are in the scene to be affected, a PBomb Space Warp could be used, perhaps with a cylindrical blast Symmetry and decayed range.

AUTOMATED DUST TRAILS

"I have noted in a Manchester newspaper…
that I have proved 'might is right' and
therefore that Napoleon is right and every
cheating tradesman is also right.

—CHARLES DARWIN, IN A LETTER TO LYELL, 1860

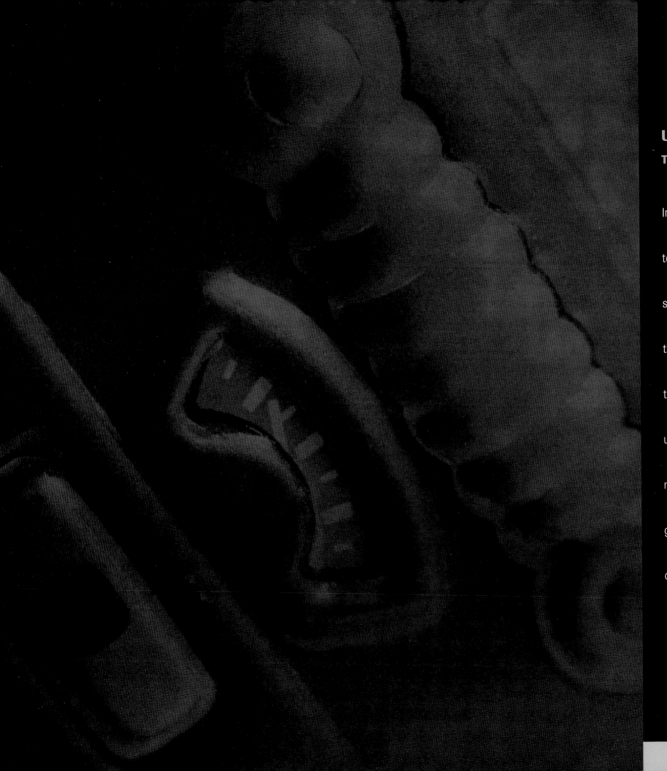

USING SUPERSPRAY PARTICLE SYSTEMS TO SIMULATE A DUST TRAIL

In this example, you'll use a simple expression to control particles emitted from a vehicle to simulate dust trails. The expression will drive the particle birthrate and speed depending on the vehicle's velocity. This technique is very useful because it allows you to simply automate particle generation and, in the long run, gives you more time to work on the animation of the vehicle.

AUTOMATED DUST TRAILS

BY BRANDON DAVIS

GETTING STARTED

In many cases, keyframing objects or their parameters is sufficient to accomplish an animation task. There are times, however, when automating certain functions can save time or add flexibility to the animation process. Imagine having the task of animating this scene: A military vehicle is supposed to cruise around a desert set. The requirements are that the vehicle move a certain way and realistic dust be kicked up from the tires accordingly. Suppose you animate it the old-fashioned way by keyframing the vehicle and then matching the particle systems to the motion of the vehicle. That's fine, but what if the task is suddenly altered, as they often are, causing your particle animation to be thrown out? You could set up a series of expressions to automate the particle motion. This would give you the flexibility to animate the vehicle however you want, change it, and change it again. Throughout this task, your particle animation is

automated and driven by the changes you make to the vehicle animation. This is the power of procedural animation.

Expressions are a great automation tool, allowing you to define a value for a parameter by referencing other parameters in the scene and adjusting them in mathematical expressions. Sound complex? It really isn't, and it doesn't take a whole lot of math ability to make use of expressions in MAX. Of course, having some basic understanding of math can't hurt.

In this exercise, you'll take the existing animation of the military vehicle, add SuperSpray particle systems to the rear wheels, and use expression controllers to automate the Birth Rate and Speed values of the particle systems.

Load the 08mem01.max file from the project's pre-load folder on the accompanying CD-ROM.

You should have a 150-frame animation of a crude fighting vehicle that speeds up and slows down as it moves about a desert landscape.

Load the 08mem01.max file. You'll see a crude military vehicle ready to tear up the desert.

CREATING AND ALIGNING THE EMITTERS

In this section, you'll create a pair of SuperSpray particle systems and align them to the rear tires of the vehicle.

1   In the Create panel, select Particle Systems and choose SuperSpray.

2   In the top viewport, click and drag to create a SuperSpray emitter.

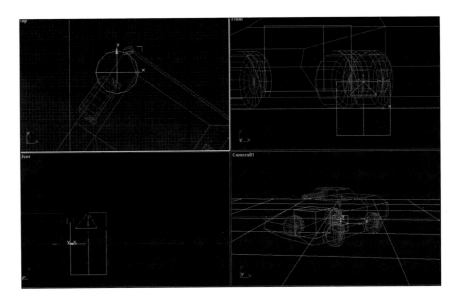

Create a SuperSpray particle system and align it to the rear of TireRearRight object.

127

3   Right-click the newly created emitter and choose
    Move from the right-click menu. This activates the
    Move tool.

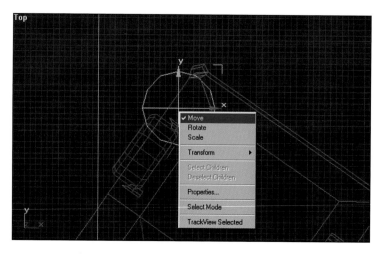

Activate the Move tool by
right-clicking the emitter.

4   Move the SuperSpray emitter to the rear of the
    TireRearRight object. Because it was created in the
    top viewport, the SuperSpray emitter should already
    be level with the ground object at zero on the
    Z-Axis.

5   Right-click the SuperSpray emitter again and choose
    Rotate from the menu.

6   Choose Local from the coordinate system dropdown
    in the Main toolbar (to the immediate right of the
    Scale icon). This will allow you to rotate on the
    object's axis, not the world or view axis.

Select the Local coordinate
system from the dropdown box.

7   Rotate the SuperSpray emitter on its X-Axis roughly
    20 degrees downward. The intention here is to point
    the particle emission out and away from the vehicle
    a bit.

8   Select the Select and Link button and link the
    SuperSpray to the Vehicle object by click-dragging
    to the Vehicle.

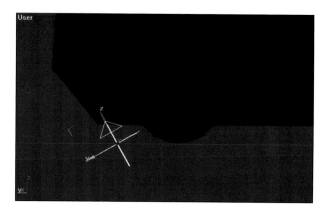

Rotate the emitter so it
points upwards and away
from the tire to the rear.

SETTING SUPERSPRAY PARAMETERS

In this section, you'll set up the basic parameters for the SuperSpray particles.

With the SuperSpray emitter selected, go to the Modify panel to access its parameters. Set them as follows:

Off Axis Spread:	60 degrees
Off Plane Spread:	180 degrees
Speed Variation:	25%
Emit Stop:	150
Display Until:	150
Life:	30
Size:	5
Size Variation:	25%
Standard Particle Type:	Facing
Object Motion Inheritance Multiplier:	0.5

The Off Axis and Off Plane controls are used to aim the particle emission in a given direction without reorienting the emitter object. In this case, you can just leave these values at zero, allowing for the more visually intuitive approach of actually pointing the emitter in the direction it should emit in. Even with the Axis and Plane values at zero, you should set their Spread values (which work independently) to positive values. This will cause the particle stream to be more conical or fan-like. The variation parameters are important so the effect is less uniform, more random, and therefore more realistic. Object motion inheritance will control how much velocity the particles receive from the emitter at birth. In this example, you'll want the particles to leave a trail behind the vehicle and not follow it every step of the way. However, to make it more realistic, you need to add a little bit of inheritance. This is consistent with the behavior of a dust trail of an actual non-streamlined vehicle in motion where the pressure in the rear is less.

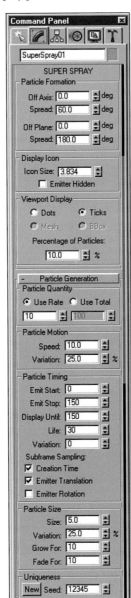

Set the SuperSpray parameters as follows.

SETTING UP THE EXPRESSION

In this section, you'll access the SuperSpray parameters in TrackView, namely Birth Rate and Speed, and assign an expression to them.

1   Select the SuperSpray and right-click to access the right-click menu. Choose TrackView Selected from the menu. This automatically opens a TrackView window and jumps to the selected object.

2   Click the plus button to the left of the SuperSpray object in TrackView to expand the tracks.

3   Click the plus button to the left of the Object (SuperSpray) track. This will reveal all of the tracks associated with SuperSpray parameters.

4   Select the Speed track. Using the Assign Controller button, assign a Float expression.

5   Right-click the Speed track and choose Properties. This will bring up the Expression Controller.

6   Create a vector variable by selecting the Vector radio button and typing V in the Name slot. Click Create. You've now created a vector variable called V, and it appears in the Vectors list. You must use a vector variable instead of a scalar because you will be dealing with position information, which is stored in an array (X,Y,Z) and not a single value.

7   Repeat step 6, except name the second variable V2. You should now have two variables in the Vectors list—V and V2.

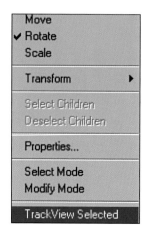

Choose TrackView Selected from the right-click menu.

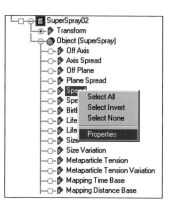

Right-click the Speed track to access the Expression Controller via the properties command.

130

8 In the Vectors list, select V. Click the Assign to Controller button below. In the Track View Pick dialog box, expand the Vehicle track so you can select its Position track. This now assigns vector variable V to the position track of the Vehicle object.

9 Repeat step 8 with the V2 variable.

10 With the V2 variable selected, set the Tick Offset to –150 in the Variable Parameters group. Though both V and V2 reference the same position track, setting the tick offset to –150 tells V2 to reference the track one frame back in time.

11 In the Expression window, type the following expression:

length(V–V2)/4

This uses the length function to determine the distance between the Vehicle object at one frame and one frame back in time. This will return a low value when the object is moving slowly and a high value when it's moving quickly. You divide this by four to lessen the amplitude of the value a bit.

12 Click the Evaluate button to activate and test the expression. If you receive any errors, go back through the previous steps to determine where you went wrong.

13 Still in TrackView, make sure the Speed track is selected and click the Copy Controller button on the TrackView toolbar.

14 Select the Birth Rate track. Click Paste on the TrackView toolbar. Choose Copy from the Paste dialog box. This will copy the Speed track and its expression to the Birth Rate track. Right-click the Birth Rate track and choose Properties to access the Expression Editor.

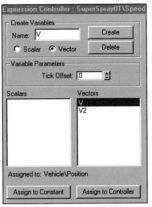

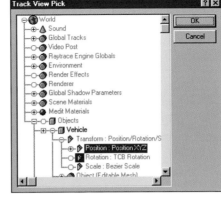

Expand the Vehicle track to select its Position track.

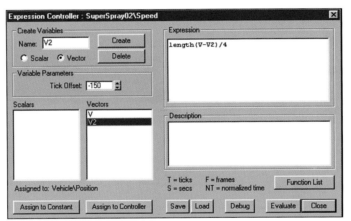

Enter length(V–V2)/4 in the Expression window.

15 Make one minor change to the expression in the window:

length(V–V2)/4*3

"*3" will take the result of "length (V–V2)/4" and multiply it by 3.

16 In the top viewport, make sure the SuperSpray is selected. Click the Move tool and, while holding the Shift button down, drag the SuperSpray over to the TireRearLeft object. This creates a clone of the first particle system. You could have done this earlier, but unfortunately you can't instance particle systems. Therefore, it makes more sense to set up one SuperSpray and then clone it when you need extra copies.

If you play the animation at this point, you'll see that as the Vehicle moves, particles are emitted from the area near the rear tires. You can adjust the Birth Rate and Speed of the particles by adjusting the expression you created earlier. For example, you could lower the "divide by" value from four to two to create more and faster-moving particles.

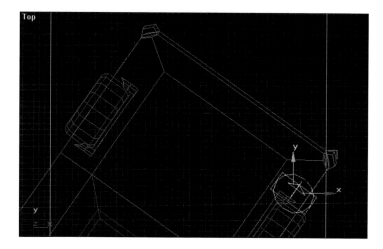

Shift-drag the SuperSpray to make a clone.

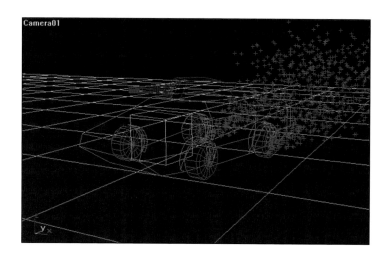

The faster the vehicle moves, the higher the speed and quantity of particles that are emitted.

CREATING A DUST MATERIAL

In this section, you'll create a simple dust material for the particles.

1 In the Material Editor, select an empty slot.

2   Create a Standard material with the following parameters:

Face Map:	Checked
Ambient Color:	(R = 169, G = 146, B = 121)
Diffuse Color:	(R = 169, G = 146, B = 121)
Opacity:	0
Specular Level:	0
Glossiness:	0

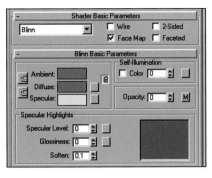

Create a Standard material with these parameters.

3   In the Maps rollout, assign a Gradient map to the Opacity slot.

4   In the Gradient map, set the following parameter:

Type:	Radial

5   Set the Opacity slot value to 25%.

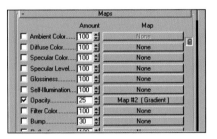

Set the Opacity value to 25%.

6   Rename the material to Dust and assign it to the two SuperSpray particle systems in the scene.

The completed scene with dust particles emitted.

PLUG-INS

There are two areas where plug-ins could help this process: particle systems and volumetric particle shaders.

- More advanced particle systems will allow you to create more complex particle motion than normally available. Examples are:

  - Particle Studio, by Orbaz Technologies and distributed by Digimation, is a very robust event-driven particle tool. It's primary advantages are its timing controls and procedural workflow.

  - Matterwaves, from Cebas Computer, is an advanced particle system that has the primary advantage of using maps to control many aspects of particle animation.

  - Particles Plus, by Peter Watje, is a freeware particle system that expands on the original Spray particle system.

- Volumetric particle shaders are excellent for making 3D smoke or dust effects. Some examples are:

  - Afterburn, by Kresimir Tkalcec, is a very powerful suite of volumetric tools. The core program allows you to shade particles with spherical, box, cylindrical, or metaball volumes. These volumes can have advanced illumination parameters to include self-shading and shadow casting. Its Raymarcher is very accurate, but can be slow when not optimized, whereas its Octane shader is an exceptionally fast volumetric shader optimized specifically for low density effects such as dust or steam. Crisp ray-traced shadows are supported, as are fast shadow maps via MAX 3's shadow API. Seven different noise types are included along with implicit surfaces with bump or displacement for effects such as liquids without the generation of vast amounts of polygons.

- PyroCluster, by Cebas Computer, is another advanced volumetric particle shader. It too can handle self-shading and shadow casting as well as implicit surfaces. PyroCluster pioneered the use of Shadow maps for shaded volumetrics in MAX. It is tightly integrated into Cebas' flagship Pro Optics Suite plug-in. A less powerful but free version of PyroCluster, called FreePyro, is also available from Cebas.

- Firestorm, from Blur Studio, is a freeware shaded volumetric plug-in. Not only does it support standard atmospheric apparatus, but also has controls for particle shading.

VARIATIONS

Expressions are highly flexible, allowing you to tweak them to no end. Some simple modifications can be made by simply adjusting the expressions. For example, you can increase the amount of particles emitted by adjusting the expression so the final value is multiplied by yet another number, or you can lessen the amount of particles by dividing the final value. You can also make much more powerful automated particles by using a Script Controller instead of expressions.

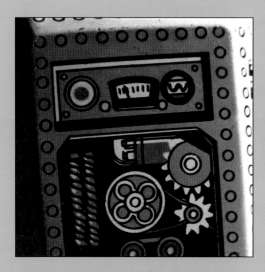

"Is there some way to make an object in MAX look like something other than plastic?"

—QUESTION POSTED ON THE DISCREET
SUPPORT WEB BOARD

SHADERS AND HIGHLIGHTS

USING LIGHTING TO ADD DETAIL AND DRAMA

Rendering is really all about light, and how

light bounces off objects in your scene to

produce color, texture, and other surface

properties. You can affect these by using

maps, changing transparency, and so on, but

the overall look of your material is usually

most affected by the type (or lack) of high-

light you have applied. In MAX 3, highlights

and the overall way a surface reflects light is

called a *shader*. In this project, we will look at

all the shader possibilities, and then how to

apply them to achieve various materials.

SHADERS AND HIGHLIGHTS

BY NEIL BLEVINS

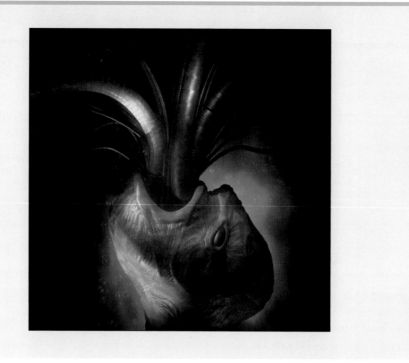

GETTING STARTED

In MAX 3, the highlight has been divided into its own plug-in class, referred to as a *shader* (the term shader in other applications has different meaning, and usually refers to a much larger selection of surface properties inherent to the material and object). Using different shaders and combinations of shaders, you can achieve many new looks in MAX that were impossible to do before, silencing the old complaint that MAX's renderer makes things look like plastic.

Before we start messing with materials, let's quickly go over what a shader is, the kinds of shaders available in MAX 3, and the other tools and plug-ins we will use for this tutorial.

1. The first example file is called 09mem01.max and can be loaded using the Open command. Inside this file, you'll find four spheres in the scene. If you open the Material Editor, you'll find that the materials applied to the spheres are in the first four slots, named 1 to 4. These will be our test spheres for our materials.

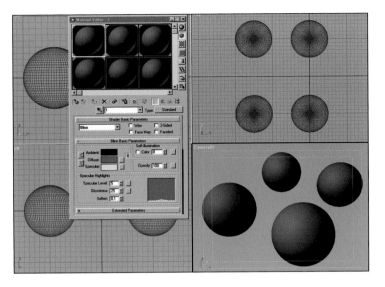

Use these four spheres to test our four materials.

2. Let's quickly learn what the different shader types are. In the first material slot, go to the section called Shader Basic Parameters and look at the drop-down list that says Blinn. These are the shader types. Below, in the Specular Highlights section, you can change the specular highlight of your material. Change the highlight to Specular Level=50, Glossiness=30. We now have that plastic look that is the default—what Blinn tends to do best.

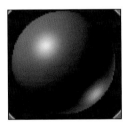

Use the Blinn shader for plastic-type materials.

3. Now change the shader type to Phong by using the drop-down list. Phong is very similar to Blinn, except its highlight is slightly more harsh (instead of a smooth gradation between the highlight and the diffuse surface, the edge between the two is slightly more defined). In most cases, using Blinn is a better idea. Blinn is slightly slower to calculate then Phong, but does tend to look a little nicer.

Use the Phong shader if you feel the Blinn shader takes too long to calculate.

4 Now change to Metal. Metal is used for most smooth metal surfaces. Change the Specular Level and Glossiness to 80. Notice how this shader does not just add a highlight on top of your surface, but as the highlight gets smaller and stronger, also causes the rest of the object to get darker.

Use the Metal shader for metallic materials.

5 Now change the highlight to Anisotropic. Here's the first of the new highlights to MAX 3. Anisotropic shaders are mainly used for brushed metals and are characterized by their long, thin oval highlight, as opposed to the purely circular highlight of Blinn or Phong shaders. To illustrate this, change the Glossiness to 30. Notice the highlight is no longer round. Notice how thin the highlight is, and how its orientation can be controlled using the Anisotropy and Orientation spinners.

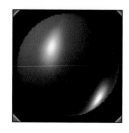

Use the Anisotropic shader for brushed metals.

6 Change to Oren-Nayer-Blinn. This is mainly used for materials such as fabrics or rubber. To illustrate the difference between this and Blinn, change the Specular Level to 20, Glossiness to 30, and the roughness to 0. Now it looks a lot like a normal Blinn sphere. Now change the roughness to 50. Notice how more of the ambient black color takes over the surface color, making the material more matte.

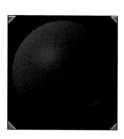

Use the Oren-Nayer-Blinn shader for materials such as fabrics and rubber.

7 Change to Strauss. This shader can change the sur-face from a Blinn to a metal using the Metalness spinner. Change Glossiness to 80 and Metalness to 80 as an example. I rarely use this shader, but it may have applications for blending between a plastic and a metal surface.

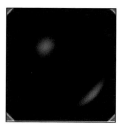

Use the Strauss shader for blending between a plastic and a metal surface.

8 Last is Multi-Layer, which is a simple way to combine
   two different highlights on top of each other.
   However, I prefer another method for mixing highlights that uses Blur studio's HighlightOnly plug-in
   (http://www.blur.com/Blurbeta/) and Shellac. I prefer
   it because it lets you layer an infinite number of
   highlights on top of one another and gives you more
   transparency control over how much of each particular
   highlight is applied to your material.

Blend highlights using
HighlightOnly.

Let's make a quick material using this technique. Make
sure you have installed the HighlightOnly plug-in and be
sure the plug-in Blurlib.dlu is also installed and loaded
before HighlightOnly is loaded. (Do this by editing your
plug-in .ini file with Notepad and making sure the blurlib
entry is before the HighlightOnly entry.) Reopen your
test file. Change the Specular Level of the first material to
7. Now click Type: Standard and choose Shellac. Choose
Keep Old Material as Submaterial. Change the Shellac
Color Blend to 100. Click the Shellac Material slot. Click
Standard; choose HighlightOnly. Change the Shader
Type to Anisotropic and change Anisotropy to 80. Now
look at the results: a strong main highlight combined with
a thin, anisotropic highlight. HighlightOnly creates a
highlight with no material properties. Shellac takes that
highlight and adds it as a layer on top of your original
material, so you can now layer several different highlights
on top of one another.

That ends our introduction. Now let's use what we've
learned to produce some interesting materials.

Change the Shellac Color
Blend to 100.

SHINY AND SMOOTH METALS

Previously, metals could only be made using the Metal shader, but now that we have Anisotropic and HighlightOnly, we can make complex metal highlights relatively easily.

1 Open 09mem01.max. Change the first material to a raytraced material. Change Shading to Metal. Place the bitmap Square Grad04.gif from the CD in the bump map slot. Change Bump Amount to 500. Under Raytraced Basic Parameters, check the FaceMap box.

2 Change the material's Diffuse Color to 154, 141, 128. Change Specular Level to 75 and Glossiness to 67. Now look at your metal material. It looks fine, but the highlight could be a bit smaller and brighter. But if you do that, you will lose illumination on most of your sphere, much as we would see if we changed the Glossiness to 90. So what we'd really like is some tighter, smaller, and brighter highlights in addition to the illumination we currently have.

The first example looks good, but the highlight could be tighter. The second example has a good strong highlight, but now we lose illumination on the rest of the sphere.

3 Change Glossiness back to 67. Click the Raytraced button and choose Shellac from the list. Choose Keep Submaterial. Change Shellac Color Blend to 100. In the Shellac slot, choose HighlightOnly. Choose Anisotropic. Set Glossiness to 35, Specular Strength to 150, and Anisotropy to 80.

4 Now go back to the parent of the material (your Shellac material). Click the Shellac Material button and choose Shellac again. Choose Keep Submaterial. Change Shellac Color Blend to 100. In the Shellac slot, choose a second HighlightOnly. Set Glossiness to 20, Specular Strength to 50, Anisotropy to 60, and Orientation to 80.

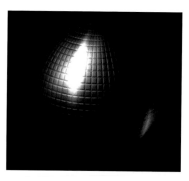

Combine the Metal shader with two Anisotropic highlights using Shellac and HighlightOnly.

Now we have our original metal highlight. Layered on top of it first is a strong small highlight (that's also narrowed due to the anisotropic calculations) and then another highlight, again anisotropic. This one is a bit softer and wider, and at a different orientation, so you achieve a criss-cross pattern on your sphere. What used to be a simple round metal highlight can now actually be quite complex, especially when mixed with Diffuse, Bump, and Reflection maps. Although it looks good on a sphere, it will look even better when applied to a complex metallic object.

WAX OR SHELLAC LAYERS

The plug-in Shellac is named after substances such as varnish that are commonly painted on top of wood to help preserve it and give it a shiny finish. Technically, a shellac is a top-level glossy layer that is still transparent enough to allow us to see the surface below. This can be used for many more things than wood, of course. This example is an alien egg covered in a layer of wax or some other smooth varnish-type material.

1 Take slot 2 and make sure it's a Standard material. Add a Bump map, choose Cellular, change Size to 5, and change Bump Amount to 20. Change Specular Level to 45 and Glossiness to 20. Set Diffuse Color to R=67, G=65, B=70 and Specular Color to R=255, G=255, B=195. Now we have our base alien egg.

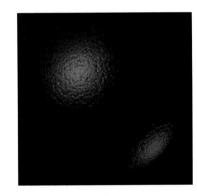

The base alien egg.

2 Now choose the Standard button. Change to Shellac. Choose Keep Old Material as Submaterial. Change Shellac Color Blend to 100. Click the Shellac Material slot. This slot currently has another Standard material in it, but we don't want that, so click the Standard button. Choose HighlightOnly and change the shader type to Anisotropic. Set Anisotropy to 0 (hence, no anisotropy), Glossiness to 55, and Specular Strength to 40.

Add Shellac.

143

3 Click Go to Parent and select the Base Material slot. Place a Falloff map in Self-Illumination. Change the amount of the mix curve to resemble the figure to the right.

We have created an egg, with a large, soft highlight that is broken up by the Bump map. Layered on top of that is a second highlight not affected by the Bump map. The second highlight appears not to be on the surface of the bump (the egg), but on a smooth surface that is covering the sphere (the wax layer). To enhance this effect, we place a Self-Illumination map that only illuminates the edges of the sphere. If you look at any object that is covered in varnish or a similar substance, you'll notice that the edges of the object reflect light differently than does the main surface. This effect can be simulated with more or less subtlety using a Falloff in the Reflection map, or, in this case, in the Self-Illumination map. Also, because Self-Illumination tends to flatten out an object by adding light to the ambient part of your material, making the material brighter, it looks like light is reflecting off the shiny and smooth wax coating on the surface of your material. These techniques can be modified to make much more realistic materials than the one I have presented. Just remember: Look carefully at real-world examples around you.

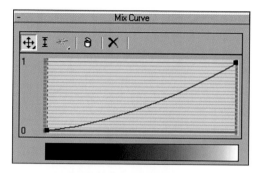

Change the amount of your mix curve to this for the Falloff map.

This waxy material was created using Shellac, HighlightOnly, and a Falloff map.

WET LOOK

How do we make an object appear to be wet? The effect is very similar to the varnish in our last example, except because the water layer is so thin, the bump of the lower material tends to affect the second highlight.

1   Change the Diffuse Color in slot 3 to 141, 102, 94.
Set Specular Color to 255, 220, 135. Set Specular
Level to 30, Glossiness to 20, and Soften to 0.5 (so
the low highlight won't be as sharp). In the Bump
map, place a Noise map, with a Noise type of
Fractal, size of 10, and levels of 4.

2   Now change the Standard material to a Shellac by
clicking the Standard button and choosing Shellac.
Shellac Color Blend should be 100. Shellac Material
should be a HighlightOnly. Set Type to Anisotropic,
Anisotropy=0, Glossiness=70, Specular Strength=55,
and click the Bump slot. Choose From Scene, get
the Noise map that was in your other material, and
choose Copy. Change bump amount to 25.

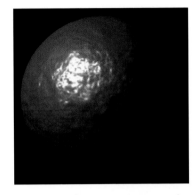

Use a thin Shellac layer to
create a wet surface.

Observe your material. First you have a large, soft-
colored highlight on your original material. Layered
on top of that is a harsh, tight, and strong white
highlight that is being affected by the Bump map on
the surface of the sphere. The top highlight is the
highlight from the water surface covering your
original sphere. For smoother water, try reducing
the number of levels in your water layer Noise. Also
try experimenting with the size of the lower-colored
highlight. See how making it larger, smaller, more
intense, and so on, affects how wet the surface looks.
It's the combination of these two highlights that help
make this and the other effects work. There's no
sure way of going about it except taking these few
suggestions to heart and tweaking parameters 'til it
looks just right.

Experiment with tweaking
settings and rerendering
until you achieve the effect
you like.

145

RUBBER

As mentioned earlier, Oren–Nayer–Blinn is useful for rubber. That's because a rubber surface, unlike plastic (Blinn and Phong), tends to not reflect as much light. Hence, the ambient color is dominant, even in areas that should be reflecting the diffuse color and illumination level (if it had been made using another material).

1   Change slot 4 to Oren–Nayer–Blinn. Set Ambient Color to 104, 42, 42 and Diffuse to 141, 141, 130. Specular Level should be 15 and Glossiness should be 40. Set Roughness equal to 0. Place in the Bump slot a cellular map of Size 3.0. Now render. Looks OK, but a little too plastic for me.

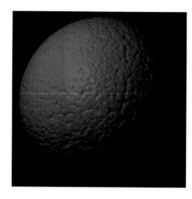

Here's the Oren-Nayer-Blinn surface before the roughness is added.

2   That's what the roughness is for. Increase it to 100 and see the difference. The object loses some of its roundness and looks much more like true rubber. The highlight that exists still gives it a little bit of shine. Reducing the highlight by reducing the Specular Level will make the object completely matte, which might be a good idea depending on the situation.

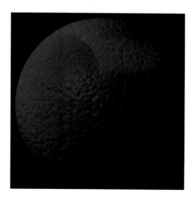

The Oren-Nayer-Blinn surface after the roughness is added.

PLUG-INS

The main plug-ins useful for changing the appearance of a material's shader are Shellac and HighlightOnly, which we have already used. Both were written by Blur Studio. For more information on the plug-ins as well as the most recent version of them, check out www.blur.com/blurbeta/.

VARIATIONS

The variations are limitless, especially when you start combining Diffuse maps, Bump maps, and of course, Shininess Strength and Glossiness maps to give you even more control over the placement of the highlight.

■ Remember that light placement in your scene will also be critical. The light position, strength, and color go hand in hand with your materials, and you can enhance any of these effects with some good lighting. You can also detract from them by using poor lighting, so be careful.

■ Lastly, observe real materials around you. Observe how their highlights react to light. See how the dust collects and dirties the glossiness, or how strong it is. Notice it's shape and how the bump interacts with the highlight to make it irregular or not. You can learn a lot from observation.

"Look like the time; bear welcome in your eye..."

—WILLIAM SHAKESPEARE, Macbeth

A REALISTIC EYE

USING SOURCE PHOTOGRAPHS TO CREATE A REALISTIC 3D EYE

In animation, eyes are portrayed as anything from black dots on white to photoreal. Of course, much expression comes from the shape of the eyelids, which range from painted circles to elaborate folds of skin between brow and cheek. However you model your characters, at some time, you'll need an eyeball. This project takes you through the steps of creating a realistic human eye.

A REALISTIC EYE

BY JEFFREY ABOUAF

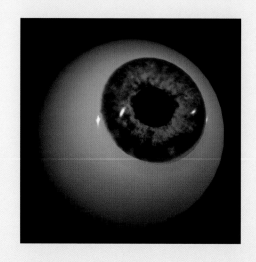
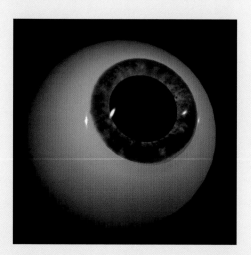

GETTING STARTED

The eye is the "window to the soul." From birth, we learn to discern the meaning of its expressive subtleties, combining this information with other thoughts and emotions expressed in the face. The shape of an eye is high on a list of easily recognizable patterns, with the human eye at the top of that list. The following exercise takes you through the steps of modeling and texturing a detailed human eye. This eye will:

- Be accurate for close-up shots (front, side, and angled)

- Include an animatable pupil

- Follow an animatable dummy object

- Be modifiable for non-human species

The project uses a source photograph scanned and imported into Photoshop, where bitmaps are isolated for use as iris and the eyeball Texture maps. In MAX R3, the working eyeball and cornea are constructed separately. With the mechanics in place, the bitmapped and nonprocedural textures are layered to create the final piece.

First, we'll scan in a photograph at high resolution and import it into Photoshop. This is the background layer. Later, we'll model the eye geometry in MAX, create a dilating pupil, and add texture.

STARTING IN PHOTOSHOP: SCANNING SOURCE MATERIAL

Best results come from a highly-detailed source image; that is, a close-up photograph of an eye. Outdoor shots in direct sunlight work best to illuminate the iris. (Take care not to injure the person posing for you by having him or her stare into the sun!)

Select the best images and scan them into your image editor (without filters) at the highest resolution. (Photoshop is the most popular and prevalent tool for this purpose, although any package that supports your scanner and layers compositing will suffice.)

The figure on the right shows the samples looked at for this project. The lower figure shows the image used as the source image, which is included for you on the accompanying CD as eye5_small.psd.

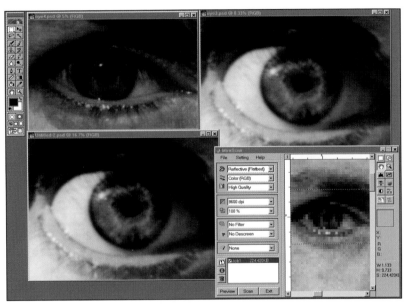

Import several high-resolution photos into Photoshop and choose the one that best reveals iris detail.

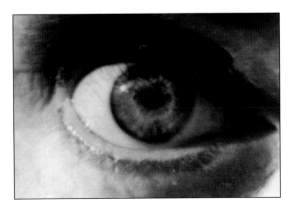

Use the best photo as the background layer. Sample and isolate the "white" area on its own layer. Select the iris and pupil and isolate them on another layer.

ISOLATING BITMAPS

1   Expand the scanned image canvas size to a resolution
of 1100×1100 pixels. (Do *not* change the image proportions—the iris must remain round.) Copy the
background layer and name it Layer 1. Select Layer 1.
Make a circular selection around the iris and feather
the selection 15 pixels. Edit, Copy the selection and
paste it into a new Layer 2, where it is isolated
against a transparent background. Using the Rubber
Stamp and Dodge tools, carefully cover any reflections
and remove any shadow effects.

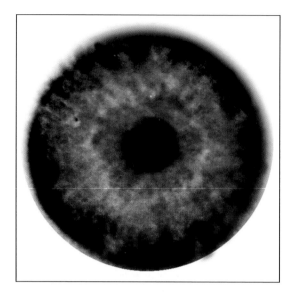

Remove any reflections,
shadows, and indications of
the cornea with Photoshop's
clone tool.

2   Create a new Layer 3. With the Eyedropper tool,
sample sections of the white area around the iris.
Alternatively, select a portion of that area, make a
pattern from it (Edit, Define Pattern), and then perform an Edit, Fill using either the sampled foreground
color or pattern. (You might use each on a separate
layer, adjust the opacity to blend the layers, and
merge them to form the new background.)

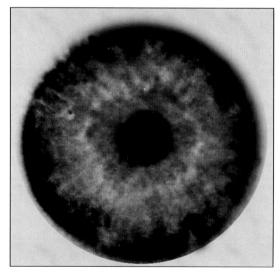

Sample the "white" area
of the eye either with
Photoshop's pattern or
eyedropper tools to arrive
at a color and pattern that
doesn't look like a cue ball.

3   Experiment isolating black-and-white images for use
    as Bump and Self-Illumination maps in MAX. In
    RGB color mode, the green alpha channel carries a
    lot of detail; in LAB mode, the Lightness channel
    contains a different kind of detail. These files
    are included on the accompanying CD as
    green_alpha.tga and lightness2.tga. There are also
    color variations for your use. Save the file for use
    in MAX.

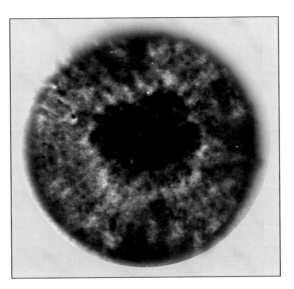

Use the green channel or
switch to LAB color mode
and use the Lightness channel
to pull black-and-white maps
you might use as Self-
Illumination and Bump maps
on the iris.

4   Open 3DS MAX R3. In the front viewport, create a
    sphere, R=50.0. (This places the polar region toward
    you.) In the top viewport, create a dummy object
    placed so the eyeball will look at it. Select Sphere01.
    Under Motion, Parameters, Assign Controller, high-
    light Transform: Position, Rotation, Scale and press
    the Assign Controller button. This brings up the
    Assign Transform Controller dialog box. Change the
    controller to Look At and press OK.

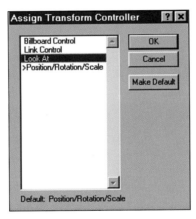

Align the polar region of the
sphere with the dummy
object, select the sphere, and
apply a Look At controller.

5 Click Pick Target and choose the dummy object. Notice the eyeball aligns with one polar axis pointing toward the dummy. That polar axis faces front in the front viewport.

Pick the dummy at the Look At target.

6 Convert eyeball to an Editable Mesh (use either the right-click menu or the Modify, Edit Stack menu). Rename it "eyeball." Check Ignore Backfacing and, in the front viewport, select the first ring around the center vertex. Label this selection set "pupil." Clear the selection and select the second ring out. Save this selection as "2 rows verts."

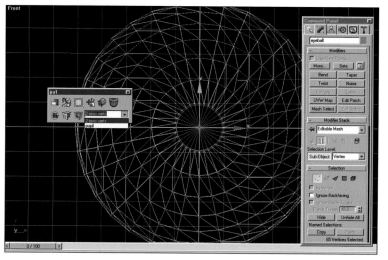

Name the innermost vertex selection set "pupil" and the next one out "2 rows verts."

7   Select and delete the faces immediately surrounding the polar region. (Do not delete isolated vertices.) This hole will remain uncapped and act as the pupil.

The "pupil" vertex selection can be uniformly scaled up or down, allowing you to animate the iris. To set the eyeball up for a slit-type iris, such as a cat, first rotate the sphere's Pivot Point 90 degrees (so the Look At controller aligns the sphere to the dummy along the equator instead of the pole). Next, remove part or all of two "slices" of adjacent sphere faces, leaving isolated vertices. Go to Vertex Sub-Object mode. Turn on 3D Snap; set it to Snap to Vertex. Take each vertex along the top and bottom three rows of the slit and snap them to the center vertex. Select and weld these vertices (that is, sew up the top and bottom of the slit so it does not run from pole to pole). Remove the isolated vertices. Select the vertices bordering the slit. Name the selection set. Create a second dummy object. Select the vertex selection and apply a Linked X-Form modifier and use the dummy as the control object. Scaling the X-Axis of the dummy scales the vertex selection bordering the slit to animate the iris expansion and contraction.

8   Next make the iris area concave. In the left viewport, select the pupil vertices and move them along the X-Axis until they are even with the second row of vertices. Select both the pupil and second row vertices (make sure the Ignore Backfacing checkbox is clear). Move them along the X-Axis until they are even or nearly even with the third row. Select the pupil vertices and move them toward the center of the eye, past the second ring of vertices. Moving the dummy makes the eye rotate.

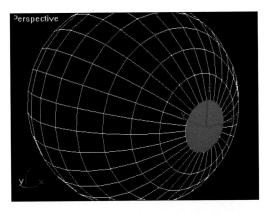

Delete the faces immediately surrounding the polar region; don't remove isolated vertices.

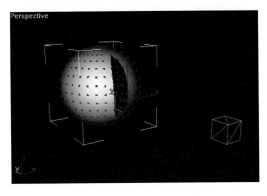

Scale the vertex to a slit to make a cat's eye.

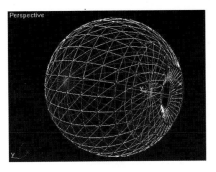

Move the pupil vertex selection toward the center of the eye past the second ring of vertices to create a concave surface. Create a second dummy and apply a Linked Xform modifier to the "pupil" vertices to animate pupil motion.

Learning Resources Centre

155

9 Select the pupil vertices and apply a Linked Xform modifier. Create a second dummy object inside the eye. Choose this dummy as the control object for the pupil vertices. Viewed from the front viewport, nonuniform scaling the dummy along the X-Y-Axes animates the pupil.

10 Because the materials for the eye are complex, it's easiest to develop them in stages. In many cases, a Double-Sided material will work. The Facing Material is the edited iris and background map created in Photoshop, and the Back Material is flat black, enabling the eye to always look black. Open the Material Editor. Select an empty slot and click the Get Material button (Browse from New), and select the Double-Sided Material.

11 Click the Facing Material button. Choose the Anisotropic shader. Under the Anisotropic Basic Parameters rollout, set Specular Level=125, Glossiness=85, Anisotropy=10, and Orientation=45.

12 Open the Maps rollout. Open the Asset Manager. Locate the color file you created in Photoshop with the edited iris and background. Drag it to the Diffuse Color channel. (Alternatively, on the CD maps directory for this project, use file eye5e_white&black.tga.) Drag-copy this file as an instance to the Specular Level and Glossiness channel buttons.

13 Locate and drag-copy one of the alpha channel bitmaps made in Photoshop to the Self-Illumination channel (alternatively, use lightness2.tga from the accompanying CD).

Choose a Double-Sided material for the eye mesh. The Back material is for the nonreflective black surface on the eye's interior; the Facing Material is the eye Texture map.

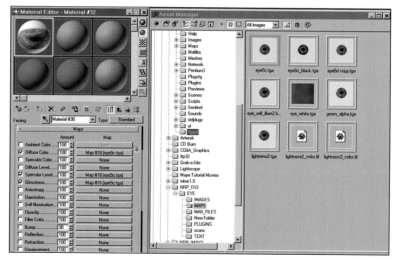

Use the retouched iris and white area bitmap in the Diffuse Color Map channel and make instance-copies in the Specular level and Glossiness map channels.

14 Copy the black-and-white image as an instance to the Bump channel.

15 Click the Self-Illumination Channel button. Click the Type button (currently reads Bitmap) and select a Composite map. Select Keep Old Map as Submap in the Replace Map dialog box and click OK. Notice the bitmap becomes Map 1.

16 Click Map 2 and select a Falloff map. Under Falloff Type, select Fresnel; under Falloff Direction, select Viewing Direction (Camera Z-Axis). Go to the top level of this material. Label this material "eyeball temp."

17 Click the Back Material button. Under Blinn Basic Parameters, click the Diffuse Color Swatch and set the color to black. Drag-copy this swatch to Ambient and Specular Color Swatches. Set Specular Level=0 and Glossiness=0. This put a black, non-reflective material inside the eyeball.

18 We now modify the material to give a sense of wet-ness and depth on the surface using the Shellac material. Click an empty slot in the Material Editor, and then click the Get Material button, and choose the Shellac Material. Now click and drag the slot for the eyeball temp material you just created and drag it to the Base Material button (as an instance).

19 Click the Shellac Material Button. Choose the Anisotropic shader. Choose a flesh tone for the Diffuse Color Swatch (for example, H=5, S=50, V=230). Set Specular Level=150, Glossiness=75, Anisotropy=85, and Orientation=0. Return to the top level.

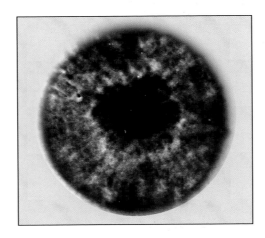

Copy one of the alpha-channel bitmaps to the Self-Illumination channel.

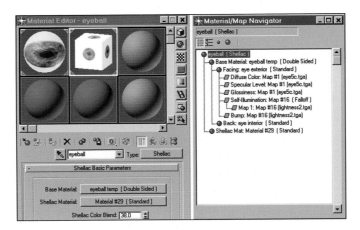

Create a Shellac material in an empty slot. Drag-copy as an instance the slot containing the Double-Sided material to Shellac's Base Material button.

20 Set Shellac Color Blend=38. Label the material "eyeball." Assign the eyeball material to the eyeball geometry. Open the Material, Map Navigator and jump to the Diffuse Color Map level. Click the Show Map in Viewport button (the blue checkered box). Select the eyeball geometry and assign this material to it.

21 You can't see the material and map you just applied without adding a UVW Map modifier to the stack. With the eyeball selected, apply a UVW Map modifier under the Modify panel. Leave Mapping set at Planar. Set the front and perspective viewports each to Smooth and Highlights. You should see the iris on the eyeball surrounding the hole.

22 Click the Sub-Object button to get to the gizmo. Move and uniformly scale the gizmo until the iris map is centered around the pupil and the iris appears to be the correct size for the geometry.

Set the Shellac Color Blend parameter to 38.

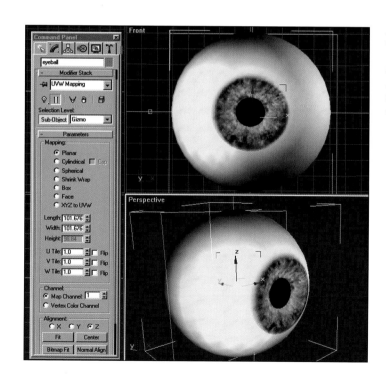

Apply the Shellac material to the eyeball mesh using planar UVW mapping. Go to the Sub-Object level of UVW Map modifier and Move, Scale the gizmo as appropriate to position the iris.

23 Next, create geometry for the cornea. In the front viewport, create a second sphere, R=33, Hemisphere=0.695. Position it in the front and left viewports so it covers the iris map and appears to blend with the eyeball geometry. You may need to adjust the eyeball vertex selections made earlier so they appear to meet the cornea properly. Choose Select and Link and link the cornea to the eyeball.

24 Pick an empty slot in the material editor for the Cornea material. Label it Cornea. Under Shader Basic Parameters, choose the Anisotropic shader and check 2-Sided.

25 Under Anisotropic Basic Parameters, make the Diffuse Color dark lavender (H=179, S=73, V=84). Set the Ambient Color to H=29, S=231, V=32 and the Specular Color to H=179, S=37, V=194. Set Specular Level=150, Glossiness=90, Anisotropy=83, and Orientation=45.

26 Under Extended Parameters, drag-copy the Specular Color Swatch to the Filter color. Set Falloff=In and Amt.=100.

27 Go to the Maps rollout. Click the Reflection channel bar and choose a Raytrace map. Click the Global Parameters button. Under Global Raytracer Settings, check Fast Adaptive Antialiaser. Leave Trace Mode at Auto-Detect. Go to the parent level and set the Reflection map amount=20. Assign the material to the cornea geometry.

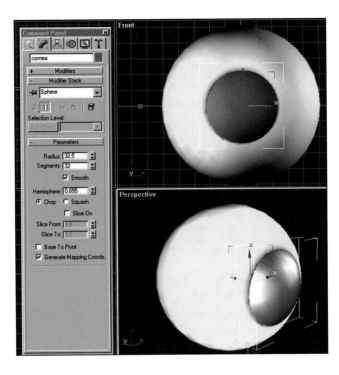

Create a hemisphere, adjusting the Hemisphere and Radius spinners to make it fit the iris, but not extend outside that area. The cornea should be transparent when viewed from the side.

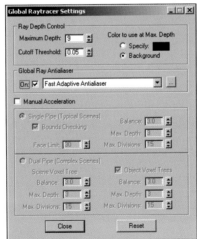

Turn on the Fast Adaptive Antialiaser in the Global Raytracer Settings dialog box.

28 Test render the scene. Everything appears too bright and self-illuminated, and much of the iris detail is lost. You can return to Photoshop and darken the iris. Alternatively, substitute file eye5c_black.tga from the CD. A third alternative is to adjust the Output settings for the eye bitmap in the Diffuse Map channel. Go to the Bitmap level, open the Output rollout, check Enable Color Map, and adjust the curves so the correct iris colors show through the cornea. This fixes the iris, but not the white area.

29 Drag the current eyeball material to an empty slot in the Material Editor. By sampling a darker part of the eyeball source and compositing that with gradients in the Diffuse channel of the Facing material, you can change the color of the eyeball white, yet keep the sense of self-illumination and gloss. Open the Material, Map Navigator and jump to the Diffuse Color channel.

30 Click the Type button, choose a Composite map, and select Keep Old Map as a Submap. Turn off the Show End Result button. The bitmap becomes Map 1 (that is, the bottom map) of the composite. To tint the white, we apply a Mask map containing two gradients. Click the Map 2 button and choose a Mask map.

31 Under Mask Parameters, click the Mask button and get the Gradient map. Set Gradient Type to Radial and set the Color 2 Position to 0.59. This makes a radial gradient—white at the center, fading to black. Note that adjusting the mask affects how much of the base layer shows through. Go to the parent level and check the Invert Mask box.

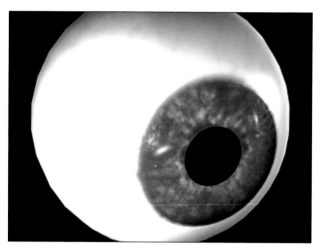

You can change the eye bitmap in Photoshop to correct the iris color in the render, or you can use the Curves adjustment at the Bitmap level of the Material Editor. This makes the iris appear correctly as seen through the cornea, but doesn't fix the whites.

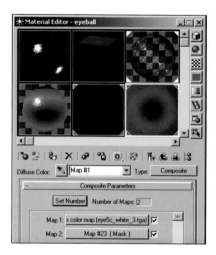

Set the Composite Map parameters for the eyeball.

32 Under the same Mask map, click the Map button. Get another Gradient map. This will colorize the composite. Set the Gradient Type to Radial. For gradient Color #1, load the file eye_white.tga from the CD. Set Color #2 to a pale yellow (for example, H=32, S=48, V=220). The color gradient and material tree should appear as in the figure on the right. The altered Diffuse Color map should appear as in the figure below it.

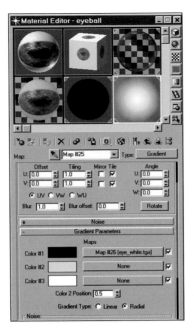

Composite a gradient on top of the eye bitmap to darken the white area as it recedes away from the iris. Use a Mask map to protect the iris area from the gradient.

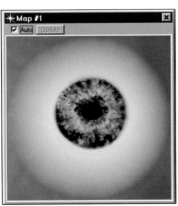

The altered "white" area picks up colors from the original photo. You can composite another layer on top of this that samples blood vessels and so on, again, radiating as a gradient.

33 Return to the top level. Set Shellac Color Blend to 10. Put the new eyeball material to scene. Render. The iris and cornea are clear, but the white falls off to an organic pink. If your character's eyes are bloodshot, you can add this to the composite by compositing a third Diffuse map with veins using the technique in steps 29 through 31, or alternatively, painting an overlay of veins onto the file eye_white.tga and reloading it into this material. The finished eyeball is in the figures to the right. The finished MAX file is included on the CD as 10mem01.max.

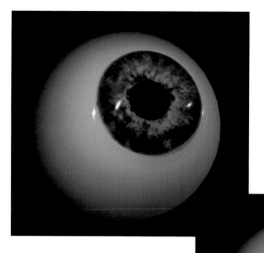

The final eye has the feeling of depth and moisture of a real eye and darkens as it recedes to the back.

Note the changes as the pupil opens and closes.

PLUG-INS

Here's a short list of plug-ins that can vary the eye effect:

- Flatten the eyeball texture for real time. There are plug-ins available to flatten these materials to a single layer for RT3D.

- Use the flexibility of the Material Tree to vary the look. This layered approach to creating the materials can be extremely useful in setting up different eyes for a cast of characters—swapping a few bitmaps changes the entire result.

VARIATIONS

Except for those inclined toward medicine or horror films, the eye is not finished until put into context:

■ Make it cartoonish: This is by placing a larger sphere around the eyeball, making sure to align their common centers, and taking advantage of the Slice function in the sphere's parameters. Using Slice To and Slice From, you can independently animate the upper and lower eyelids. You can also add cartoonish expressions by selecting the eyeball and lid together and applying Stretch, Taper or FFD modifiers and animating those parameters.

■ Make it real: For realistic models, whether built using NURBS, patches, or polygons, be sure the eyeball sits far enough into the head that the eyelid has proper thickness and that it protrudes far enough to cast appropriate shadows on the eye surface. Many attempts at realism fail because the eyelid is either too small or thin, and because its elasticity, volume, and articulation are underestimated. If you have any doubts, refer to the enclosed reference shot or examine your own face in a mirror.

■ Add bloodshot and tears: This model lacks visible veins and tears. As noted previously, you can either composite or paint veins into the Diffuse channel of this material structure. You control the entire range of looks, from hyper-realistic to grotesque, with a single bitmap. For extreme close-ups, consider adding a raytraced Refraction map to the cornea material. Metaparticles with gravity and deflector Space Warps work well for tears—either welling up within the eye or running down the cheek. The cornea material works well for tears.

■ Animate it: The eye is physically in motion at all times. In addition to the Look At controller, you can experiment with a toned-down noise controller in the rotation track. You can extend the current iris animation setup with MAXScript; for example, by placing the scale event on a slider.

*"Fortunately, I keep my feathers numbered,
for just such emergency."*

—FOGHORN LEGHORN

PROJECTILE
FIRE STREAM

CREATING A STREAM OF FIRE

In this project, we will create a scene that depicts one character shooting fire at another. The second character, a superhero, will be able to deflect the fire with his chest. This effect will also work if you want an object to repel the fire. This effect will work well for fire-breathing characters as well as supernatural forces.

To create this effect, we will use SuperSpray particles with motion blur, glow effects, particle deflectors, and lighting. The scene is set with the two characters and some basic lighting so we can focus on the effect itself.

PROJECTILE FIRE
STREAM

BY DOUGLAS KING

GETTING STARTED

We have created a basic scene with a hero and a villain so you can focus on the effect itself.

1 Load the 11mem01.max file from the project's preloaded subdirectory on the accompanying CD-ROM.

Load the MAX file from the project's preloaded subdirectory on the accompanying CD.

CREATING THE PARTICLE SYSTEM

The particle system makes up almost the entire effect, so we will begin with it.

1   Create a SuperSpray particle system in the scene. Place the SuperSpray directly in front of our villain character near his outstretched hands. Make sure the spray is pointing towards the hero character.

2   With the SuperSpray selected, set the Basic parameters as follows (though you can experiment to create your own unique effects):

Create a SuperSpray particle system in front of the villain.

Particle Formation

Off Axis:	0.0
Spread:	8.0
Off Plane:	0.0
Spread:	75.0
Viewport Display	
Percentage of Particles:	10

3   Set the Particle Generation parameters as follows:

Create a SuperSpray with these parameters.

Use Rate :	20

Particle Motion

Speed:	20.0
Variation:	0.0

Particle Timing

Emit Start:	15
Emit Stop:	120
Display Until:	151
Life:	30
Variation:	0

Particle Size

Size:	9.0
Variation:	0.0
Grow for:	2
Fade for:	10

Make sure all the subframe sampling boxes are checked.

167

4 Set the Particle Type parameters as follows for the best results:

Particle Types: Standard Particles

Standard Particles: Tetra

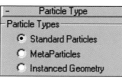 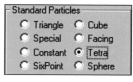

Set the Particle Type parameters.

5 Set the Rotation and Collision parameters as follows:

Spin Speed Controls

Spin Time: 50

Spin Axis Controls: Random

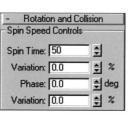 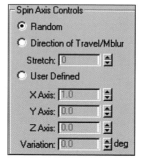

Set the Rotation and Collision parameters.

6 Set the Particle Spawn parameters as follows:

Particle Spawning Effects

Check: Spawn on Collision

Spawns: 1

Affects: 100

Multiplier: 1

Variation: 50.0

Direction Chaos: 5.0

Speed Chaos Factor: 10.0

Speed Chaos

Check: Slow

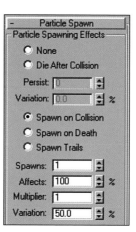 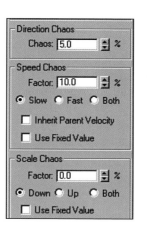

Set the particle spawning parameters to those shown in the figure.

7 Right-click the SuperSpray icon to open the Object Properties dialog box. Select Image Motion Blur and set the multiplier to 2.0.

8 To make the firestream appear less uniform, we will create a second SuperSpray and slightly adjust the parameters. Create a copy of the SuperSpray by holding Shift and clicking the SuperSpray icon. You can offset the new SuperSpray backward by a few units.

9   Under the Modify panel, change only the following
    parameters on the SuperSpray02:

    Off Axis: 0.0
    Spread: 9.0
    Off Plane: 0.0
    Spread: 85
    Particle size: 10.0
    Variation: 10

    As with any effect, you can experiment with some of
    the settings above to create your own personalized
    look. Experiment with different Axis and Plane
    Spread settings as well as particle size. Or, change the
    particle spawn settings to see what unique looks you
    can create.

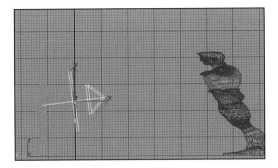

Create the second particle
array offset a little from the
first with different parameters.

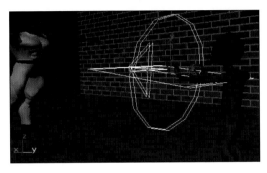

SETTING UP THE DEFLECTOR

The Particle Deflector adds one more dimension to the effect and gives our
hero some superpowers.

1   Under the Particles tab, select the UDeflector Space
    Warp. Place it in the scene facing the SuperSpray
    icons and in front of the hero character.

2   Set the Basic parameters to:

    Object Based Deflector
    Click the Pick Object button and select Chest mesh.

3   Select SuperSpray01 and then click the Bind Space
    Warp button in the Main toolbar. Drag from the
    SuperSpray icon to the UDeflector icon to bind
    the two.

Note: The placement of the UDeflector is not important
because the object selected will be doing the deflecting.
Although the actual physical placement of the deflector is
not important, you may wish to place it at or near the point
of contact just for visual reference and to keep the scene
clean-looking and organized.

4   Repeat step 3 to bind SuperSpray02.

You can experiment with different particle deflectors to get different looks, or try the scene without the deflector.

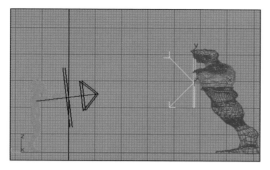 

Create a UDeflector in the scene.

CREATING THE MATERIALS

We need some basic materials for our particles to approximate the appearance of flame.

1   In the Materials Editor, create a bright-red material.
    Set the Basic parameters as follows:

    Ambient: (R–46,G–17, B–17)
    Diffuse Color: (R=255, G=50, B=50)
    Specular: (R=255, G=255,B=255)
    Set Self Illumination: 100
    Set the Material effects channel to 1.

2   Apply to SuperSpray01.

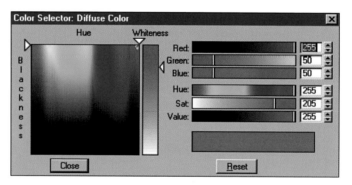

Set the Diffuse Color to bright red.

3   Create another material that is bright yellow/orange.
    Set the Basic parameters as follows:

    Ambient: (R=237, G=162,B=0)
    Diffuse Color: (R=255, G=204, B=0)
    Specular: (R=255, G=255, B=255)
    Set Self-Illumination: 100.
    Set Effects channel to 1.

4   Apply to SuperSpray02.

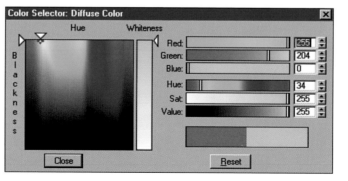

Set the Diffuse Color to bright yellow.

Setting Up the Post Effect

The Post effect gives the punch we need to make this effect work. By adding a glow to the particle stream, we enhance the realism of the effect. This will be enhanced even more by the addition of lighting.

1 Under the Rendering tab, select Effects to open the Rendering Effects dialog box.

2 Click Add and select Lens Effect.

3 Under Lens Effect parameters, select Glow.

4 Under the Glow Element rollout, set the Glow parameters to:

Size:	2.0
Intensity:	100.0
Use Source Color:	100.0

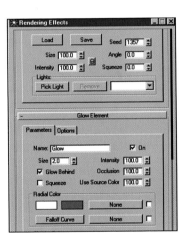

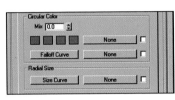

Set up a Glow in your scene.

5 Set the Glow Element options to

Apply Element To:	Image (Deselect Lights and Image Centers if necessary.)
Image Sources:	Effects ID 1
Image Filters:	All

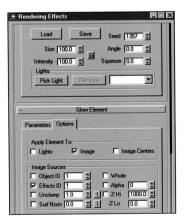

Set the Glow Element options.

SETTING UP THE LIGHTING

Lighting is integral for any effect to work. Good lighting can make a scene and an effect, whereas bad lighting will completely destroy even the best effect.

The scene comes with a target directional light with basic settings of:

Color:	(R=134, G=140, B=187)
Hotspot:	700
Falloff:	1800

1 We now need a light to represent the light coming from the firestream. Create an Omni light and position it in the middle of the SuperSpray icon.

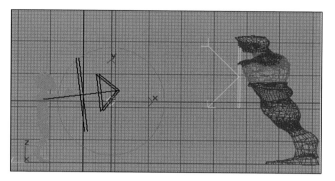

Create an Omni light in the scene.

2 At first we want the light to be off because there is no fire in the scene yet. Set the Basic parameters as follows:

R=0, G=0, B=0

Turn Cast Shadow ON

Exclude SuperSpray01 and 02

Set the Attenuation parameters as follows:

Near Start:	0.0
End:	164.0
Use:	ON
Far Start:	725
End:	1189
Use:	ON
Decay:	None
Start:	40.0

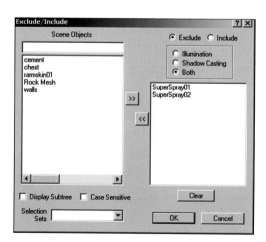

Exclude SuperSpray01 and SuperSpray02.

Set the Attentuation parameters.

3   After the firestream is activated, we want the light to reflect this. Scrub to frame 33. Turn on the Animate button. Set the Basic parameters as follows:

R=252, G=192, B=10

4   Scrub to frame 40 and move the light along the X-Axis in the Left view so the light moves toward the Hero character. Turn Animate off.

Change the color of the Omni light.

5   Right-click the Omni light and click on TrackView Selected. Select the keys at frame 0 for position and color and Copy/Move them to frame 19.

Render a few frames at various times to make sure you are satisfied with your result. When you've tweaked everything to your satisfaction, render the scene as an AVI or a series of TGA images to view in the new MAX RAM Player.

Superheroes and villains should always have super special effects. Projectile objects such as a stream of fire fit that bill perfectly. The finished effect is on the CD-ROM as 11mem02.max.

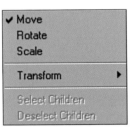

Click on TrackView Selected.

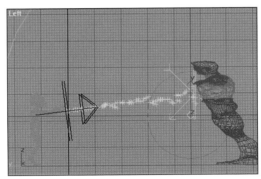
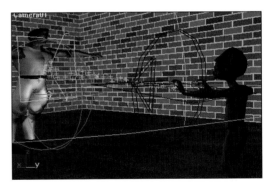

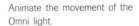

Animate the movement of the Omni light.

Plug-Ins

A few plug-ins can be used to enhance this effect further. With ProOptic Suite, you can add different glow and optical effects to make the firestream more magical or supernatural. With Particle Studio, you can control your particles in much finer detail to create some truly amazing effects.

- ProOptic Suite (Trinity)
- Particle Studio (Digimation)
- Ultrashock (Digimation)
- AfterBurn (ID8)
- ProOptic Suite (Trinity) and Particle Studio (Digimation)

The last two plug-ins will allow you to create more realistic (as opposed to the more magical) firestream effects in this scene.

Finally, if you wanted more realism, you could use plug-ins such as UltraShock (Digimation) or AfterBurn (ID8) for the firestream. These allow you to have trailing smoke from the last particles. This is a completely different look for the effect, but could work if done properly.

Variations

Now that you have created your scene, try different settings on the Particle Streams to achieve unique looks for your effect. For instance, change the speed of the particle stream for a faster spray. Change the spread settings for a more narrow, pin-pointed stream. Alternatively, change the material colors to create some other-worldly fire streams. Finally, if you want your superhero to deflect the particles with something other than his body, check out the different deflectors offered with MAX. You can use a standard Deflector or an SDeflector to produce different effects and looks. Enjoy experimenting with all the different options:

- Change the speed of the particles
- Change the spread of the particles
- Experiment with different materials for the particles
- Use other deflectors such as the SDeflector

TERRAIN

"A power is passing from the earth
To breathless Nature's dark abyss."

—WORDSWORTH

.

USING TEXTURES AND DISPLACEMENT MAPPING TO CREATE REALISTIC TERRAIN

Realistic environments are often created for

use in pre-rendered animations, as back-

grounds for live-action and CG characters,

and in visualization. Using the tools available

in MAX, you can model and texture highly

detailed terrain, water surfaces, and sky-scapes.

In this tutorial, you will create a section of

mountainous terrain and texture it to reflect

the different surfaces found in such a natural

environment.

TERRAIN

BY SEAN BONNEY

GETTING STARTED

Displacement mapping is an essential tool in this project. By using precise displacement to define the topology of the terrain, you can reference this displacement when placing objects such as trees and rocks, alleviating the tedium of placing these articles manually. You will augment this scene with a small body of water and a sky filled with clouds generated from Combustion effects.

Before beginning this project, you must ensure that MAX will be able to find the project map files.

1   Copy the Terrain project map files from the accompanying CD-ROM to the MAX Maps subdirectory.

2   Open the file 12mem01.max from this project's Preload directory on the accompanying CD-ROM.

This scene may not appear to contain much. However, several objects are hidden and materials are present that will be used in this chapter. A camera has been set up to look into the expected center of the scene.

Note: If you prefer not to copy the files, you can configure MAX to find the map files on the CD-ROM. To set this up, go to Customize, Configure Paths. Go to the Bitmaps tab and click Add. Navigate to the Chapter 12 project directory and click Use Path.

CREATING THE SKY

The color and atmosphere of the sky in a scene are crucially important to setting a scene's emotional tone, as well as communicating the desired time of day, climate, and weather pattern. Before beginning on the actual geometry in this scene, you will create an appropriate background and atmosphere, including a few clouds.

First, create a texture for a background map.

1   Open the Material Editor, select a new material, and name it Sky. Go to the Diffuse channel, select Composite as the map type, and name this map Sky Color.

2   Map 1 will represent the background gradient of the sky. Select Map 1, choose Gradient as the map type, and name this map Sky Gradient. Set the following values for this map:

Note: Obviously, the exact naming conventions used for materials/maps have no bearing on their function. Names are suggested in this chapter as a means for maintaining organization. Feel free to use whichever system makes sense to you and be glad you stuck to it when you're searching for Sky Background instead of Gradient #21.

Coordinates		Noise	
Type:	Environ	Type:	Fractal
Mapping:	Spherical Environment	Amount:	0.2
		Size:	0.5

Gradient Parameters

Color #1: (R=65, G=110, B=125)

Color #2: (R=125, G=170, B=185)

Color #3: (R=190, G=230, B=230)

3 Go up one level to the Diffuse channel to continue.

4 Map 2 will represent a cloudy layer in the sky. Select Map 2, choose Mask as the map type, and name this map Cloud Layer.

5 Select Map, choose Noise as the map type, and name this map Cloud Color. Set the following values for this map:

Noise Parameters

Noise Type: Regular

Size: 5

Noise Threshold

High: 0.65

Low: 0.15

The sky gradient, as rendered from the Material Editor.

6 Go up one level to the Cloud Layer map to continue.

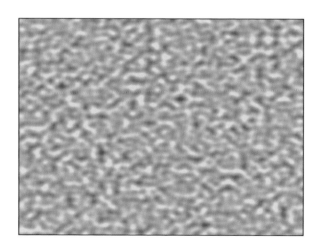

The Cloud Color map, which will be masked to create a cloudy layer.

7 Select Mask, choose Noise as the map type, and name this map Cloud Mask. Set the following values for this map:

Noise Parameters		**Noise Threshold**	
Noise Type:	Fractal	High:	0.85
Size:	7.5	Low:	0.45

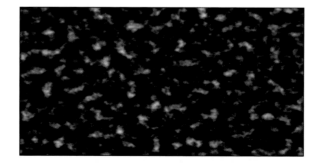

The Cloud Mask map, which determines which areas of the sky appear clouded.

8 Go up to the Sky material. To apply this material as a
background, open the Environment dialog box and
drag the Diffuse map, either from the small M button next to the Diffuse Color box or from Map column of the Maps rollout, to the Environment Map
button in the Background area of the Environment
dialog box. Choose Instance as the method.

Now you will add atmosphere using Fog and Combustion.

Render a still frame from the
Camera viewport to see how
the sky is taking shape.

ADDING ATMOSPHERE

1 Go to the Atmosphere rollout of the Environment
dialog, click the Add button, and choose Fog from
the list. Set the following values in the Fog
Parameters rollout:

Fog

Color: (R=240, G=245, B=200)

Standard

Near %:   5

Far %:   35

2 Create a spherical atmospheric apparatus with
Radius=40. Move it to X=–60, Y=100, Z=100. This
gizmo will contain a discrete cloud.

Render a still frame to see the
effect of distance-based fog.

181

3 Select Non-Uniform Scale and scale the apparatus 50% on the View Z-Axis.

4 Go to the Atmospheres rollout of the gizmo's modifier panel, click the Add button, and add a Combustion effect.

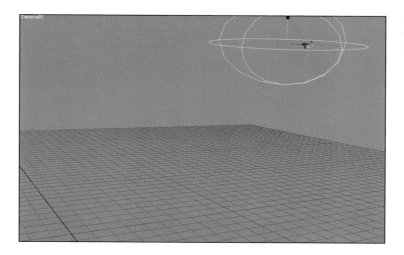

Create a spherical atmospheric apparatus to contain a discrete cloud.

5 Select the new Combustion effect and click the Setup button to go directly to this effect's setup panel in the Environment dialog box. Set the following values in the Combustion Parameters rollout:

Colors

Inner Color: (R=215, G=230, B=235)
Outer Color: (R=120, G=150, B=145)

Shape

Regularity: 0.9

Characteristics

Flame Size: 60
Flame Detail: 6
Density: 7
Samples: 30

Render a still to see the effect of adding this combustion effect.

6 To animate the slow churning of this cloud, turn the Animate button on, go to frame 100, and set Phase=20.

7 Turn the Animate button off and go to frame 0 to continue.

8 Now you will create several duplicates of this cloud. Clone the SphereGizmo01 apparatus using Copy as the method. Move the copy to X=−36, Y=18, Z=95. To prevent this gizmo from producing results identical to the original, click the New Seed button on the modifier panel. Use this button on each duplicate you create.

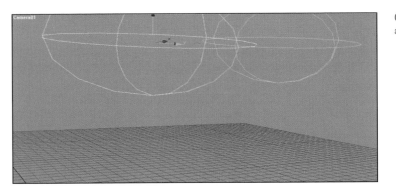

Clone the apparatus to create a second cloud.

9 Create another copy, moving it to X=−110, Y=0, Z=90.

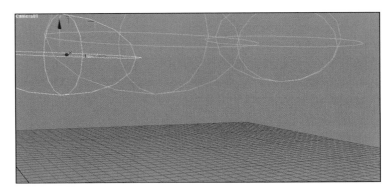

Clone the apparatus to create a third cloud.

10 Create another copy, moving it to X=−130, Y=75, Z=90.

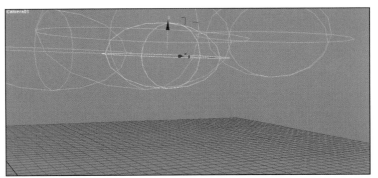

The fourth and final cloud gizmo.

11 To produce a slow movement across the camera frame, select all four spherical gizmos and turn the Animate button on. Go to frame 100 and move the selection approximately 25 units on the View X-Axis and 20 units on the View Y-Axis.

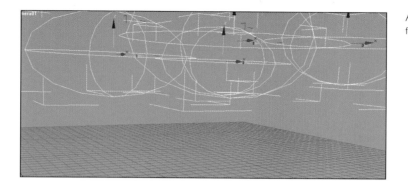

Animate a slow drifting motion for the four cloud gizmos.

12 Turn the Animate button off and go to frame 0 to continue.

Note that each Combustion effect adds a significant burden at render time, so you may wish to deactivate atmospheric effects for test renders throughout this chapter. You can do this either globally in the Options section of the Render Scene dialog box, or specifically in the Environment dialog box.

The four clouds, rendered as they appear at frame 0.

MODELING THE TERRAIN

You will model the main body of ground using the Displacement modifier. Note that MAX R3 provides the ability to apply Displacement maps directly in a Maps slot. This option, however, only provides displacement at render time, so it is not useful for situations where mapping and object intersection depend on geometric displacement at the editing stage.

1   Go to a top viewport and create a Plane at X=0, Y=0, Z=0. Set the following values for the object's creation:

Length: 300   Length Segs: 35
Width: 300   Width Segs: 35

2   Name this object ground_plane.

3   Apply a Displace modifier with a Strength setting of 95.

4   To create the map that will provide the displacement values, open the Material Editor, and select a new material. Name this material Ground Displace. Go to the Diffuse channel, select Mix as the map type, and name this map Displacement.

5   Color #1 will represent the displacement of the mountains. Select Noise as the map type for Color #1 and name this map Mountains. Set the following values for this map:

Coordinates

Source: Explicit Map Channel

Noise Parameters		**Noise Threshold**	
Noise Type:	Fractal	High:	0.9
Size:	0.2	Low:	0.1

6   Go up one level to the Diffuse Color map to continue.

7   Color #2 will represent the displacement of the valley area. Select Noise as the map type for Color #2 and name this map Valley. Set the following values for this map:

Coordinates

Source: Explicit Map Channel

Noise Parameters		**Noise Threshold**	
Noise Type:	Regular	High:	0.8
Size:	3.0	Low:	0.45

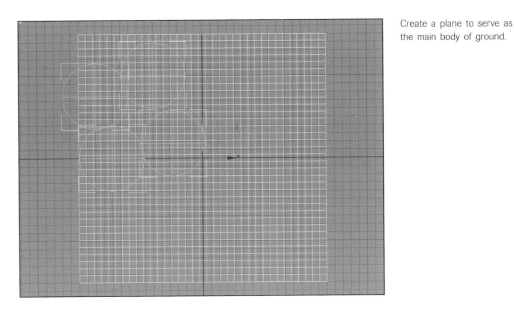

Create a plane to serve as the main body of ground.

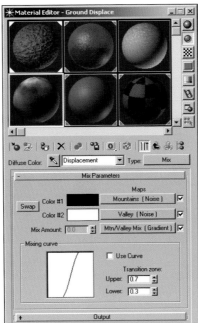

Create a map to be used with the Displace Modifier.

8 Go up one level to the Diffuse Color map to continue.

9 These two maps will be mixed according to a circular gradient, which will provide a soft valley region in the center of a circle of sharp mountains. Select Gradient as the map type for Mix Amount and name this map Mtn/Valley Mix. Set the following values for this map:

Coordinates

Mapping: Explicit Map Channel

Tiling		**Tile**	
U:	1.5	U:	Off
V:	2.0	V:	Off

Gradient Parameters

Color 2 Position: 0.2

Gradient Type: Radial

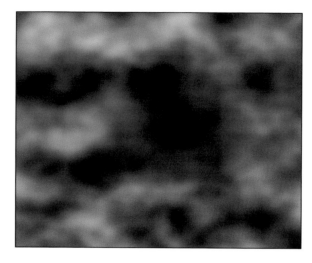

The Displacement map, as rendered from the Material Editor.

10 To apply this material as a Displacement map, go up to the Ground Displace material and drag the Diffuse map, either from the small M button next to the Diffuse Color box or from the Map column of the Maps rollout, to the button labeled None under Image: Map in the Displacement modifier. Select Instance as the method. Go to the Camera viewport to see the ground plane being displaced to create a rough mountainous terrain surrounding a small valley.

Drag the map to the Displacement modifier to use it to determine the shape of the ground plane.

11 The final step in modeling this piece of terrain is to smooth over the displacement. Apply a MeshSmooth modifier to the ground_plane object. It is advisable that you activate Inactive in Viewport for this modifier in order to avoid screen refresh delays.

Apply a MeshSmooth modifier to give the ground a more organic contour.

TEXTURING THE TERRAIN

Before creating the texture maps for this terrain, you must provide additional UVW mapping. One of the benefits of using the modifier version of Displacement is that UVW maps can be applied across the displaced geometry. This is an important feature because it allows you to access the height value of the terrain and apply appropriate textures.

1 Select the ground_plane object and apply a UVW Mapping modifier. Set Alignment equal to Y and click the Fit button to fit the UVW gizmo to the Y-Axis extents of the object.

2 To begin creating a texture for this object, go to the Material Editor, select a new material, and name it Ground. Apply this material to the ground_plane object.

3 Go to the Diffuse Color channel, select Mix as the map type, and name this map Ground Color. In this map, you will apply grass textures and rock surfaces according to the terrain height.

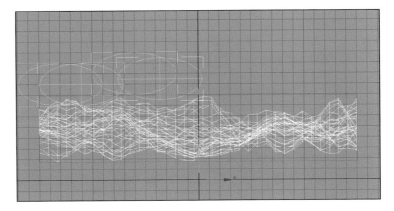

Apply UVW mapping along the ground plane's vertical access.

187

4 Color #1 will represent the rock areas. Select Noise as the map type for Color #1 and name this map Rock. Set the following values for this map:

Noise Parameters		Noise Threshold	
Noise Type:	Fractal	High:	0.65
Size:	.002	Low:	0.18
Color #1:	(R=155, G=90, B=50)		
Color #2:	(R=50, G=95, B=125)		

5 Go up one level to the Diffuse Color map to continue.

6 Color #2 will represent the grass areas. Select Noise as the map type for Color #2 and name this map Grass. Set the following values for this map:

Noise Parameters		Noise Threshold	
Noise Type:	Regular	High:	0.8
Size:	15	Low:	0.0
Color #1:	(R=175, G=100, B=45)		
Color #2:	(R=45, G=135, B=45)		

7 Go up one level to the Diffuse Color map to continue.

8 These two maps will be mixed according to the UVW channel you provided along the ground plane's vertical axis. Select Gradient as the map type for Mix Amount and name this map Grass/Rock Mix. Set the following values for this map:

Coordinates

Source: Explicit Map Channel

Noise Parameters

Noise Type: Fractal
Amount: 0.5
Size: 0.7

Noise Threshold

High: 0.8
Low: 0.45

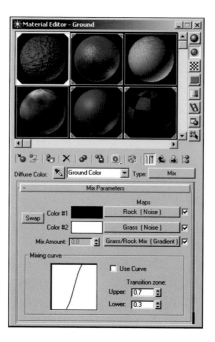

Use a Mix map to represent the look of grass and rocks on the ground object.

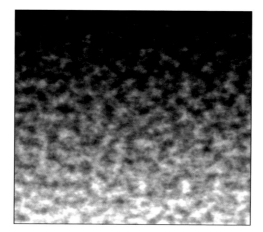

The Grass/Rock Mix map, which will divide the terrain color into different regions.

The effect of mixing the Grass and Rock maps together.

9   Go to the Specular channel, select Gradient as the map type, and name this map Ground Shine. In this map, you will make the rocky areas shinier than the grass-covered portions. Set the following values for this map:

Coordinates

Source: Explicit Map Channel

Gradient Parameters

Color #1:   (R=55, G=55, B=55)
Color #2:   (R=23, G=23, B=23)
Color #3:   (R=18, G=18, B=18)

Noise

Noise Type: Fractal
Amount: 0.5
Size: 0.35

10   Go to the Bump channel, set Amount=50, select Mask as the map type, and name this map Ground Bump. In this map, you will apply a combination of procedural bumps according to ground height.

11   Select the Map channel, select Mix as the map type, and name this map Bump Mix.

12   Select the Color #1 channel, select Gradient as the map type, and name this map Ground Bump #1. Set the following values for this map:

Coordinates

Source: Explicit Map Channel

Gradient Parameters

Noise
Noise Type: Fractal
Amount: 0.05
Size: 0.7

13   Go up one level to the Bump Mix map to continue.

The Specular map, showing the shiny areas at the top of the map that will represent rockier terrain.

The Ground Bump #1 map, one half of the basic bump mix.

14 Select the Color #2 channel, select Dent as the map type, and name this map Ground Bump #2. Set the following values for this map:

Dent Parameters

Size: 400

Strength: 10

Iterations: 4

15 Go up one level to the Bump Mix map to continue.

16 Select the Mix Amount channel, select Noise as the map type, and name this map Bump #1/#2 Mix. Set the following value for this map:

Noise Parameters

Noise Threshold

Low: 0.2

17 Go up two levels to the Ground Bump map to continue.

18 Select the Mask channel, select Gradient as the map type, and name this map Bump Mask. Set the following values for this map:

Coordinates

Source: Explicit Map Channel

Gradient Parameters

Color #1:   (R=255, G=255, B=255)

Color #2:   (R=191, G=191, B=191)

Color #3:   (R=82, G=82, B=82)

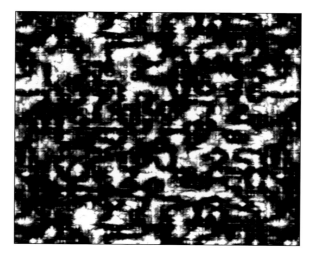

The Ground Bump #2 map, the other half of the basic bump mix.

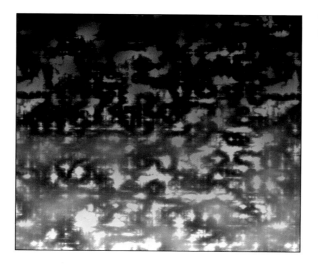

The two Bump maps mixed together.

CREATING THE WATER

Now you will create a small mountain lake and fit it into the depression provided for in the Displacement map.

1   Go to a top viewport and create a Plane at X=0, Y=55, Z=30. Set the following values for the object's creation:

Length:	165	Length Segs:	5
Width:	100	Width Segs:	5
Generate Mapping Coords:	on		

2   Name this object Water.

3   To begin creating a texture for this object, go to the Material Editor, select a new material, and name it Water. Apply this material to the Water object. Set the following values for this map:

Blinn Basic Parameters

Ambient:	(R=40, G=25, B=115)
Diffuse:	(R=60, G=90, B=200)
Opacity:	40
Specular Level:	40
Glossiness:	30

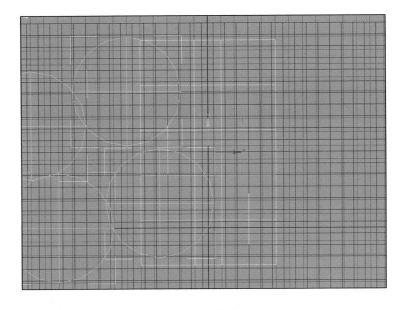

Create a plane to represent the surface of a small body of water.

4   Go to the Bump channel, set Amount=30, select Noise as the map type, and name this map Water Bump. Set the following values for this map:

Noise Parameters

Noise Type:	Turbulence
Size:	2.0

5   To animate this texture, turn the Animate button on, go to frame 100, and set Phase=5.

The Water Bump map, which will provide the water's surface texture.

6 Turn the Animate button off and go to frame 0 to continue.

7 Go to the Reflection channel, set Amount=20, select Bitmap as the map type, and name this map Water Reflect. Go to the Bitmap Parameters rollout and assign sky_map.tga as the bitmap.

8 Set the following values for this map:

Coordinates

Type: Environ

Mapping: Spherical

Note: It is relatively easy to create a simple reflection map. The map included with this project was created from a small render of the basic scene (ground and sky), which was edited so it would wrap horizontally.

Render a still to see the water added to this scene.

ADDING DETAILS TO THE LANDSCAPE: ADDING TREES

This landscape will not be complete with the natural details we expect in such a scene, such as foliage and rock formations.

Simple brush can be easily added to this scene using cloned geometry. By using the same Displacement map that was used to create the terrain, trees and bushes can be automatically placed on the ground's surface. This time, displacement will be implemented using a Space Warp so bound objects can be moved without affecting the alignment of the Displacement map.

1 Unhide the object Tree01. This object is placed near to Z=0, where the original ground_plane object was placed.

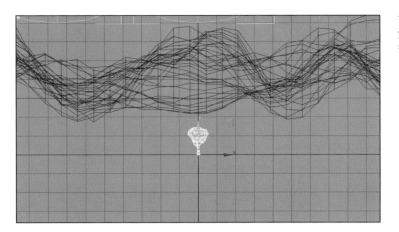

The low polygon tree that you will distribute across the surface of the terrain.

2 Now you will create the Space Warp that will be applied to this and several other objects. Go to a top viewport and create a Displace Space Warp at X=0, Y=0, Z=0. Set the following values for this modifier:

Strength: 95
Length: 150
Width: 150

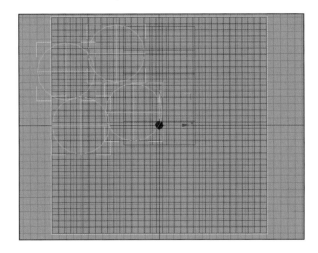

Create a Displace Space Warp to match the Displace modifier used for the terrain.

3 This Space Warp will use the same map used for the original terrain displacement. Go to the Ground Displace material and drag the Diffuse map to the button labeled None under Image: Map in the Displacement modifier. Select Instance as the method.

4 Select the Bind to Space Warp button and drag from the Tree01 object to the Displace Space Warp.

Note that when you bind the tree to the Space Warp, it immediately moves to the level of the ground (underwater in this case).

5 Select the Move button and move the tree around the viewport. Note that it automatically follows the contours of the terrain. Move this object to X=−50, Y=72. Note that you can still change the Z value, although this most likely will not be necessary.

6 Clone this object, using Copy as the method. Move Tree02 to X=21, Y=65.

Move the tree to a picturesque spot. Note that the Z-Axis value of the tree's pivot point does not change because you are not actually moving the object on the Z-Axis, only displacing geometry.

7 Clone Tree02, using Copy as the method. Move
   Tree03 to X=27, Y=50.

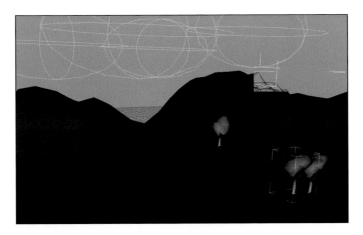

Place two cloned trees
across the water to start on
a small cluster.

8 This tree looks a little odd next to the previous one
   because they are obviously identical. Select Rotate,
   turn on Angle Snap, and rotate this object 20
   degrees on the View Z-Axis. Select Non-Uniform
   Scale and scale this object 120 degrees on the View
   Z-Axis.

Rotate and scale one of the
trees to make it look less
like a clone of the original.

9 Now you will add a small forest of trees. Clone
   Tree03, using Copy as the method. Move Tree04 to
   X=−80, Y=0.

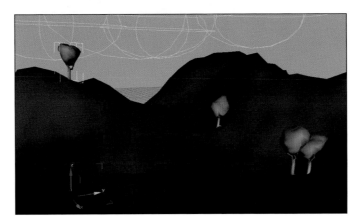

Place a cloned tree as the
source object for a small
group of trees.

10 Create a Scatter compound object. Under Distribution, select Use Transforms only. Set the following parameters for this modifier:

Duplicates:	25	**Local Translation**	
Transforms		X:	800
Rotation		Y:	800
X:	5		
Y:	5		
Z:	180		

11 If you are not immediately satisfied with the arrangement of these trees, go to the Display panel and click on the button labeled New to generate a new random seed.

Note: You may wish to activate Proxy display or reduce the Display% value to improve screen refresh times.

Create a small group of randomly placed trees using Scatter.

ADDING BUSHES

You can add bushes using similar methods to those used for the trees. In this case, however, the bushes consist of general ground cover, not individual plants.

1 Unhide the object Bush01. Select the Bind to Space Warp button and drag from the Bush01 object to the Displace Space Warp.

The low polygon bush you will place around the scene as ground cover.

2 Move this bush to X=–48, Y=75 to accompany the first tree you placed.

3 Clone this object using Copy as the method and move it into the small forest. Placing it near or under trees will enhance the realism.

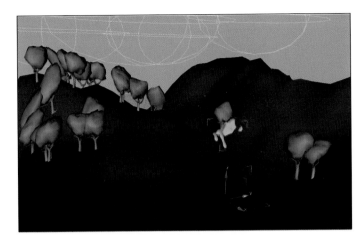

Move the bush to complement the first tree. Note that the vagaries of displacement mean that the bush object will intersect the ground plane differently at different locations, contributing to the sense of randomness.

4 Don't forget that you can still rotate, scale, and move bushes to achieve the exact placement you need.

Render a still to see how much character these trees and bushes add to the scene.

ADDING A CLUSTER OF ROCKS

In this section, you will add a cluster of rocks along a curve of your mountain lake. As large rock formations do not generally follow curve of softer terrain, you will not use displacement to place these rocks. Instead, you will manually place them, and then use Noise, Smooth, and MeshSmooth modifiers to add the necessary random element.

1 Unhide the object Rock01. Go to a top viewport, zoom in on the lake, and go to Smooth Shaded mode to see how this rock is placed along the shoreline.

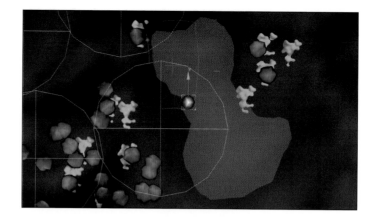

The first of several rocks that you will place along the shoreline.

2 Clone Rock01, using Copy as the method, and move the clone (rock02) to X=−25, Y=40, Z=24.

3 Clone rock02, again using Copy as the method, and move the clone (rock03) to X=−33, Y=46, Z=24.

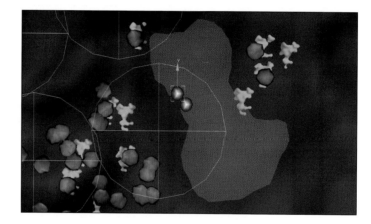

The second rock, following the curve of the shoreline.

4 Continue placing clones along the lake shore to resemble the figure to the right.

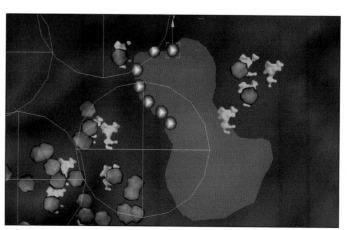

Create an arc of rocks around the edge of the lake.

5   Go to the Camera viewport. To apply a large-scale randomizing effect to these formations, select all rock objects and apply a Noise modifier. Set the following values for this modifier:

Noise

Seed: 2

Scale: 20

Strength

X: 5

Y: 5

Z: 15

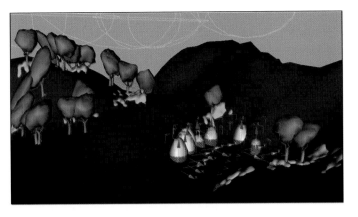

Apply large-scale noise to these rocks to randomize their overall layout.

6   Now you will apply small-scale noise to individualize each rock even further. Apply another Noise modifier to the selection and set the following values for this modifier:

Noise		**Strength**	
Seed:	4	X:	5
Scale:	1.5	Y:	5
Fractal:	on	Z:	7.5
Roughness:	0.4		
Iterations:	6		

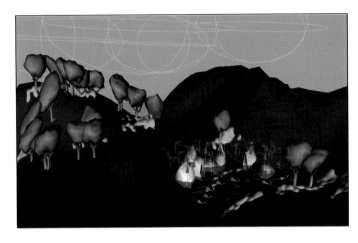

Small-scale noise adds roughness to the faces of individual objects.

7   To apply appropriate smoothing over these wild perturbations, apply a Smooth modifier to the selected objects and set the following values:

Auto Smooth:	On
Prevent Indirect Smoothing:	On
Threshold:	40

8 Finally, you will smooth the geometry using MeshSmooth. Apply a MeshSmooth modifier. You may wish to make this modifier Inactive in Viewport in order to avoid screen refresh delays.

Render a still to see how these rocks enhance the curve of the shoreline.

PLUG-INS

The techniques explored in this chapter can be augmented by plug-ins that provide advanced procedural textures, trees, and other objects found in nature, or methods for placing detail onto organic surfaces.

Here is a list of commercial plug-ins:

- DarkTree Textures ($345), from Digimation. A sophisticated engine for producing and layering procedural textures.

- Four Elements ($295), from Digimation. Produces amazing texture effects for weather, fire effects, and realistic environments.

- Glider ($95), from Digimation. A pair of Space Warps for conforming objects, particles, and even cameras to the surface topology of another object.

- Spray Master ($95), from Digimation. A tool that allows geometry to be applied as a particle stream and to accumulate on a surface.

- Tree Factory ($195), from Digimation. Generate a variety of tree types or customize your own.

- Tree Still ($395), from Digimation. Model elaborate trees in real time.

- Tree Storm ($695), from Digimation. Affect your Tree Still trees with highly customizable wind effects.

For more information on Digimation plug-ins, see its site at http://digimation.com/.

Here is a list of free and shareware plug-ins. Note that free or shareware plug-ins often represent side-projects or hobbies, and as such, are not always entirely stable.

- Blob Mod, from Peter Watje/Spectral Imaging. A metaball modifier that turns all of an object's vertices into metaballs.

- Deform Paint, from Peter Watje/Spectral Imaging. Displace geometry with a paintbrush-like tool.

- Digimation Gradient, from Digimation. A Gradient map with as many as 100 channels.

- Dirt, from Blur Studio. A procedural dirt map.
- Distance Blender, from Blur Studio. Blurs textures based on distance from camera.
- Mercury, from Harry Denholm/Ishani. Powerful fractal map generator with a library of dramatic presets.

A nearly complete list of free/shareware MAX plug-ins is available at the Virtual Republic Boboland site at http://gfxcentral.com/bobo/.

VARIATIONS

The terrain modeling/texturing techniques in this chapter can be expanded in a variety of ways:

- Try displacing several mesh objects to create different parts of the terrain.
- Planes and other geometry used to create terrain can be linked to various Space Warps to create effects from earthquake tremors to surreal distortions.
- For man-made terrain details such as roads, add a Mask material on top of both the Displacement map and the terrain material.

The creation and placement of natural details such as rocks and foliage could be elaborated on:

- For a densely populated field of boulders, use displaced terrain geometry as the Distribution object of a Scatter compound object.
- More detailed trees and shrubbery can be created using Super Spray particle systems to emit either instanced leaf geometry or masked Facing particles. Snapshot the particles to create a custom cloud of leaves.

Atmospheric effects can be animated in a variety of ways, both by using standard MAX parameters, as well as the above-mentioned plug-ins:

- The arrival of inclement weather can be simulated by animating the Combustion parameters of cloud-producing atmospheric apparatuses. Try increasing Density, accelerating Phase, and animating Inner/Outer Color towards darker tones to imply threatening storm clouds.
- The lighting of an outdoor scene can be made more atmospheric with the inclusion of denser fog and volume light. New to MAX 3 is the capability for creating atmospheric effects such as Combustion clouds to cast shadows.

"Harmony of form consists in the proper balancing, and contrast of, the straight, the inclined, and the curved."

—OWEN JONES,
GRAMMAR OF ORNAMENT

DIMENSIONAL ORNATE TEXTURE ART

Using MAX and Photoshop to Create Ornamental Texture Art

Ornament is an intrinsic part of good texture art, and as such, plays a fundamental role in establishing the character of a 3D scene. However, it is often difficult for the 3D artist to find the perfect texture, one that will combine art, ornament, design, and dimensional qualities. For those specialty projects, the artist has the option of creating a unique piece of dimensional ornate texture art using 3D Studio MAX, combined with a bit of design and a painting program such as Photoshop.

DIMENSIONAL

ORNATE

TEXTURE ART

BY ENI OKEN

This chapter, including text, imagery, and all files relevant to the chapter included on this book's CD-ROM copyright© 2000 by Eni Oken. All rights reserved.

GETTING STARTED

In this project, you will create texture art using 3D Studio MAX, combined with a bit of design and a painting program such as Photoshop. Mind you, this technique is not for a quick project. It involves creating 3D models, retouching in Photoshop, and finally, extracting a flat piece of art to be used over yet another 3D model. The advantages, though, are extremely high-quality results and unique designs.

In this exercise, you will execute the following steps: First, you will choose an ornamental design and prepare it to use as a template. Next, you will model the geometric parts and assemble the 3D models over the template. Last, you will render the image in frontal view and retouch it using Photoshop, converting the image into a seamless piece of texture art.

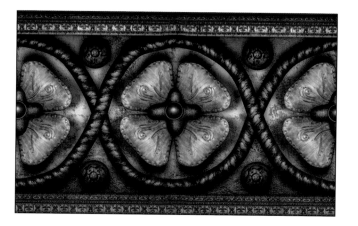

Before starting to model, it is necessary to choose an ornamental design to work upon as a template. You can design the ornament yourself or you can copy it from a history book. Either way, you will need to do some drawing. You can use Photoshop with a tablet or scan a drawing.

1 Open Photoshop. From the Magic Effects CD, open the file 13flowerpattern.tif, which is the ornamental design used for this exercise. At this point, the size of the image doesn't matter; it will not influence the final art.

2 Notice how the main lines of the pattern are reinforced, showing only the main lines of the pattern.

3 When using your own designs, it is preferable (but not absolutely required) that you choose a pattern that is repetitive; that is, that can form a texture that can be tiled. You should reinforce the main lines so they will be visible in 3D Studio MAX.

4 Decide which elements are going to stand out; that is, that will be dimensional against the background. For this exercise, use the colored image in this book as a guide (see the color gallery at the beginning of the book for the colored image).

5 Create new layers over 13flowerpattern and paint roughly over the shapes that will stand out in a different color. These colors will also serve as a main color guide when creating the art.

6 Flatten the art by choosing Layer, Flatten Image and saving it as flowertemplate.tif. You can also skip the coloring phase and just use the file 13flowertemplate.tif that comes with the CD.

Open 13flowerpattern.tif.

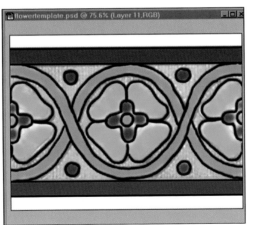

Create new layers in 13flowerpattern and paint out the main shapes.

LOADING THE TEMPLATE INSIDE MAX

The next step is to call the template from inside 3D Studio MAX 3 and create the first geometry.

1   Open 3D Studio MAX 3 and reset it. In the front viewport, set the viewport background to be the file 13flowertemplate.tif (use the file from the CD) by using the command Views, Viewport Background or pressing Alt+B.

2   Click Files and browse through the dialog box to load the template file, and then be sure to use:

Aspect Ratio: Match Bitmap
Lock Zoom/Pan: Checked
Viewport: Front

3   Go to the Render Scene dialog box and assign the Output Size to the following:

Width: 500
Height: 500
Image Aspect: 1.0

Close the dialog box without rendering. Don't worry if you want a high-resolution texture.

These are only working values and can be adjusted later.

4   On the Front icon, right-click and be sure that Show Grid, Show Background, and Show Safe Frame are all checked.

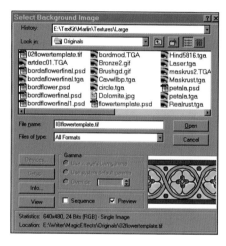

Choose the file 13flowertemplate.tif as the background.

Note: While working on the image, it is important to not zoom, pan, or move the image, or the reference to the whole background image will be lost. If you want to work closer, use another viewport with the same background and without the Safe Frame option checked.

CREATING THE BACKGROUND

The next step is to model the major elements present in the pattern. There are six major elements: the pattern background, the upper and lower borders, the curly borders, the flower, the flower center, and the decorative circles.

1   Create a Rectangle by using Create, Shapes, Rectangle, following the outside perimeter of the upper and lower brown borders. Change its name to Background. Convert the rectangle to an editable mesh by selecting it and right-clicking. Choose the option Convert to Editable Mesh.

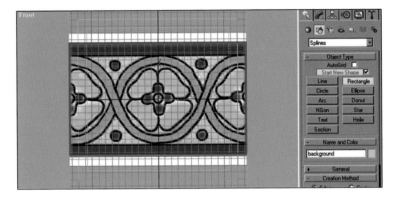

Create a spline rectangle following the template.

2   Apply UVW map, choosing the Planar type with View Align and Fit options.

3   Open the Material Editor and create a new material, using the following parameters and assigning the material to the rectangle.

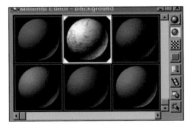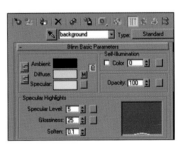

Create a material for the background object.

Name:	Background
Shader:	Blinn
Ambient Color:	Black
Diffuse Color:	RGB 240,225,180 (Beige)
Specular Color:	White
Specular Level:	5
Glossiness:	25
Soften:	0.1
Diffuse Map:	13background.tif
Diffuse Amount:	55
Bump Map:	13background.tif
Bump Amount:	30

Assign the material to the background rectangle by choosing the command Assign Material to Selection.

CREATING THE UPPER AND LOWER BORDERS

The next step is to create the upper and lower borders, which are identical.

1 Create a box on the front viewport (using the Create, Geometry, Box following the upper markings on the template) with the following parameters. Change the name to upperborder.

Length segments: 5
Width segments: 19
Height segments: 5

The numeric length, width, and height of the box do not really matter, as long as the box is positioned considerably to the front of the background rectangle.

2 Apply a MeshSmooth modifier to upperborder, making sure that the NURMS option is checked and that it will operate on polygons instead of faces. This will give the box a rounded edge.

3 On the front viewport, apply a frontal UVW map coordinate, assigning the following parameters:

Mapping: Planar
U Tile: 3.0
Alignment: View Align and then Fit

This will repeat the tiling three times across the box.

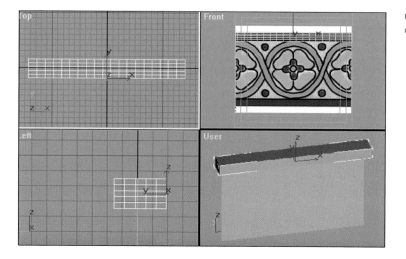

Create the upperborder object following the template.

4 Create a material in the Material Editor using the following parameters and assign it to the upperborder:

Material Name: Border
Shader: Blinn
Ambient Color: Black (0,0,0)
Diffuse Color: RGB 244,206,116 (light yellow)
Specular Color: White
Specular Level: 35

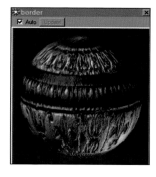

Create the ornamental material for the upperborder object.

Glossiness: 14
Soften: 0.1
Diffuse Map: 13borderintricate.tif
Diffuse Amount: 100
Bump Map: 13borderintricatebmp.tif
Bump Amount: 160

5   Clone the upperborder into a new border, naming
    it lowerborder and moving it on the Y-Axis down
    into place.

CREATING THE CURLY BORDERS

The next step is to create the curly yellow borders that surround the blue flowers by
creating a loft.

1   Create a spline in the center of the yellow markings
    of one of the curly borders and name it CurlyPath. It
    doesn't have to be perfect. Be sure that the ends go
    beyond the Safe frame. In the Modify panel, choose
    the Spline Sub-Object, right-click the spline, and
    choose Curve (even if it's checked, click on it again).
    The spline will be changed to a curve.

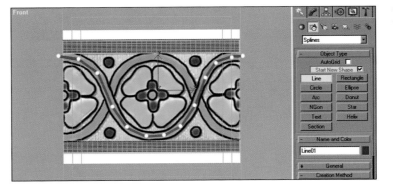

Create a spline following the
template.

2   Create a circle from the Create, Shapes menu that is
    the same diameter as the thickness of the border and
    name it CurlyShape. You can create it anywhere
    you like.

3   Select the spline CurlyPath and choose Loft from the
    Create, Geometry, Compound Objects. Choose Get
    Shape from the Creation Method menu and click on
    the circle CurlyShape. The surface will appear.

4 Under the Skin Parameters, adjust the Shape Steps to 2 and the Path Steps to 7. Under the Surface parameters, check Apply mapping and use 25.0 for the Length Repeat and 1.0 for the Width Repeat. Change the name to CurlyBorder1.

5 Go to the Material Editor and create a material called Gold Border with the following parameters and apply it to the CurlyBorder1 object:

Shader:	Metal
Ambient Color:	Black
Diffuse Color:	RGB 155,139,61 (gold)
Specular Level:	46
Glossiness:	75
Diffuse Map:	13goldbord.tif
Diffuse Amount:	100
Bump Map:	13stripes.tif
Bump Amount:	140
Reflection Map:	13sunset.jpg
Reflection Amount:	25

In the Diffuse and Bump submenus, use Coordinates Angle W as 45 to make the map go sideways, simulating a twisted cord.

6 Move CurlyBorder1 on the left viewport in front of the object Background, aligned with lower and upper borders. Use the mirror command to create an instance of CurlyBorder1, mirroring on the Y-Axis and name it CurlyBorder2. Move the new object into place, aligning with the template, and slightly behind CurlyBorder1.

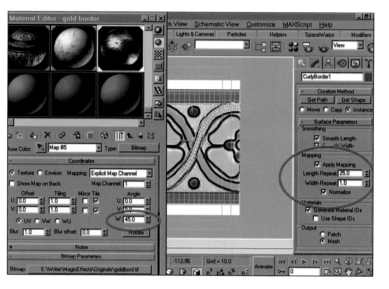

Adjust the Length repeat to 25.0 and the map angle to 45.0.

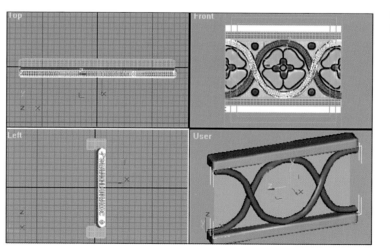

Duplicate the object CurlyBorder1 and mirror.

CREATING THE LARGE FLOWERS

The larger flowers are made out of four identical petals: Just create the first one with texture and copy it three more times.

1   Create a spline, using the template as guide, for the basic shape of the flower. It is important to have the Interpolation Steps set to 0, under the General parameters, before creating the Spline. It does not have to be perfect. Use only 8 to 10 vertices, approximately. Name the object Petal1. Be sure to continue the petal towards the center and close the spline. Use the Extrude modifier with a low value (values will vary, depending on your model) to convert the spline to a thin mesh.

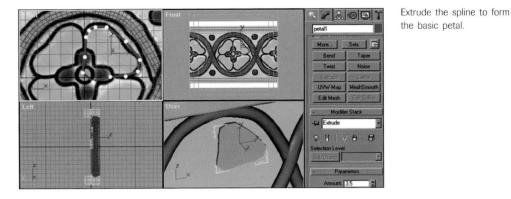

Extrude the spline to form the basic petal.

2   Apply an Edit Mesh modifier. On the front viewport, select the top vertices of the petal. Move the vertices on the left viewport towards the front of the model.

3   Apply a MeshSmooth modifier to the petal, with NURMS and Polygon options checked.

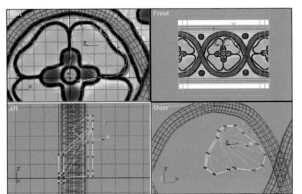

Select the vertices and move them towards the front of the model.

4   On the front viewport, apply a UVW Mapping modifier set to Planar mapping coordinates. Manipulate the gizmo until the icon is fitted onto the petal and rotated at a 45-degree angle.

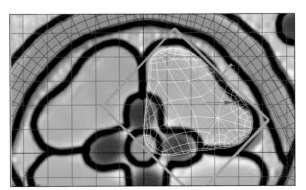

Manipulate the Map gizmo until it fits the petal.

5   In the Material Editor, create a material called Petal
    with the following parameters and apply it to the
    petal object.

Shader:	Blinn	Soften:	0.1
Ambient Color:	Black	Diffuse Map:	13petal.tif
Diffuse Color:	RGB 128,219,205		
Specular Color:	White	Diffuse Amount:	83
Specular Level:	29	Bump Map:	13petal.tif
Glossiness:	40	Bump Amount:	81

Apply the Petal material to
the petal geometry.

6   Copy the petal object three times, rotating each time
    90 degrees, and placing the petals on top of the
    template.

CREATING THE FLOWER CENTER PIECE

To disguise the center of the petals, create a smaller flower using a technique similar to
that of the larger petal: Combine extruded spline with MeshSmooth.

1   Create a simple spline with 0 steps of interpolation
    following the center smaller flower and name it
    flowercenter. Apply an Extrude modifier using a
    value that will make the flower extrude beyond the
    petals. Apply a MeshSmooth modifier to it with the
    following options:

MeshSmooth Type: NURMS
Operate On: Polygons
Keep Faces Convex: Checked

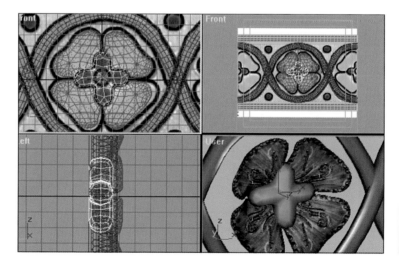

Create a center to disguise
the petals using a spline and
MeshSmooth.

2   On the front view, apply a Planar UVW map onto
     flowercenter, fitted to the object. In the Material
     Editor, create a material with the following properties
     and apply it to the flowercenter object:

Name: Gold
Shader: Metal
Ambient Color: RGB 26,0,86 (dark blue)
Diffuse Color: RGB 155,139,61 (gold)
Specular Level: 77
Glossiness: 63
Diffuse Map: 13gold.tif
Diffuse Amount: 100
Bump Map: 13gold.tif
Bump Amount: 23
Reflection Map: 13Sunset.jpg
Reflection Amount: 34

3   To finish the center of the flower, create a sphere
     with 24 segments following the template and name it
     centersphere. Create a material called blue metal
     with the following parameters and apply to the
     sphere:

Shader: Metal
Ambient Color: Black
Diffuse Color: RGB 48,142,150
Specular Level: 56
Glossiness: 75

4   Create a small torus just outside of the centersphere,
     with 24 segments and 12 sides, checking the option
     Generate Mapping Coordinates, and apply the Gold
     material to it (the same used for the flowercenter
     object).

     Don't worry if the shapes look irregular. Organic-
     looking irregularities are highly desirable in a piece
     of texture art.

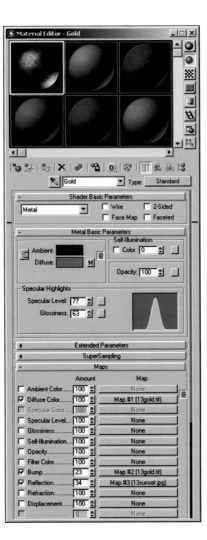

Create a gold material and apply it
to the flowercenter object.

5 Move both torus and sphere in the left viewport so the center of the sphere is roughly in front of the flowercenter object.

Move the torus and sphere so they are positioned in front of the flowercenter.

DUPLICATING THE FLOWER

The next step is to group the flower elements and duplicate the group to the sides to form the other two half flowers.

1 Select the four petals, the flowercenter object, the centersphere object, and torus. Use the command Group from the Group menu and name the new group FlowerTotal1.

2 Clone the group FlowerTotal1 twice by moving it to the side on the X–Axis while pressing the Shift button. Choose Instance when presented with the dialog box and name the groups FlowerTotal2 and FlowerTotal3.

Be sure that the center of each group is well aligned with the edge of the template.

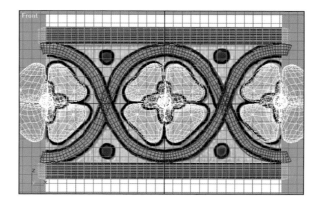

Create duplicates of FlowerTotal1 group twice, moving to the sides.

CREATING THE SMALLER CIRCLES

The final touch to the texture is to create the four small circles that adorn the background. Up to now, the template has been followed almost perfectly. Sometimes, however, it becomes necessary for the artist to modify elements so they are more in balance with the final design, as you will see in this case.

1 Create a sphere with 24 segments following the template. Leave the name as Sphere01.

2 Apply a Planar UVW Mapping modifier using the front viewport as reference. Check the options View Align and then Fit.

3 Using the following parameters, create a material in the Material Editor called circle and apply to Sphere01.

Shader:	Metal
Ambient Color:	RGB 150,96,80 (brown)
Diffuse Color:	RGB 150,129,80 (light brown)
Specular Level:	37
Glossiness:	69
Diffuse Map:	13circle.tif
Diffuse Amount:	90
Bump Map:	13circle.tif
Bump Amount:	110

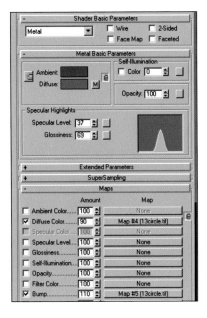

Create the material for Sphere01.

4 Speaking artistically, the Sphere01 object turned out to be a bit small, so feel free to rescale and move the sphere element so it almost touches the curly borders and the upper border. This way, the background barely shows through: It is almost entirely covered by the ornate objects.

5 Clone Sphere01 three times, using the Instance option. Move the new spheres into position next to the flowers.

Allow artistic freedom by modifying Sphere01 to be larger than the template.

CREATING LIGHTS

Up to now, no special lights were used besides the default lighting. However, for the texture to acquire a more dimensional feel, it is necessary to create lights with shadows.

1. Create one Omni light in the front viewport by choosing from the menu Create, Lights and place it just in front of the center of the flower. On the left viewport, move the light so it is in front of the geometry approximately the same distance as the total height of the model. The parameters for the light are the following:

Light Color:	RGB 255,237,228 (light pink)
Cast Shadows:	Checked
Multiplier:	1.1
Far Attenuation:	Check Use
Object Shadows:	Shadow Map
Shadow Map Bias:	0.1
Shadow Map Size:	500
Sample Range:	10.5

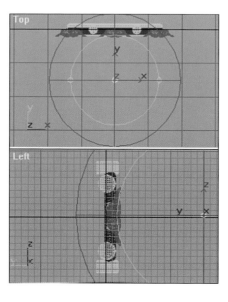

Move the light and adjust the attenuation parameters to fit the model.

2. Set the Far Attenuation Start and End manually until the Start is barely touching the petals of the flower on the left viewport and the End is covering the entire geometry. The top viewport should show the attenuation Start intersecting with the other two Omni lights.

3. Create two more instances of the Omni light and position them in the center of the neighboring flowers.

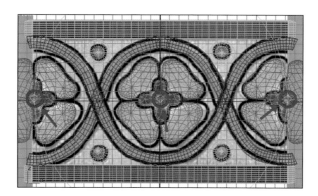

Duplicate the light and align with the center of the flowers.

EXTRACTING AND PREPARING THE TEXTURE

Finally, the project is ready to be rendered. You will extract the texture by rendering it to a flat piece of art that will then be manipulated in Photoshop.

1 If you have turned the Safe frame off to be able to work more comfortably, turn it on again on the front viewport. In the Render Scene parameters, assign the following parameters, but do not render just yet:

Time Output: Single
Output Size Width: 1024
Output Size Height: 1024
Image Aspect: 1.0
Anti-Aliasing: Checked
Filter Maps: Checked
Filter: Catmull-Rom

2 While still in the Render Scene dialog box, click on Render Output/Files and choose 13texture01.tif. Choose Color from the Tif Image control.

3 Use the Zoom and Pan tool to position the geometry so the centers of the two side flowers are just matching the edges of the Safe Frame and render.

Please note that because adjusting the safe frame position is not a precise operation, it is preferable to show a bit more of the side flowers than less (you can always crop the image). Also, you can assign other values for the Width and Height, according to your needs.

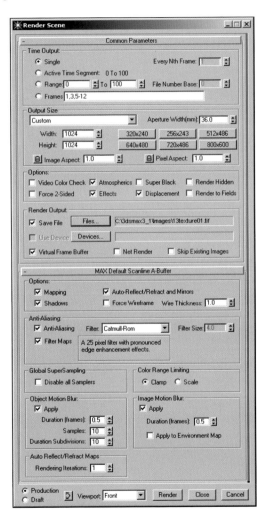

Set the parameters to render the texture.

4 Start Photoshop and open the file 13texture01.tif (you can use the one from the CD, if you prefer). In the Channels window, you will notice that the TIF file was saved with an Alpha channel. Drag the Alpha channel Alpha 1 to the Load Alpha Channel as Selection button.

5 Loading the Alpha channel Alpha 1 will cause the black area of the image to be selected. In the Layers panel, double-click the layer Background to make it into a floating layer. Choose command Select, Inverse and press Delete to clear the black area. Deselect all by pressing Alt+D.

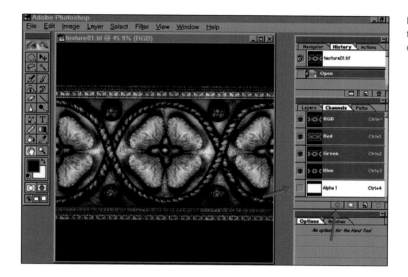

Drag the Alpha channel to the Selection button to select only the art.

FINALIZING THE TEXTURE ART

With the image extracted and ported to Photoshop, it is necessary to transform the texture into a seamless piece of art so it can be repeated multiple times for use in other 3D projects. You will use the offset command to correct the small seam caused by rendering.

1 The image is 1024×1024. Choose the command Filter, Other, Offset with the following parameters:

Horizontal: 256 Pixels Right
Vertical: 0 Pixels Down
Undefined Areas: Wrap Around

2 You will notice that although the two flowers seem identical, there is a slight seam on the left one.

Use Offset to display the seam clearly.

3 Click on the Edit button in Quick Mask Mode from the Tools panel. Choose the airbrush with a brush approximately 85 pixels wide and start painting down the center of the flower on the right. You will see the painted area turn red.

4 Choose the Edit in Standard mode from the Tools box. The red area is converted into a selection. Choose Edit, Copy and Edit, Paste to create a copy of that soft selection into a new layer.

5 Move the contents of the new layer sideways until it covers the seams of the left flower. Choose Layer, Merge Down to group the two layers. Select the contents of Layer 0 by clicking the layer while pressing Ctrl.

6 Choose Edit, Copy and File, New. The Width and Height should be exactly the size of the selected area. Choose Edit, Paste and flatten the layer. Save the file as 13texture01.psd.

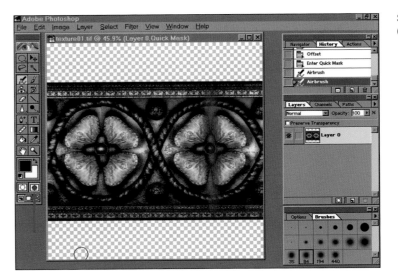

Select the right flower using Quick Mask.

MANIPULATING AND USING THE TEXTURE

With the main texture created, you can now create various types of textures for your 3D projects.

1 Select All of 13texture01.psd. Choose Edit, Define Pattern. Create a new file that is 2048×657 pixels. Choose Edit, Fill, Pattern, with 100% Opacity. You have now created a border that can be used in various situations.

2 Create a new image, this time 2048×2048 or larger. Fill in with the pattern. This is a different variation that can also be used as a Texture map.

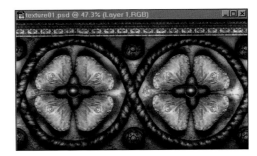

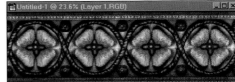

Create a longer border by duplicating the art.

PLUG-INS

There are no plug-ins that apply to this effect.

VARIATIONS

As mentioned before, you are not limited to the template. Feel free to add new elements to the geometry or change existing ones. It is important that you let your creativity loose. A variation may consist of adding elements that are outside the geometry, changing the color of petals or other elements, and moving light positioning.

One suggestion to find good ornamental templates is to consult art history books, especially those that cover the art of ornament or textiles. They offer a variety of suggestions in different historical themes.

It is important to notice how the combination of these two elements, ornament and depth, create a rich resulting texture. Even a simple box can become so much more interesting by applying an ornamental piece of texture art onto it.

Change the lighting or add extra elements for interesting variations.

Make a simple box more interesting by using ornate texture art.

"To have arrived on this earth as a product of a biological accident, only to depart through human arrogance, would be the ultimate irony."

—R. LEAKY, *ORIGINS*, 1977

PLANET WITH ATMOSPHERE AND CIVILIZATION

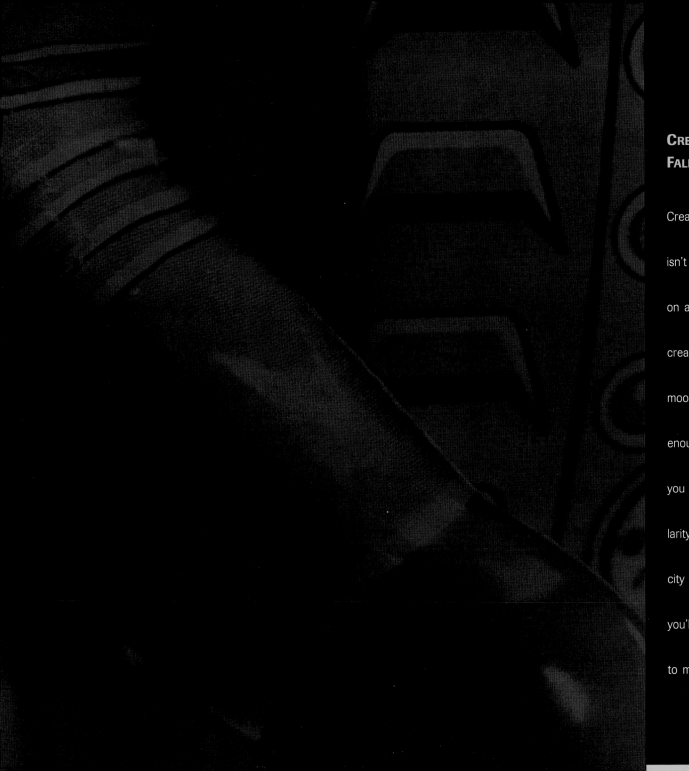

CREATING A REALISTIC PLANET WITH FALLOFF MAPS

Creating a realistic planet for a space scene isn't as simple as just slapping a Texture map on a sphere. This might suffice if you were creating the dead, airless wasteland of a moon, but for just about anything else, it's not enough. To create a living, breathing planet, you need to add a hint of atmosphere, specularity to oceans, and perhaps a suggestion of city lights from civilization. For this project, you'll use falloff masks to create the elements to make a living, breathing planet.

PLANET WITH ATMOSPHERE AND CIVILIZATION

BY BRANDON DAVIS

GETTING STARTED

To create a realistic planet, you must add atmosphere: for example, specularity to oceans and a suggestion of city lights from civilization. These elements are like layers in an image. Take this approach and apply it to creating a single material that encompasses all elements. You will use a map for the color of the planet (including the land and seas). This will be applied to a NURBS sphere along with a specularity mask so only the seas catch specular highlights. You'll also populate the planet with city lights in the form of another bitmap. This will be restricted to the shadow regions only by use of the new Falloff map. Finally, you'll add a subtle blue atmosphere limited to the lit regions only.

In this chapter, you'll create a NURBS sphere for the planet that uses adaptive tesselation to control the surface detail, depending on the distance to the camera. Then you'll create a light source for the sun that casts parallel rays, much like those from a massive light source. Next, you'll create a map for the planet surface, utilizing mask maps to isolate the oceans and land. You'll also create city lights that only appear in the shadows via a Falloff map using the Shadow/Light option. Lastly, you'll create an atmosphere with a similar NURBS sphere. You'll also use a Falloff map to limit the opacity of the atmosphere to the very edges of the object.

In this section, you'll create the planet with a NURBS sphere.

1 Start by creating a Sphere primitive in the top viewport. Set the radius to 40.

2 Now convert the sphere to a NURBS sphere by right-clicking the sphere and selecting Convert to NURBS. Another way to do this is to go to the Modifier panel and click the Convert To/Edit Stack button and choose NURBS.

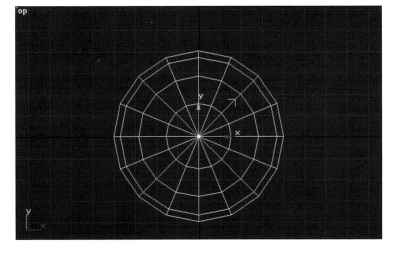

Create a Sphere primitive

3 Go to the Modify panel and open the Surface Approximation rollout. Select the Renderer radio button and set the Tessellation Presets to High. This will automatically set the Tessellation Method to Spatial and Curvature with high-quality settings. Also, check the View-Dependent checkbox.

4 Rename the NURBS Sphere to Planet.

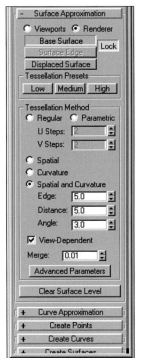

Set the NURBS Surface Approximation rollout to Spatial and Curvature for the Renderer.

Note: Why should you convert from a polygon mesh to NURBS surface? NURBS have the added advantage of being multiresolutional. This means that the surface detail is adaptive or dynamic (able to change on the fly). This is because NURBS aren't a set of points in space connected by edges to form polygons. Instead, they are a complex set of mathematical surfaces defined by curves. By setting the Tessellation Preset to High, you've basically told the sphere to remain very smooth without noticeable faceting. This is important because as you approach a surface, you must add more polygonal detail to avoid this faceting. With a standard mesh, this amount of tesselation would have to be set and remain constant. So, what if you are moving towards or away from the object? Why have extra detail when you don't need it? This is the advantage of using a NURBS surface with View-Dependent Tesselation. The surface will build detail when and where it needs it. For this reason, it's a good rule of thumb to use this technique when creating planets.

CREATING THE SUN

In this section, you'll use a Directional light to play the role of the sun. You'll also use a helpful tool to automatically align the light to a chosen spot on the planet to create the perfect highlight.

1   In the top viewport, click and drag out a target direct light. Start in the upper-left corner of the viewport and drag it to the center of the sphere. It doesn't have to be exact because we'll be realigning it soon. Set the lights parameters to the following settings:

Cast Shadows: Checked

Contrast: 50

Soften Diff. Edge: 100

Hotspot: 72

Falloff: 74

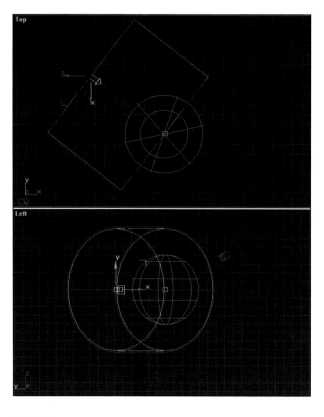

Create and align a target direct light towards the Planet object.

2   With the target direct light selected, activate the PlaceHighlight tool. Now, go to the Perspective viewport (make sure it's shaded by pressing F3) and click-drag on the surface of the Planet object. You'll notice that as you drag the cursor across the surface of the object, the light automatically adjusts to center the highlight over your cursor. Try to find a location

Use the PlaceHighlight tool to automatically align the light to a given point on the Planet object to create a specular highlight.

(for example, the upper-left side of the object) where you'll see both the lit and shadowed areas of the object. This is important because in this Perspective viewport, you'll want to be able to see how the object is shaded so we can eventually see both city lights and atmosphere in the same image.

Note: There are a couple of different ways to activate the PlaceHighlight tool. First, you can click and hold the Align button to open the flyout panel. This will reveal more tools underneath the Align tool. The PlaceHighlight tool looks like a shaded sphere with an arrow pointing to it. If you get lost, you can also select PlaceHighlight from the Tools menu. After you've activated the PlaceHighlight tool, your cursor should change to a crosshair with the PlaceHighlight tool icon.

CREATING THE PLANET MATERIAL

In this section, you'll create the material for the planet. Not only will you be using a texture to define the color of the planet, you'll also use maps to limit specularity to the ocean as well as control the self-illumination of lights in the planet's shadow.

1   First activate an empty slot in the Material Editor and set the parameters as follows:

Shading Method: Oren-Nayer-Blinn

Ambient Color: (R=19, G=25, B=36)

Specular Color: (R=255, G=255, B=255)

Roughness: 100   Glossiness: 40

Using the Oren–Nayer-Blinn shading method gives you more control over the surface of the material. It's often very helpful when creating rough surfaces that diffuse or spread out reflecting light. It also adds a Diffuse Level value, giving you more control over the diffuse output.

2   Name the material Planet.

3   Go to the Maps rollout. Assign a Bitmap map to the Diffuse Color slot. Choose the map planet-color.jpg, which can be found on the accompanying CD. This will apply a Texture map with detailed land and ocean regions to the Diffuse Color of the material.

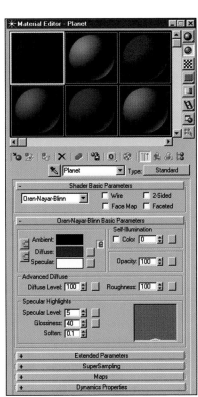

Create a Standard material using the Oren-Nayer-Blinn shading model.

4   Assign a Bitmap map to the Specular Level slot. Choose the map planet-oceanmask.jpg. This will apply a black-and-white image to define the specularity or shininess of the object. Areas that are dark will be less specular and areas that are light will be very shiny. This black-and-white image or mask has been painted to show the ocean areas as white and the land areas as black.

5   Next, assign a Falloff map to the Self-Illumination slot with the following parameters:

    Falloff Type: Shadow/Light

6   In the Falloff map's parameters, select the slot next to the Black Swatch and assign a Mask map.

7   In the Mask Map rollout, select the Map slot and assign a Bitmap map. Choose city-lights.jpg from the CD enclosed with this book. This is a rather arbitrary map with city lights strewn about randomly. You need to limit these city lights to just the landscape, not the ocean.

8   Go back to the Mask Map rollout and select the Mask slot. In the resulting Material/Map Browser dialog box, instead of selecting a new Bitmap map, you'll choose the already existing planet-oceanmask.jpg from the Material Editor. In the Browse From group of the Material/Map Browser, change the radio button selection from New to Mtl Editor. This will display all of the maps currently used in the Material Editor. From this list, choose planet-oceanmask.jpg. In the resulting dialog box, choose Copy.

9   On the Mask Map rollout, check Invert Mask. Unlike what you did with specularity, this time you'll be masking out the ocean, not the land.

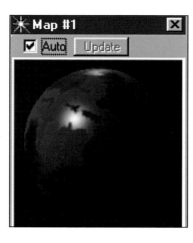

Assign the planet-oceanmask.jpg map to the Specular Level slot.

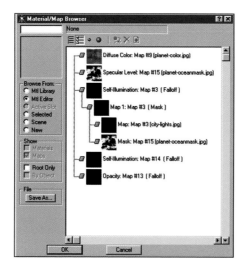

Use the Material/Map Browser to grab the already existing Bitmap map containing planet-oceanmask.jpg instead of creating a new one.

10 As it stands right now, you've got a map for the Diffuse Color, a map to control specularity, and now a map of city lights that will only show up on the land portions as well as only in the shadows. However, you need to tweak the Shadow/Light curve a bit so the city lights make a more abrupt transition in the shadows. Go back to the Falloff map parameters and take a look at the Mix Curve rollout. You'll need to adjust the gradient a bit by bringing both the white and black points inward.

11 Assign the Planet material to the Planet object.

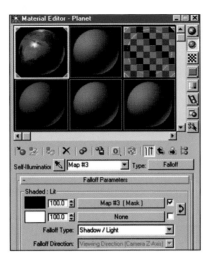

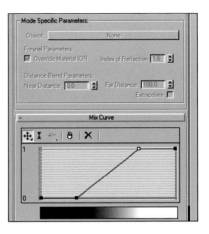

Adjust the Mix Curve so you clamp both ends, creating a tighter gradient.

Note: This method of using the Material/Map Browser is a very powerful way to access or share common maps among materials, and you aren't limited to a single map. You can grab an entire tree and copy or instance it to another map or material. This workflow is much less tedious and linear than going one by one to each slot and assigning maps or groups of maps. Why assign the same map in different locations when you can have them share the exact same map?

CREATING THE ATMOSPHERE

In this section, you'll create the atmosphere visible around the edges of the planet. You'll need to use the Falloff map to control the opacity and self-illumination.

1 Start by selecting the Planet object in any viewport.

2 With the Uniform Scale tool, shift–drag on the selected Planet object to create a clone that's larger than the original object. In the Clone Options dialog box, rename the new object to Atmosphere and choose Copy as the cloning method. This will create an independent copy of the Planet object, complete with materials and any animation.

3 Right-click over the Scale button in the Main tool-bar or press F12 to bring up the Scale Transform Type-In dialog box. This displays the selected object's scale values numerically. Adjust all three axes (X,Y,Z) to 101. This will make the Atmosphere object slightly larger than the planet.

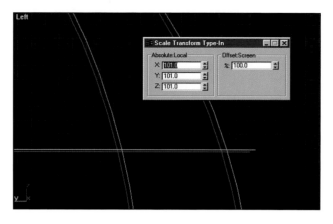

Use the Scale Transform Type-In tool to make the Atmosphere object only slightly larger than the planet.

4 Activate a new slot in the Material Editor. Create a Standard material with the following parameters:

Shading Method:	Blinn
Ambient Color:	(R=23, G=16, B=46)
Diffuse Color:	(R=49, G=162, B=249)
Self-Illumination	
Color checkbox:	Checked
Specular Level:	0
Glossiness:	0

Checking the Color option in the Self-Illumination group activates illumination based on non-uniform RGB values. This allows you to fake tinting and translucency on objects. By default, Self-Illumination is based on 256 levels of gray.

5 In the Maps rollout, assign a Falloff map to the Self-Illumination slot. Set the Falloff parameters as follows:

Falloff Type:	Shadow/Light
Lit Color:	(R=49, G=162, B=249)

By default, the Falloff map uses black-and-white colors. Adjust the light color (white) to the same color as the atmosphere material's Diffuse Color. You can type the values in individually or use the Color Clipboard utility. It can be found in the Utility panel and allows you to "store" color swatches you can drag and drop anywhere in the Material Editor.

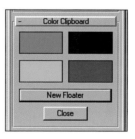

Use the Color Clipboard utility to copy and paste color swatches in the Material Editor.

6   Go back to the Maps rollout. Assign a Falloff map to the Opacity slot. Set the Falloff parameters as follows:

Falloff Type: Fresnel

Index of Refraction: 1.1

This will limit the opacity to the very edges of the atmosphere without any spillover.

7   Rename the material as Atmosphere and assign it to the Atmosphere object.

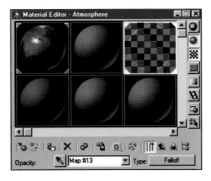 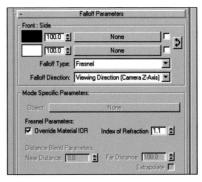

Assign a Falloff map to the Opacity slot of the Atmosphere to limit its transparency to the edges only.

You now have a planet with a blue atmosphere that is fully self-illuminated when lit by the sun and visible only at the horizon.

PLUG-INS

Not many plug-ins can help you in a situation such as this. The two areas in planet creation that plug-ins can help with are Materials and Image Effects. Procedural maps are incredibly useful when creating maps for planets, whether it's gas giants such as Jupiter or eroded surfaces such as that of our own moon. Planets with atmosphere can also be enhanced with image effects such as glows, flares, and highlights.

■ Texture Lab from Digimation is an excellent set of powerful procedural maps based on complex algorithms. Each map is broken down into specific themes for which it's best used such as earth, fire, water, and fog.

■ Worely Labs' Essential Textures, also distributed by Digimation, is by far the largest, most flexible, and powerful set of procedural maps available as a plug-in to MAX artists. It consists of 48 maps that have been ported over and greatly enhanced from the venerable Imagine Essence Textures. Each map contains several rollouts of "tweakability" such as Fractal Coordinate Transformations, Output Normal, RGB, and HSV Adjustments. The Essential Textures also have the unique ability to be antialised, an often-needed function when a detailed procedural map is viewed from a distance.

■ Darkling Simulations has created DarkTree Textures as an advanced procedural texture factory. It's a standalone app that hooks into MAX via material plug-ins. In DarkTree Textures, you use a series of operations to create a procedural map, much like how you create objects and animation in MAX via the Modifier Stack. This very adept network operator workflow makes it exceptionally flexible, giving you limitless options and room to experiment.

■ Pro Optics Suite from Cebas Computer is the flagship optical effects package for 3D Studio MAX. POS is a suite of several tightly integrated tools centered around Real Lens Flare. RLF is a flare, glow, and highlight tool of exceptional speed. Cebas has also added several workflow enhancements to MAX via its plug-ins.

VARIATIONS

In this chapter, you created a somewhat earth-like planet with atmosphere and city lights. But this isn't necessarily Earth, so experiment with it. Create your own maps for the land and oceans or create a different colored atmosphere. If you're very close to the surface, you might try using a Bump or Displacement map to bring out the land more. You could also add a cloud layer to the atmosphere. The Internet is a valuable tool—use it to hunt down reference images or even maps to use in your planet creation endeavors.

MOVING CROWD

"The crowds upon the pavement
Were fields of harvest wheat."

—W. H. AUDEN

USING PARTICLE SYSTEMS AND UNIVERSAL DEFLECTORS TO CREATE A CROWD OF MOVING PEOPLE

One of the most exciting applications of computer graphics in recent films has been the creation of vast crowds of living creatures. From the milling insects in Pixar's *A Bug's Life* and Disney's *Antz* to the Battle Droids of LucasFilms' *Star Wars: The Phantom Menace*, large crowds add a sense of community and depth to CG-enhanced storylines. In this section, you will create a mass of walking and running characters, based on two preanimated figures.

PROJECT 15

MOVING CROWD

BY SEAN BONNEY

GETTING STARTED

Quite often, particle systems are used to control large numbers of independent entities because the pseudo-random movements of particles are a good fit for the chaotic, yet organic, milling of crowds. MAX's native particle systems are well suited for creating this kind of motion, and when paired with appropriate instanced geometry, can produce a believable crowd scene.

In this section, you will create a crowd of walking and running characters. There are several ways to control the movement of this crowd. In this case, you want to send your virtual crowd along a specific walkway. The easiest way to restrict particle movement to a confined space is with the use of a universal deflector (UDeflector), which will allow you to specify any object geometry as a particle deflector.

234

By modeling a narrow channel, you will be able to restrict particles to a specific path. The direction and speed of the walking and running figures will be determined by the friction qualities of the deflector, as well as the velocity with which the particles are originally emitted. Particle motion will be tweaked using several Space Warps to give directional influence to the moving mass. Before beginning this project, you must ensure that MAX will be able to find the project map files.

1   Copy the Chapter 15 project map files from the accompanying CD-ROM to the MAX Maps subdirectory.

2   Open the file 15mem01.max from this project's Preload directory on the accompanying CD-ROM.

Note: If you prefer not to copy the files, you can configure MAX to find the map files on the CD-ROM. To set this up, go to Customize, Configure Paths. Go to the Bitmaps tab and click Add. Navigate to the Chapter 15 project directory and click Use Path.

This scene contains a long walkway that begins in a small structure (at the top of the top viewport) and ends with two smaller walkways. A camera has been provided to pan/dolly along the walkway throughout the course of this sequence, which is set to 1000 frames (33 1/3 seconds.)

SETTING UP THE PARTICLE SYSTEMS

1   Go to a front viewport and zoom in on the start_building object that your virtual characters will start from.

Two preanimated low-polygon characters have been provided, one with a 24-frame run cycle, and the other with a 44-frame walk cycle. By pairing these characters with particle generators, you will create a large mass of clones walking and running along the walkway. To examine these characters, view the AVI file movingcrowd.avi in the Chapter 15 project directory.

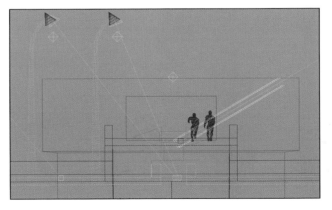

Zoom in on the structure containing the two original characters.

2 Select one of the low-polygon characters and note that its axis is located near the figure's waist. The particle systems you will create should be aligned on the View Y-Axis (World Z-Axis) with the characters' axes.

When using instanced geometry in particle systems, the geometry's axis is aligned with the point(s) that represent the particles. In a crowd simulation, it is important to maintain the particles at the proper distance from the ground plane in order to create the illusion of contact.

3 While still in a front viewport, create a SuperSpray emitter centered on the View X-Axis with the start_building and on the Y-Axis with the characters. To finalize the position of this emitter, open the Transform Type-In dialog box and enter the following coordinates: X=0, Y=950, Z=90.

4 Name this emitter SuperSpray_walker. You will use this emitter to create a mass of walking figures.

5 To get a feel for the default particle distribution of this emitter, go to frame 50 and view the emitter from a top viewport.

Note the location of the character's axis; the particle system must align with this point.

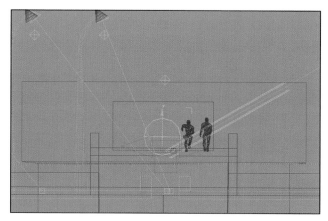

Place the first particle emitter in line with the characters' axes.

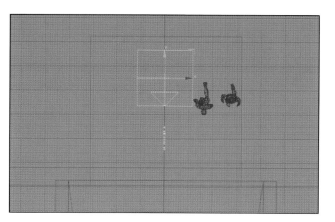

Note that the default particle distribution is a small burst in a straight line from the emitter.

6 To achieve the proper dispersion, set the following values:

Particle Formation		Particle Quantity	
Off Axis:	0	Use Total:	35
Spread:	55		

Particle Timing			
Emit Start:	100	Display Until:	1000
Emit Stop:	450	Life:	1000

By default, only 10% of the total number of particles are displayed onscreen. To get a more accurate rendition of how this particle system will function, increase Percentage of Particles to 100%.

Go to frame 300 and zoom out a bit to see the new distribution pattern.

This will result in the emission of 35 particles over the lifetime of this particle system, between frames 100–450, spread over a 110 degree arc in the XY plane. Particles will have a lifetime of 1000 frames and be displayed through frame 1000, ensuring that they will be visible throughout the animation. Note that the Particle Timing default values will result in short-lived particles, which will disappear after frame 100. Keep this in mind when troubleshooting particle emitters.

7 Set particle motion using the following values:

Particle Motion

Speed:	6
Variation:	5

Later in this exercise, you will augment the speed of these particles using Space Warps and reduce this Speed value to compensate, but at this point a value of Speed=6 will give you a good feel for how this system will behave.

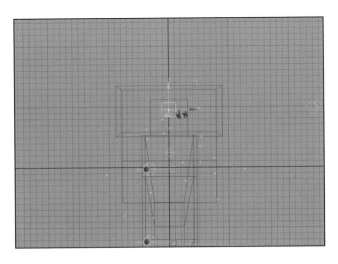

Modify the particle settings to create a wider, more random dispersion.

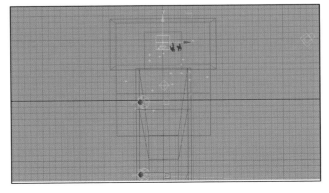

Decrease particle speed to produce a tighter grouping of particles.

8   To substitute the character geometry for the particles, go to the Particle Types rollout and select Instanced Geometry. Under Instancing Parameters, click the Pick Object button and select the Walker character.

9   To see the instanced figures displayed, go to the Viewport Display rollout and select Mesh.

    Displaying this quantity of mesh objects may result in significant display refresh delays. Depending on your system speed, you may wish to reduce the Percentage of Particles value or even set Viewport Display to BBox (bounding box) before continuing.

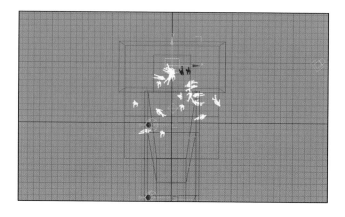

Use the Instanced Geometry type to replace particles with copies of scene objects.

10 The figures are rotated in ways that would be very unnatural for walking figures. This is due to the default rotation settings. To remove random particle spin, set Spin Time=0.

    It is not recommended that you enable inter-particle collisions. Collision calculations are very intensive and will not take into account the actual dimensions of the figures.

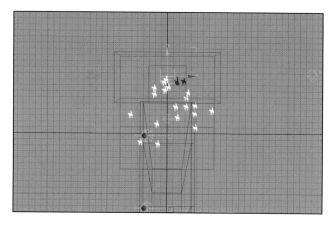

Remove random particle rotations to produce a more natural walking orientation.

Note: If at any point you are dissatisfied with the distribution of particles, simply use the New Seed button to generate a new random setting.

11 You will note that the figures look exactly alike; they are all at the same frame of their animation loop. To allow each figure to start at a random frame, set Animation Offset Keying=Random, and Frame Offset=44 (the length of the animation loop.)

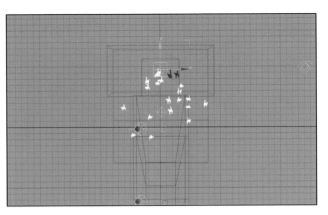

Randomize the walking animation for less obvious clones.

12 To begin creating the emitter for the running group, clone the SuperSpray_walker emitter and name the copy SuperSpray_runner. To make it easier to work with multiple emitters, go to a top viewport and move the new emitter approximately −200 units on the View Y-Axis. Changing the icon color will also help differentiate between particle systems, although this will have no impact at render time.

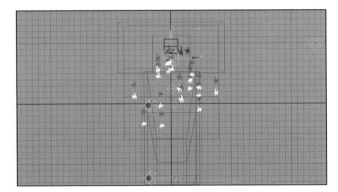

Copy the original emitter to create the system that will generate the running characters.

13 To tweak the SuperSpray_runner emitter for the generation of running characters, change the following values:

Particle Quantity		Particle Timing	
Use Total:	15	Emit Start:	0
		Emit Stop:	200
Particle Motion			
Speed:	10		

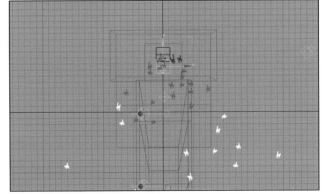

Increase the speed and decrease the quantity of characters for a smaller, faster group of runners.

14 In the Particle Type rollout, replace the walker figure with the runner figure as the instanced object and set Frame Offset=24.

If you scrub the Time Slider, you should see a crowd of running characters bursting forth between frames 0–200, followed by a larger, slower crowd of walking characters. Of course, these characters are dispersing all over because they are not yet confined to the walkway.

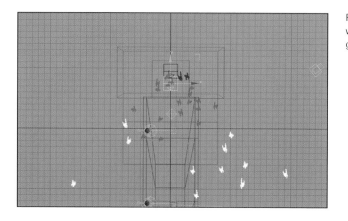

Replace the walking figure with the running one as the geometry source.

CREATING THE MAIN DEFLECTOR

To restrict a particle to a confined space, you will use a universal deflector (UDeflector), which allows any geometry to function as a particle deflector.

1 Create a box with the following dimensions: Length=2300, Width=700, Height=20. To anticipate the splitting of the walkway, set WidthSegs=2. Position this box at X=0, Y=–90, Z=90. Rename this object Channel.

Note that the volume of this object corresponds to the confines of the walkway, at approximately waist-level for the figures.

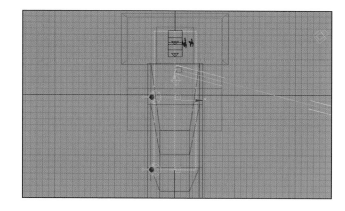

Create a box to begin modeling the primary particle deflector.

2   To extend this object down the ramp, apply an EditMesh modifier and go to Polygon Sub-Object mode. Go to a top viewport and select the row of polygons that make up the bottom of the box.

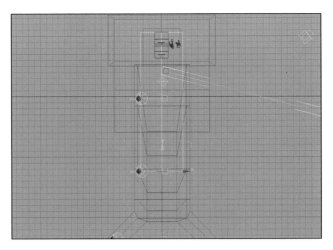

Select the bottom row of polygons to begin extending the channel.

3   Enter a value of 475 next to the Extrude button and press Enter to perform the extrusion.

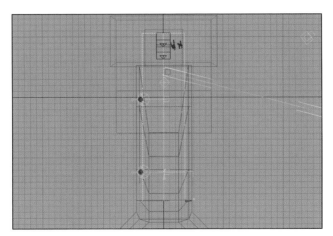

Extrude the selected polygons to cover the length of the ramp.

4   Go to the left viewport and move the selection −250 units on the View Y-Axis to conform to the slope of the ramp.

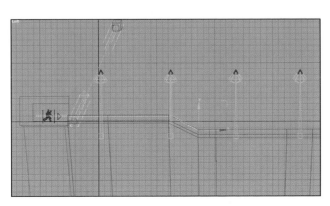

Move the extruded faces down to follow the walkway's profile.

5 Go to a top viewport and extrude the selection 1975 units.

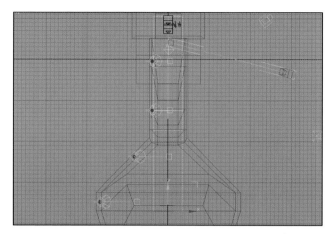

Extrude the selection to bring the channel into the main plaza area.

6 Non-Uniformly Scale the selection 430% on the View X-Axis so the particles can spread out into the large plaza-like area.

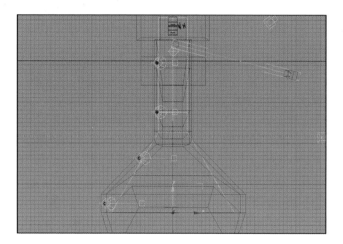

Scale the selection to match the widening walkway.

7 At this point, the channel needs to branch out as the walkway divides. Deselect the polygon on the left side of the object and extrude the remaining selection 960 units.

Note that you are dividing the channel well before the walkway divides. This is to avoid particle deflection at acute angles, which will result in unnatural backwards movement.

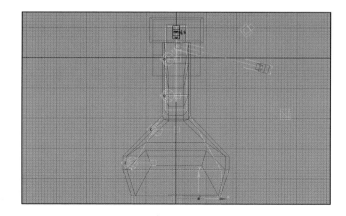

Extrude only the right half of the object to create a branching path.

8   Non-uniformly Scale the selection 65% on the View X-Axis to center the channel within the right-hand walkway.

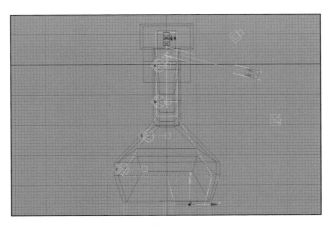

Scale the extruded polygons to match the narrowing walkway.

9   Extrude the selection 10,000 units to extend the channel beyond the end of the walkway.

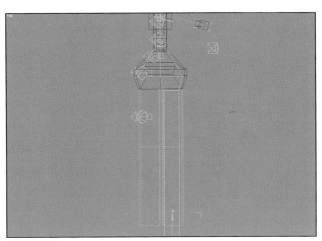

Extrude the selection to give your crowd plenty of space to walk off into.

10 To create a matching channel for the left-hand side of the walkway, select the polygons you deselected in step 7 and repeat steps 7–9.

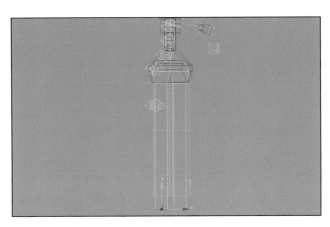

Create the left-hand branch of your particle channel.

11 In order for universal deflectors to function properly, their face normals must point toward the incoming particles. For this object to contain particles within it, all face normals must be pointing toward the interior of the shape. Select all polygons and Flip them. Exit out of Sub-Object mode.

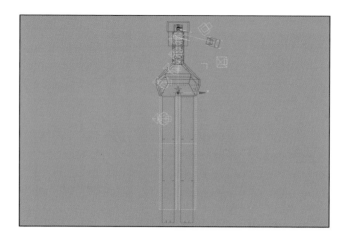

Flip all polygons so they are pointing toward the interior of the object (shown with Show Normals turned on).

ACTIVATING THE MAIN DEFLECTOR

To use this object as a deflector, you must create the appropriate Space Warp. Using simple mesh objects for particle deflection works pretty well, although sometimes an additional deflector needs to be used to catch escaping particles.

1 Create a UDeflector Space Warp, found in the Particles Only section of the Space Warps panel. The position and orientation of the Space Warp have no bearing on its function.

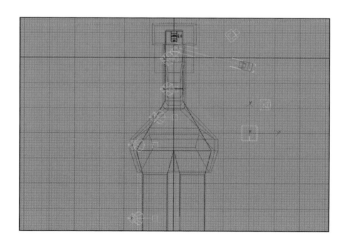

Create a UDeflector Space Warp to link the channel object to the particles.

2   Click on the Pick Object button and choose the channel object. To use this deflector with the two particle emitters, select Bind to Space Warp and drag a link from the UDeflector to each emitter. You may have to refresh your display or scrub the Time Slider to see the particles become confined to the channel object.

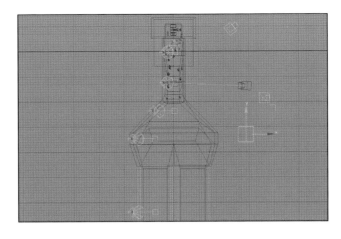

Link the UDeflector to the particle emitters to use the channel object as a deflector (shown at frame 300).

3   To ensure that the channel object does not interfere with renders, right-click the object, select Properties, and clear the Renderable box.

Make the channel object non-rendering.

4   Scrub the Time Slider to test for particle containment. You will most likely observe, in the top or left viewports, several particles escaping the deflector. You should set Percentage of Particles=100% for this test.

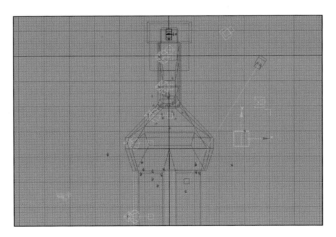

Several particles have failed the collision test and escaped the deflector (shown at frame 900).

5 The most straightforward method of dealing with the problem of escaping particles is to create a backup deflector. Select the channel object and make a copy of it, naming the copy channel_backup.

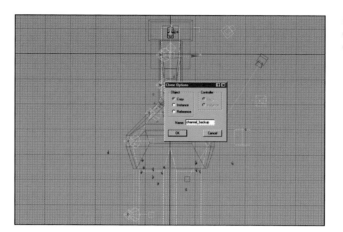

Make a copy of the channel object to use as a backup deflector.

6 This object needs to be a little bigger than the original deflector, so apply a Push modifier, setting the Push value to −10. As the Push modifier moves object faces according to face normals, a negative value will move each face 10 units farther from the interior of the object.

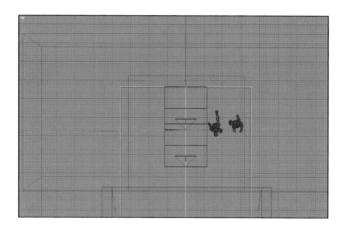

Use the Push modifier to make this backup deflector 10 units larger along face normals (shown here zoomed in for emphasis).

7 Create another UDeflector, select channel_backup as the deflecting object, and bind to both emitters. Any particles that escape the first deflector should be caught and deflected by the backup. If a few particles continue to escape, try decreasing the Push value (towards −11 or −12) until all particles are contained.

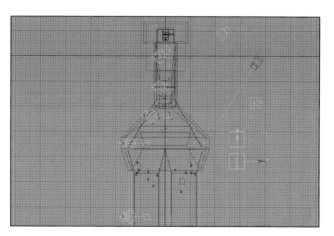

Particles that escape the first deflector are caught by the second (shown at frame 900).

ADDING MOMENTUM USING A PUSH SPACE WARP

The movement of the particles at this point involves a lot of side-to-side bouncing. Although random movement adds a natural feel to crowd movement, excessive bouncing detracts from the forward momentum of walking or running. By augmenting particle motion with a Push Space Warp, this bouncing can be reduced.

1   Go to the top viewport and create a Push Space Warp, found in the Particles and Dynamics section of the Space Warps panel.

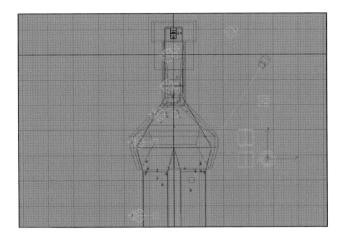

Create a Push Space Warp to add linear momentum.

2   Turn on Angle Snap and rotate this object 90 degrees on the View X-Axis so it is pointing in the direction of particle travel.

3   Set Off Time=1000 so this effect will last the duration of the animation. Set Basic Force=2.

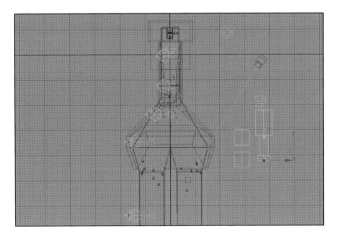

Rotate the Push Space Warp to align with the direction of travel.

4   To apply this force to the particles, select Bind to Space Warp and drag a link from the Push Space Warp to each emitter. The immediate effect will be exaggerated because the particle emission speed has not yet been reduced to compensate.

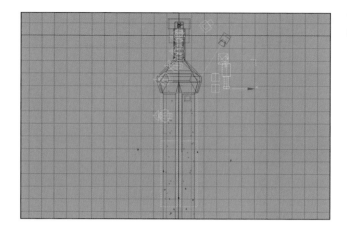

The Push Space Warp adds a great deal of momentum.

5   For the SuperSpray_walker emitter, set Speed=0.5. For the SuperSpray_runner emitter, set Speed=6.0. If you scrub the Time Slider, you will see that the figures are following straighter trajectories, and spending less time bouncing side-to-side.

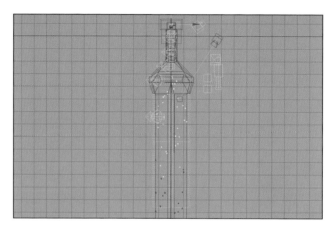

Reduce particle speed to compensate for the added momentum from the Push Space Warp.

INFLUENCING SPECIFIC PARTICLES USING PLANAR DEFLECTORS

Suppose you need to influence one set of particles to move in a particular direction. One method of accomplishing this is to add a POmniFlect (planar deflector) Space Warp to the scene.

1   Go to a left viewport and create a POmniFlect Space
    Warp, found in the Particles Only section of the
    Space Warps panel. Set Width=2000 and
    Height=1000.

2   Set Time Off=1000 so this effect will last the duration
    of the animation.

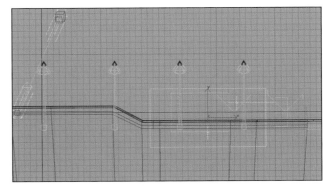

Create a planar deflector to
influence particle direction.

3   Go to a top viewport, open the Type In-Transform
    dialog box, and move the Space Warp to X=0,
    Y=−3600, Z=100.

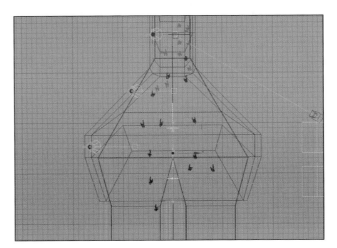

Move the deflector to the
center of the walkway,
where it branches (shown
at frame 300).

4   Rotate the Space Warp −15 degrees on the View
    Z-Axis. Note that you are still avoiding any acute
    deflections; it is important that the characters never
    appear to be walking backward.

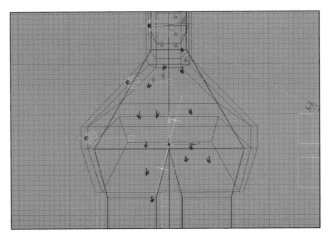

Rotate the deflector to provide
an obtuse angle of reflection.

5 To apply this force to the running figures, select Bind to Space Warp and drag a link from the POmniFlect Space Warp to the SuperSpray_runner emitter.

This deflector will cause all of the characters that intersect it to move toward the left walkway. In this way, the running figures will appear to favor that corridor.

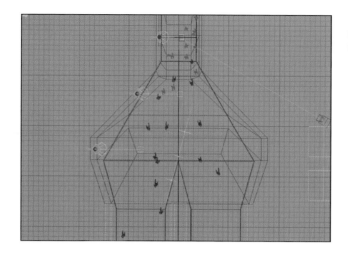

Link the deflector to the running figures to nudge them toward the left walkway.

ADDING AREA SPECIFIC MOMENTUM

If you view a rendered AVI of this effect or scrub the Time Slider in a Smooth-Shaded top viewport, you will note that one walkway has an animated conveyor belt texture applied. Figures that enter that walkway should appear to accelerate due to the moving walkway. This can be done with another planar deflector—this time set to refract and accelerate particles, rather than to reflect them.

1 Go to a front viewport and create another POmniFlect Space Warp. Set Width=1500 and Height=1000.

2 Set Time Off=1000 so this effect will last the duration of the animation.

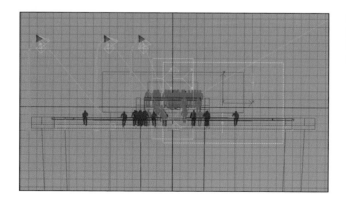

Create another planar deflector to alter the figures' speed as they enter the moving walkway.

3   Go to a top viewport, open the Type In-Transform dialog box, and move the Space Warp to X=800, Y=–4700, Z=100.

4   To prevent this Space Warp from deflecting any particles, set Reflects=0. To allow all particles to pass through and be affected by refraction, leave Refracts=100. To add velocity to refracted particles consistent with the conveyor belt effect, set Pass Vel.=2.0. To keep this deflector from changing the direction of particles that pass through it, set Distortion=0.

    This Space Warp will have the effect of doubling the velocity of all particles that pass through it. By leaving Variation=0, the direction in which the particles are traveling will not be affected.

5   To apply this Space Warp to the particles, select Bind to Space Warp and drag a link from the POmniFlect Space Warp to each emitter.

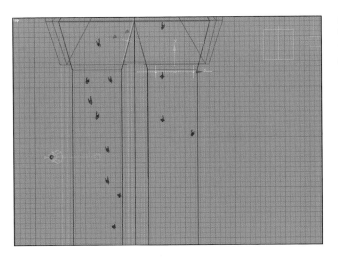

Move this deflector to the beginning of the moving walkway (shown at frame 600).

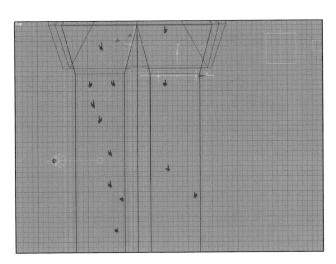

Link this deflector to both emitters so any particles that pass this way will have their speed increased.

PLUG-INS

This crowd-generating technique can be augmented by any plug-in that provides advanced particle features or Space Warps.

Here's a list of commercial plug-ins:

- Digipeople ($95), from Digimation. A collection of premapped low-polygon figures.

- Glider ($95), from Digimation. A pair of Space Warps that works with geometry, lights, cameras, and particle systems, to constrain movement to the surface topology of another object.

- Multires ($295), from Digimation. A level-of-detail plug-in that changes mesh density.

- Pandora ($150), from Digimation. Particles can change properties over time and be emitted from spheres and splines. Included are several new Space Warps.

- Particle Studio ($595), from Digimation. Control particles with unique particle events. Also includes solid assembly and disassembly of objects, realistic flocking and swarming, particle targets, particle spawning, and dynamic materials.

- Spray Master ($95), from Digimation. Allows the user to spray geometry, both 2D and 3D, as particles on or around other objects with an easy-to-use freehand brush.

For more information on Digimation plug-ins, see its site at http://digimation.com/.

Here's a list of freeware or shareware plug-ins. Note that freeware or shareware plug-ins often represent side-projects or hobbies and, as such, are not always entirely stable.

- BlurDeflector, from Blur Studios. A deflector with variable speeds.

- BlurPartForce, from Blur Studios. Includes two particle warps—BlurWind and RandomWalk.

- Chase Gravity, from Peter Watje/Spectral Imaging. A Space Warp that causes particles to chase the Space Warp or chase the vertices of another object.

- Deflector +, from Peter Watje/Spectral Imaging. Supports friction and energy transfer, and affects stationary particles.

- Maelstrom, from Blur Studios. Space Warp that creates a whirlpool effect.

- Particle Gravity, from Peter Watje/Spectral Imaging. A Space Warp that allows for inter-particle attraction/repulsion.

- Particle Spline, from Peter Watje/Spectral Imaging. Connects all particles with splines.

- Particles + 2.0, from Peter Watje/Spectral Imaging. Adds new particle types, emitter shapes, a particle position dump, and stream velocity and motion.

A nearly complete list of free/shareware MAX plug-ins is available at the Virtual Republic Boboland site at http://gfxcentral.com/bobo/.

Variations

The movement of the characters in this effect could be enhanced for a variety of projects:

■ Animate the Force value of a Push Space Warp to simulate the effects of an earthquake or other variable gravity environment.

■ Add a PBomb warp to coincide with a dramatic explosion or energy effect.

■ Refracting planar deflectors could be used to accelerate/decelerate walking characters depending on the slope of the walking surface.

Natural character variations could be added simply by dividing the particles among more emitters and linking those emitters to distinct figures.

Universal deflectors work with non-stationary geometry as well. To simulate characters walking about the surface of a moving object, such as a boat, simply animate the position of the deflecting geometry, and the particles will follow.

As the characters are *instanced* geometry, any modifiers applied to the original will be passed on to the clones. Some possibilities include:

■ For close-up shots, apply a MeshSmooth modifier (smoothing separated by materials.) It is recommended that you enable Inactive in Viewport to avoid sluggish screen redraws as each particle instance is MeshSmoothed.

■ The Morpher modifier could be used to alter the appearance of crowd figures over time, to show the influence of age, the environment, or some special effect.

■ Animate the character's materials. For example, turn an entire host of characters into ghosts using animated Opacity maps.

STANDING CROWD

"Where the crowd came from he didn't know...the crowd faces hemmed in upon him, hung over him like the large glowing leaves of down-bent trees. They were a ring of shifting, compressing, changing faces...looking down, looking down, reading the time of his life or death by his face, making his face into a moondial...to tell the time of breathing or not breathing more ever."

—RAY BRADBURY, "THE CROWD"

USING PARTICLE SYSTEMS, OBJECT ARRAYS, AND THE SCATTER COMPOUND OBJECT TO CREATE A REALISTIC STANDING CROWD OF PEOPLE

The prospect of creating large masses of characters for crowd scenes can be a daunting one for several considerations. People, for instance, tend to collect in clusters rather than in large, coherent groups. To make the crowd look less artificial, it's important to vary the individual characters' appearances and to control the interaction of the characters with the geometry of the scene. In this project, you will create a realistic standing crowd of people.

PROJECT 16

STANDING
CROWD

BY SEAN BONNEY

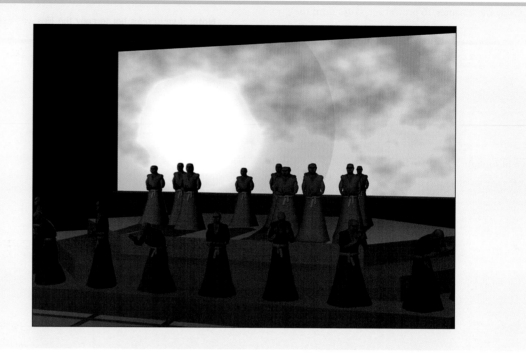

GETTING STARTED

In this tutorial, you will create crowds using a variety of techniques. You will use the Scatter compound object and object arrays to create small and large clusters of characters, shaping the crowd using a custom shape. Particle systems will be used to create a walking procession of characters, whose path will be determined by a curving spline. Small tweaks and variations will be added to differentiate between the crowd members, and their respective animation loops will be randomized as well.

Before beginning this project, you must ensure that MAX will be able to find the project map files.

256

1   Copy the Chapter 16 project map files from the accompanying CD-ROM to the MAX Maps subdirectory.

2   Open the file 16mem01.MAX from this project's Preload directory on the accompanying CD-ROM.

Note: If you prefer not to copy the files, you can configure MAX to find the map files on the CD-ROM. To set this up, go to Customize, Configure Paths. Go to the Bitmaps tab and click Add. Navigate to the Chapter 16 project directory and click Use Path.

This scene contains a large cylindrical temple-like structure, ringed with columns, and lit primarily from an outside source of sunlight. A three-tiered dais provides a focal point for the scene. A camera has been provided to pan around the chamber throughout the course of this sequence, which is set to 1000 frames (33 1/3 seconds.)

Four variations on a low-polygon monk character have been provided: one with a 60-frame walk cycle (monk_walking), one with a 64-frame gesturing cycle (monk_talking), one with an 84-frame bowing cycle (monk_bowing), and one without any animation at all. To examine these characters, view the AVI file monkcycles.avi in the MovingCrowd project directory. By using these characters within Scatter objects, object arrays, and particle systems, you will populate this temple setting with a large mass of devotees.

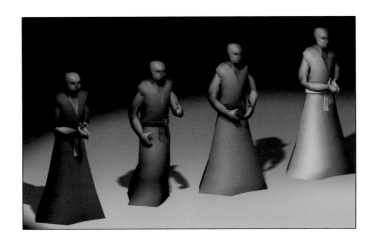

You will populate this scene using four versions of this character.

CREATING A GROUP OF HIGH PRIESTS

You will begin the populating of this scene with a cluster of high priests assembled on the dais. These figures will not be animated, but should be placed and scaled to create a moderate sense of individuality.

1 Go to the camera viewport and note the hexagonal dais in the middle of the frame. This is where you will place your first group of figures.

2 Open the Select Objects dialog box, choose the monk_still object, and click Select. Clone this object using Copy as the method, naming the clone high_priests.

The high priests will be placed on this dais.

3 Move this figure to the center of the dais, at the following coordinates: X=0, Y=−1500, Z=−30.

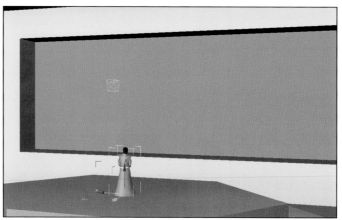

Move the cloned high priest to the center of the dais.

4 Ensure that Angle Snap is turned on and rotate the figure 180 degrees on the View Z-Axis so it will face the interior of the temple.

5 Create a Scatter object, found in the Compound Objects section of the Geometry tab. Turn on Use Transforms Only to distribute the Scatter objects without using a distribution object. This will allow you to create duplicates based solely on transformational ranges.

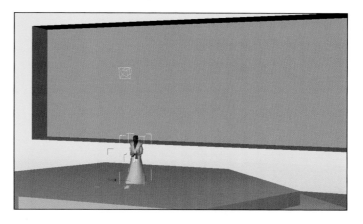

Rotate the priest to face towards the temple.

6 Go to a top viewport and zoom in on the dais to more clearly see the distribution of the Scatter objects.

7 To create a cluster of high priests centered around the source figure, set the following values:

Source Object Parameters

Duplicates: 12

Transforms

Local Translation

X: 400

Y: 300

Z: 0

These settings will distribute 12 duplicates of the source figure over an area ranging +–200 units on the World X-Axis and +–150 units on the World Y-Axis.

8 Go to the camera viewport to see this cluster of figures assembled. If the arrangement is not satisfactory, try changing the Seed value.

9 To add an element of individuality to the figures, change the scaling ranges to the following settings:

Transforms

Scaling

X: 25

Y: 25

Z: 10

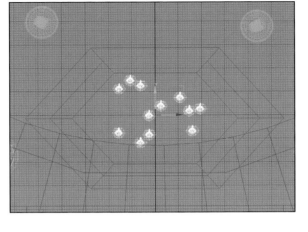

Create a Scatter object using the high priest as the source object.

Use the New Seed Value button to randomize the figures to your liking.

Adding small Scale ranges to duplicate transforms will contribute a subtle randomizing.

259

For maximum flexibility, leave these figures as a dynamic Scatter object. This will allow you to change the parameters at will, such as the number of figures or the range over which they are scattered. Also, this allows you to use the Display Proxy and Display % functions, which can reduce display refresh time by substituting a low-polygon version of the figure in the viewport or displaying only a percentage of the duplicates.

If, however, you need to alter the individual figures, apply varying materials, and so on, you can collapse the Scatter object to an editable mesh. Note that you must disable the Display Proxy and Display % functions prior to collapsing the stack.

Use the Display Proxy and Display% functions if necessary to reduce the display refresh time.

CREATING AN ARRAY OF BOWING PRIESTS

The next group of figures will be an arc of bowing priests, arranged on the lower tier of the dais by use of the Array function.

1   Select the monk_bowing object. Clone this object using Copy as the method, naming the clone middle_priest01.

2   Go to frame 45, where the camera pulls back enough to clearly show the lower levels of the dais. Move this figure to the center of the lower tier of the dais, at the following coordinates: X=0, Y=–1250, Z=–90.

Move the clone of the bowing monk to the lower tier of the dais.

3   Turn on Angle Snap and rotate the figure 180 degrees on the View Z-Axis so that it will face the interior of the temple.

4   Go to the top viewport and zoom in on the dais.

Rotate the character to face toward the temple interior.

5   To create a row of figures along the right half of the tier, click the Array button, enter the following settings, and click OK.

Incremental
Move
X: 83
Rotate
Z: −15
Array Dimensions
Count: 4

This will create a total of four bowing priests, spaced 83 units apart on the View X-Axis, and each rotated −15 degrees cumulatively on the View Z-Axis.

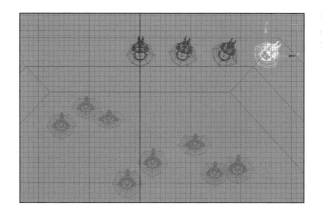

Use an Array to create three evenly spaced duplicates of the middle priest.

6   To continue the curve of figures along the tier, leave the selection set to the middle_priest04 object, click the Array button, and enter the following settings:

Incremental
Move
X: 60
Y: −60
Rotate
Z: 10
Array Dimensions
Count: 5

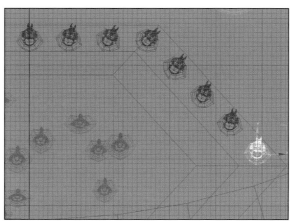

Continue the line of figures by creating another array, based on the last duplicate.

To create a duplicate set of bowing figures for the left half of the tier, you could repeat the two Array operation, reversing the sign of the Move X and Rotate Z values, but it is easier to simply Clone them.

7   Select all of the middle_priest objects with the exception of middle_priest_01. Click the Mirror Selected Objects button, set the following values, and click OK.

    Mirror Axis: X
    Offset: −600
    Clone Selection: Copy

You have now created a row of 15 identical priests along the lower tier. Of course, they look more like automatons with identical animation and scaling. Adding individual characteristics to these figures will lessen the "cloned" look.

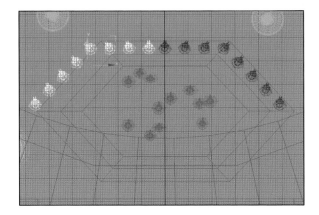

Clone the figures for the left half of the formation.

ADDING VARIATION TO THE BOWING PRIESTS

An easy method of adding variation to this array is to change the proportions of individual figures using the Squash tool.

1   Go to the camera viewport, open the Select Objects dialog box, and select five of the middle_priest objects at random.

2   Activate the Select and Squash tool. For Reference Coordinate System, choose Use Pivot Point Center.

3   Squash the selected objects 90% on the View Z-Axis to make these figures shorter and heavier than their counterparts.

4   Select five other middle_priest objects at random.

Squash the clones randomly to add scale variations.

262

5   Squash the selected objects 110% on the View Z-Axis to make these figures taller and thinner than their counterparts.

Feel free to Squash individual figures until the variation in size looks acceptable.

The bowing animation of these figures remains unchanged. Even at different scales, they will bow at the same rate.

6   To add variation to the bowing animation, select all 15 middle_priest objects and open TrackView. Ensure that your TrackView Filters are set to the following values:

Show Only

Animated Tracks: On
Selected Objects: On
Selected Tracks: Off
Visible Objects: On

7   Expand Objects to show the main track ranges for the 15 middle_priest objects.

8   Use the Zoom Region tool to zoom in on the track bars. Click and drag the middle of a range to change the begin/end times for each figure's animation cycle. Note that the Parameter Curve Out-of-Range Types for these animations have been set to Loop, so these animations will run continuously, regardless of how the track ranges are aligned.

9   To change the animation rate for some of these cycles, click either the beginning or end nodes and drag to rescale the bar. Longer bars will result in slower bowing motion, whereas shorter bars mean quicker movements. Continue until you have randomized all of the track ranges.

Squash some of the clones in the opposite direction.

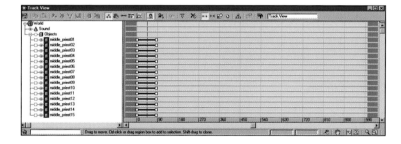

Use TrackView to examine the animation ranges for the middle priest clones.

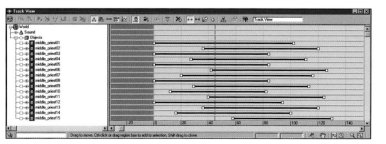

Individualize the bowing figures by varying the length and position of their track ranges.

263

You may wish to hide these figures or set them to
Display as Box, using the Display Properties rollout
of the Display Panel, before continuing with this
tutorial. This will not affect renders, but will greatly
improve display refresh.

CREATING A CROWD PERIMETER SHAPE

Now it is time to fill the temple with a large number of monks. You will use Scatter to
create the duplicates, after creating a specialized shape to determine how the duplicates
will be placed.

1   Go to a top viewport and zoom out to view the
    entire temple. The large mass of devotees needs to fill
    the circular room without intersecting the dais or the
    columns. A corridor down the middle of the crowd
    needs to be left open to accommodate a walking
    group of monks to be created in a later section.

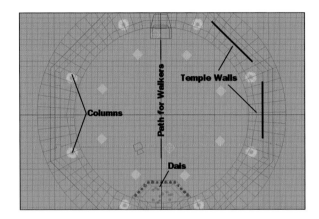

The large crowd must fit
within these boundaries.

2   Create a circular spline at X=0, Y=0, Z=0, with
    Radius=2000. This will encompass the entire floor
    space. Name this object crowd_shape.

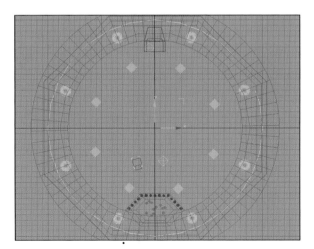

Create a circular spline to
define the overall limits of the
floor area.

264

3 Create a second circular spline at X=0, Y=−2000, Z=0, with Radius=1000. This shape will occlude the dais and the two nearby columns.

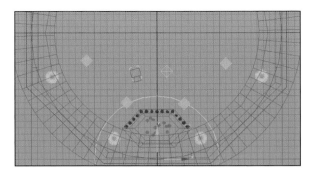

The second circular spline will be used to block out the dais and two columns.

4 Create a third circular spline with Radius=200. Select the Align tool and click the Column08 object. Check X Position and Y Position and click OK. This shape will keep figures from intersecting with the column.

5 Copy this shape and align it with the Column01 object.

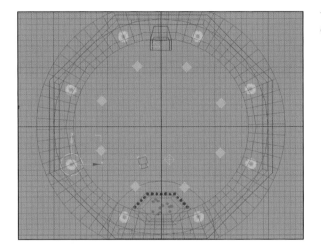

The third circular spline covers one of the columns.

6 Repeat step 5 for the remaining four columns so each column has a corresponding shape.

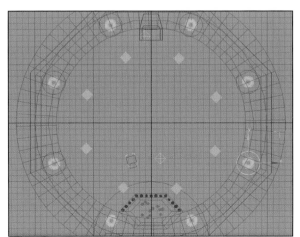

Create duplicate splines for each column.

7 Create a rectangular spline at X=0, Y=500, Z=0, with Length=3200 and Width=375. This shape will provide a corridor for marching figures.

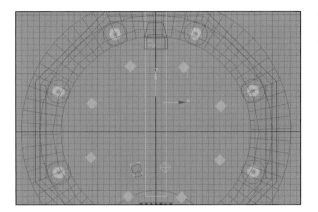

Create a rectangular spline to block out a corridor for some walking figures to be added later.

8 Select the shape named crowd_shape and apply Edit Spline. Click the Attach Multiple button, choose all the listed shapes, and click Attach. All of the circular splines are now joined into a single shape.

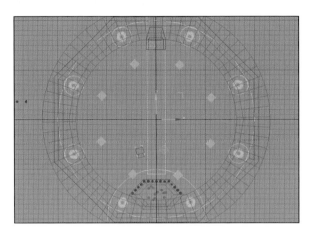

Attach all of the splines together into one shape.

9 To cut the smaller, occluding splines from the larger, first go to Spline, Sub-Object mode and select the largest spline.

10 Turn on the Subtract option next to the Boolean button in the Geometry rollout.

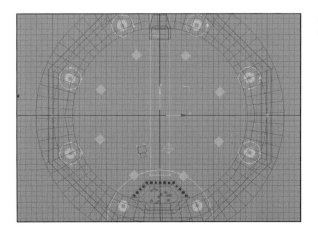

Select the largest spline as the basis for the upcoming Boolean operation.

11 Click on the Boolean button and click the remaining eight splines in turn. The result of this operation is a complex shape that will determine the placement of the larger crowd of figures.

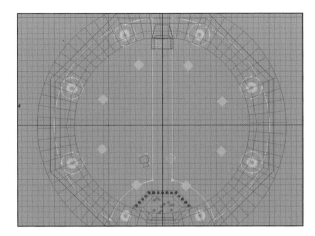

Boolean subtract the remaining splines.

12 Exit Sub-Object mode, go to a left viewport, and move the shape to Z=−70 so it will be aligned with the midpoint of the original monk figures. When using distribution objects with Scatter, duplicates are centered on the distribution objects.

13 Finally, apply an Edit Mesh modifier so this shape will be selectable as a Scatter distribution object. Go to a top viewport to continue.

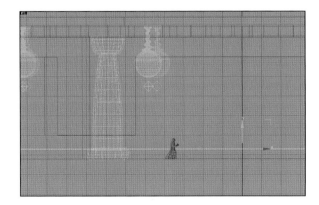

Move the shape to the Z-Axis midpoint of the original monk characters.

FILLING A SHAPE WITH FIGURES

Now that you have created your custom crowd shape, you will use it to limit the placement of scattered characters. Several distribution schemes are available for this operation. By using a scheme that distributes according to area, the space will be filled in a natural, clumping pattern. Minor variations will then be added to individual characters to lessen the cloned appearance.

1 To fill the crowd_shape object with figures, first select the monk_talking object. Clone this object, naming the copy crowd. Create a Scatter compound object, click the Pick Distribution Object button, and choose crowd_shape. Select Move as the clone type.

2 To start with 100 figures, set Duplicates=100.

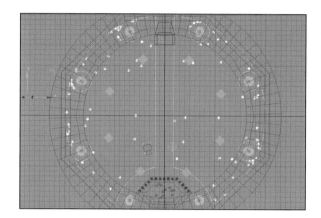

Distribute the monk_talking characters over the surface of the crowd_shape object, using a Scatter compound object.

3 Go to the camera viewport around frame 225 and note that the figures are not all facing toward the front of the temple. To force these duplicates to face in the same direction as the source object, clear Perpendicular, in the Distribution Object Parameters section. Go to a top viewport to continue.

4 Note how the duplicates are being distributed. Using the default Distribute Using setting of Even results in duplicates being evenly divided among faces in the distribution object.

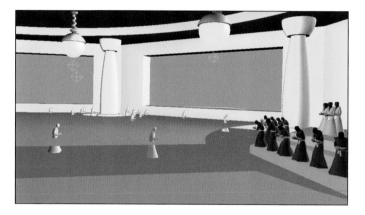

Clearing the Perpendicular checkbox causes each duplicate to maintain the orientation of the Source object.

5 If you were to turn on hidden edge display by clearing Edges Only in the Display Panel (default hotkey=E), you would see that faces in the distribution object are concentrated in the corners, where the geometry is more complex.

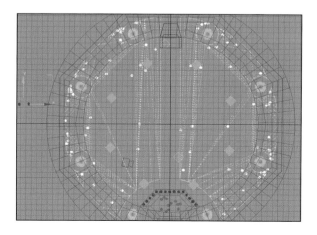

The default distribution scheme places most of the duplicates in the denser areas of the distribution object.

6 To more evenly distribute duplicates, set Distribute Using: to Area. This is the optimal setting for instances where you wish the duplicates to be evenly spread over a distribution object's surface area.

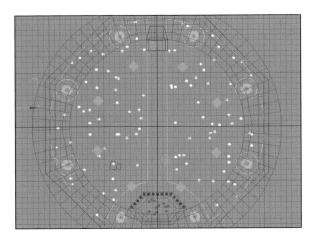

The Area distribution scheme results in more even distribution.

7 To vary the animation cycles of each duplicate, set Animation Offset=10. This will result in the animation range of each subsequent duplicate being offset 10 frames from the previous.

8 To add variation to the transforms applied to the duplicated objects, set the following values:

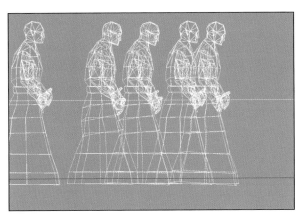

Use Animation Offset to vary the timing of each duplicate's animation.

Transforms

Rotation

X: 10

Y: 10

Z: 45

Local Translation

Z: 20

Scaling

X: 10

Y: 10

Z: 10

9 To really fill the available space, you will need to increase the Duplicates setting. You should activate Display Proxy first. For a dense crowd, try Duplicates=350.

10 Finally, to prevent the distribution object from rendering, turn on Hide Distribution Object in the Display Options section of the Display rollout.

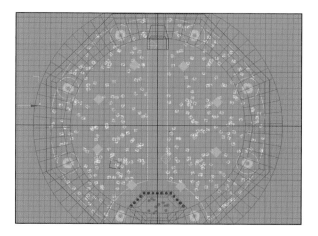

Increase the Duplicates setting to fill the distribution object (shown here with Display Proxy enabled).

CREATING A WALKING PROCESSION OF MONKS

You will insert a procession of walking devotees in the open space down the middle of the large crowd of monks. A particle emitter will make a good source for a stream of walkers, whereas a Path Follow Space Warp will allow you to bind the walkers to a specific path.

1 Go to a front viewport and create a SuperSpray emitter at X=0, Y=1500, Z=–70. This emitter will be used to spawn walking figures in the place of particles.

2 To create the proper number of particles, set the following values in the Particle Generation rollout:

Particle Quantity

Use Total: 25

Particle Timing

Emit Start: 0

Emit Stop: 1000

Create a SuperSpray particle emitter to generate a column of walking figures.

3 Also, set Percentage of Particles to 100 so all particles generated will be displayed in the viewport. Scrub the Time Slider forward to around frame 200 to see the appearance of this particle system.

4 To ensure that spawned particles last for the duration of the animation, set the following values:

Display Until: 1000
Life: 1000

5 To use walking figures as particles for this system, go to the Particle Type rollout and choose Instanced Geometry under Particle Types.

6 To select the specific walking figure, click the Pick Object button in the Instancing Parameters section and choose monk_walking.

7 The instanced mesh will not automatically use the material from the original object. To assign this material, click the Get Material From button.

8 Initially, particles will still be represented with small crosses in the viewport. To display the actual objects that will be rendered, go to the Basic Parameters rollout and set Viewport Display to Mesh.

9 Note that the default size variable results in enlarged figures. Remedy this by setting Size=0.5.

10 Moreover, as you will not want these figures to vary their dimensions as standard particles might, set Grow For=0 and Fade For=0.

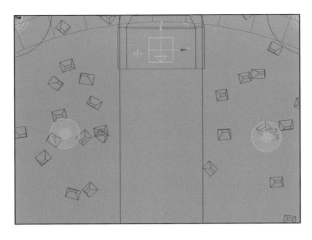

The timing parameters you set appear to result in very widely spaced particles, until they are bound to a path later.

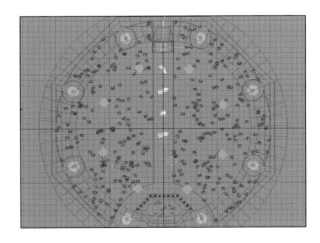

Replace the particles with instanced walking figures.

11 The stream of figures still looks odd because of the
    default spin values assigned. Go to the Rotation and
    Collision rollout and set Spin Time=0.

    The speed and motion of the figures will be
    determined by a Path Follow Space Warp and the
    path used.

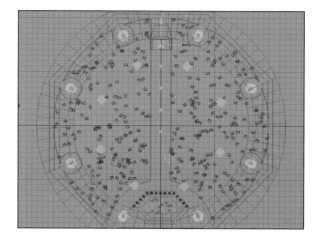

Adjust the Size, Grow/Fade,
and Spin parameters to
produce more realistic
walking figures.

12 Go to a top viewport and unhide the object
    walking_path. This shape curves through the center
    of the temple, beginning at the entryway at the top
    of the viewport, and ending at the dais at the bottom
    of the screen.

13 Create a Path Follow Space Warp. The size and
    position of the Space Warp have no bearing on its
    function.

14 To use the walking_path shape, click the Pick Shape
    Object button and choose the walking_path object.

15 The speed at which the bound particles will traverse
    the path is set by the Travel Time variable. Set
    Travel Time=2500.

16 To force the path binding to remain in effect for the
    duration of the animation, set Last Frame=1000.

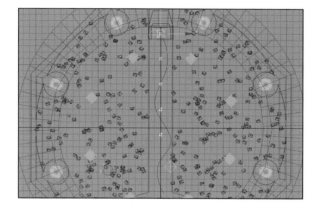

This curving line will determine
the path the walking figures
will follow.

17 In order for this Space Warp to affect the walking figures, it must be bound to the emitter. Click the Bind to Space Warp button and drag from the Path Follow Space Warp to the emitter.

18 The motion of this walking procession is complete, but needs variation to look a little more natural. Select the emitter and go in the stack to the original SuperSpray parameters. To add a random factor to the overall size of the figures, go to the Particle Generation rollout and set the following value:

Particle Size

Variation: 10

19 To add variation to the animation cycles of the individual walkers, go to the Particle Type rollout and set the following values:

Instancing Parameters

Animation Offset Keying: Random
Frame Offset: 64

Note that rendering a scene with a large number of animated figures will be very computationally expensive. Rendering this 1000-frame animation to a 320¥240 AVI (see standingcrowd.avi in this project's directory on the accompanying CD-ROM) took nearly 100 hours on a 400 MHz Pentium II with 512MB RAM.

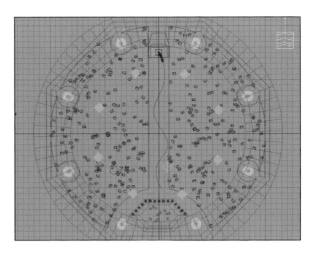

The travel time parameters determine how quickly the particles move along the path.

Use Animation Offset to vary the timing of individual walkers.

273

PLUG-INS

The techniques used in this chapter can be augmented by a number of plug-ins that provide advanced particle features or Space Warps.

Here's a list of commercial plug-ins:

- Digipeople ($95), from Digimation. A collection of premapped low-polygon figures.

- Glider ($95), from Digimation. A pair of Space Warps that works with geometry, lights, cameras, and particle systems to constrain movement to the surface topology of another object.

- Multires ($295), from Digimation. A level-of-detail plug-in that changes mesh density.

- Pandora ($150), from Digimation. Particles can change properties over time and be emitted from spheres and splines. Included are several new Space Warps.

- Particle Studio ($595), from Digimation. Control particles with unique particle events. Also includes solid assembly and disassembly of objects, realistic flocking and swarming, particle targets, particle spawning, and dynamic materials.

- Spray Master ($95), from Digimation. Allows the user to spray geometry, both 2D and 3D, as particles on or around other objects with an easy-to-use freehand brush.

For more information on Digimation plug-ins, see their site at http://digimation.com/.

Here's a list of free- or shareware plug-ins. Note that free- or shareware plug-ins often represent side-projects or hobbies, and as such are not always entirely stable.

- BlurDeflector, from Blur Studios. A deflector with variable speeds.

- BlurPartForce, from Blur Studios. Includes two particle warps—BlurWind and RandomWalk.

- Chase Gravity, from Peter Watje/Spectral Imaging. A Space Warp that causes particles to chase the Space Warp or chase the vertices of another object.

- Deflector +, from Peter Watje/Spectral Imaging. Supports friction, energy transfer, and affects stationary particles.

- Maelstrom, from Blur Studios. Space Warp that creates a whirlpool effect.

- Particle Gravity, from Peter Watje/Spectral Imaging. A Space Warp that allows for inter-particle attraction/repulsion.

- Particle Spline, from Peter Watje/Spectral Imaging. Connects all particles with splines.

- Particles + 2.0, from Peter Watje/Spectral Imaging. Adds new particle types, emitter shapes, a particle position dump, and stream velocity and motion.

A nearly complete list of free- and shareware MAX plug-ins is available at the Virtual Republic Boboland site at http://gfxcentral.com/bobo/.

VARIATIONS

The movement of the characters in this effect can be enhanced for a variety of projects:

■ Animate the Force value of a Push Space Warp to simulate the effects of an earthquake or other variable gravity environment.

■ Add a PBomb Warp to coincide with a dramatic explosion or energy effect.

■ Refracting planar deflectors could be used to accelerate/decelerate walking characters depending on the slope of the walking surface.

Natural character variations could be added simply by dividing the particles among more emitters and linking those emitters to distinct figures.

As the characters are *instanced* geometry, any modifiers applied to the original will be passed on to the clones. Some possibilities include:

■ For close-up shots, apply a MeshSmooth modifier (smoothing separated by materials). Enable Inactive in Viewport to avoid sluggish screen redraws as each particle instance is MeshSmoothed.

■ The Morpher modifier could be used to alter the appearance of crowd figures over time, to show the influence of age, the environment, or some special effect.

■ Animate the character's materials. For example, turn an entire host of characters into ghosts using animated Opacity maps.

MATRIX-STYLE EXPLOSION

"Whoa."

—NEO (KEANU REEVES), *THE MATRIX*

USING MULTIPLE CAMERAS TO CREATE 360-DEGREE EFFECTS

In this project, you'll create an explosion in which the camera rotates 360 degrees around a freeze-framed exploding object, much like the effect in the film THE MATRIX. In filmmaking, this is achieved by placing many cameras around the object, and at the desired instant, pressing the shutter to create the 360-degree freeze-frame. In computer animation, the concept is the same, but instead of pushing a shutter, the object is rendered at this instant. At first glance, it appears we could achieve this by rotating the camera 360 degrees around the object. However, with an exploding object, simply rotating the camera won't work because the explosion process relies on time-based rendering.

PROJECT 17

MATRIX-STYLE EXPLOSION

BY SUNG-WOOK SU

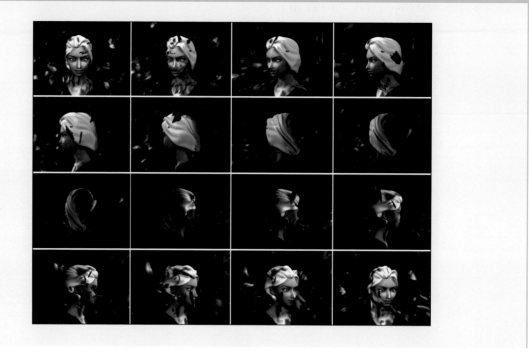

GETTING STARTED

Before we start this tutorial, we must configure the location of the mapping file to open the MAX scene file.

1 Launch 3D Studio MAX 3.

2 At the Customize menu, choose Configure Paths…, and click the Bitmaps tab. Press the Add button and select the Chapter 17 folder on the CD-ROM. Another way to access on the Chapter 17 folder is to copy it onto your hard drive and assign the path above.

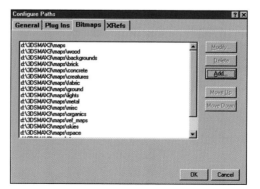

Open the Configure Paths window to add the location of the mapping file.

3   From the CD-ROM, open 17mem01.max. (If a
    Missing Mapping error message comes up, check the
    Maps path or add it if you haven't already done so.)

4   The robotic character that has been opened wears a
    mask. The explosion destroys the mask and reveals a
    human face within.

5   For convenience, hide the body object (Normal-face).

Open 17mem01.max from
the CD-ROM.

THE EXPLOSION

You will make three explosion emitters, repeating a similar process for each body part:
head, helmet, and headphones.

1   To create the explosion of the helmet, face, and
    headphones, go to Create, Geometry, Particle
    Systems, PArray. Click the viewport and drag the
    cursor to make an emitter. Name it PArray01.

2   After creating the emitter, click the Pick Object but-
    ton and click the character's face, named Ex_Face.

Make the character's face the emitter
for the Particle array.

279

3   Change the parameters to those in the example on
    the right.

    Icon size: 20
    Viewport Display: Mesh
    Speed: 0.3, Variation: 0, Divergence: 20
    Emit start: 300, Display Until: 1000, Life: 90,
    Variation: 5
    Particle Type: Object Fragments
    Thickness: 0.15
    Number of Chunks
    Minimum: 40
    Mat'l Mapping and Source: Picked Emitter

4   Click the Get Material From button on the menu to
    get the same mapping coordinates after the explosion
    as before.

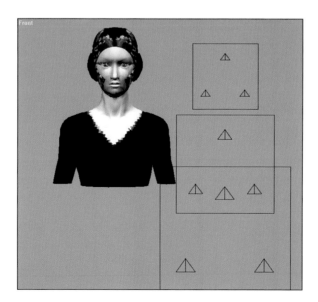

Make a PArray emitter and
change the parameters.

5   To copy the emitter, click the Select and Move icon
    on the toolbar. Holding down Shift, click and drag
    down the emitter. Name this new emitter PArray02.

6   Go to Modify and select the Pick Object button.
    Click the Helmet object on the character.

7   Change the parameters to:

Icon Size:	30	**Object Fragment Controls**	
Particle Motion		Thickness:	3.0
Speed:	1.0	**Number of Chunks**	
Divergence:	20	Minimum:	80
Particle Timing			
Life:	120		
Variation:	20		

Make two more PArray
emitters, as shown.

Then click the Get Material From button on the menu to get the same mapping coordinates after the explosion as before, this time, for the helmet.

8 Create a new emitter using PArray01. Again, to copy the emitter, click the Select and Move icon on the toolbar. Holding down Shift, click and drag down the emitter.

9 Go to Modify and select the Pick Object button. Click the Headphone object (named Sphere01) on the character.

Click the Get Material From: button again to assign the material from the helmet to the second Particle Array.

10 Change the parameters to those shown below:

Display Icon
Icon Size: 40

Particle Timing
Variation: 20

Object Fragment Controls
Thickness: 4.0

Number of Chunks
Minimum: 10

11 Click the Get Material From button on the menu to get the same mapping coordinates after the explosion as before, this time, for the headphones.

Set the final parameters for the third Particle Array using the headphones as the emitter.

THE DIRECTION OF THE EXPLODING FRAGMENTS

These instructions will set up the direction of the exploding fragments. If you want to start from here, open 17mem02.max from the CD-ROM.

1　At Create, Space Warps, Particles & Dynamics, select the Wind button and click and drag on the viewport twice to create two wind gizmos. Change the position of these gizmos as shown in the figure at the right.

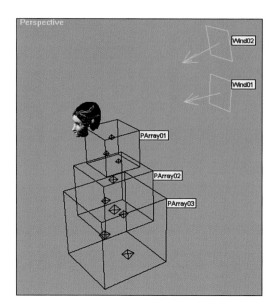

Place the Wind gizmos behind the head.

2　Change the Wind parameters as shown in the figure at the right.

3　Click Bind to Space Warps on the Main toolbar.

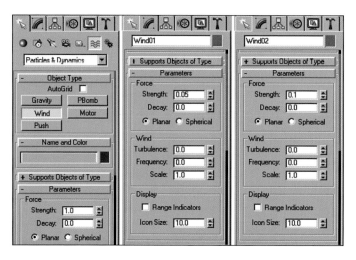

Change the Wind parameters (strength=0.05 for Wind01, 0.1 for Wind02).

4   Click and drag PArray01 to Wind01 to bind them.
    Repeat the process for binding PArray02 to Wind02.

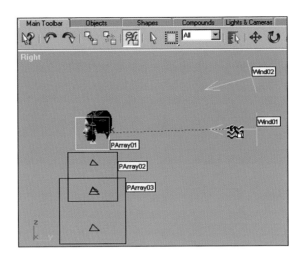

Bind PArray emitter to Wind gizmo with Bind to Space Warps on the Main toolbar.

HIDE ANIMATION

When the face has exploded, the original face will remain after the fragments fly out.
It is necessary to hide the original face to reveal the human face under the mask.

If you want to start from here, open 17mem03.max from the CD-ROM.

1   Select Ex_Face and right-click to open a menu.
    Click TrackView Selected to open the TrackView.

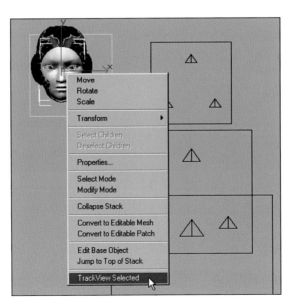

Click Ex_Face, right-click to access a menu, and select TrackView Selected.

2 Click the Filter icon on the TrackView toolbar. In the new window, make sure the Selected Objects option is turned on in the Show Only field.

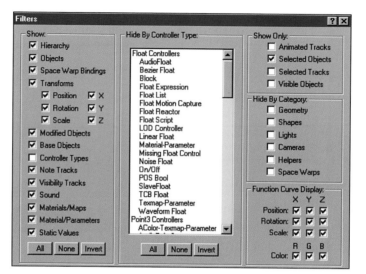

Check the option in the Filters dialog box.

3 In the TrackView, click the Ex_Face in the directory on the left so it is highlighted. Click the Edit Keys icon on the toolbar. The Add Visibility Track icon should now be enabled.

4 Click the Add Visibility Track icon.

Open TrackView window and highlight Ex_Face.

5 Click Visibility on the directory on the left to highlight it. The Assign Controller icon should now be enabled.

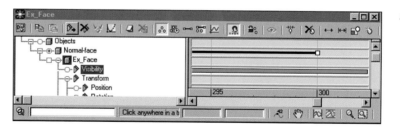

Add the Visibility track.

6 Click the Assign Controller icon. The Assign Float Controller pop-up menu should come up. Choose the On/Off option. A blue horizontal line will be shown on the Visibility track.

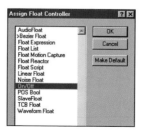

Select On/Off controller.

284

7 Click the Add Keys button on the TrackView toolbar
   and click on frame 300 of the blue horizontal bar to
   add a key. (Use the Zoom region icon to zoom in on
   the window.)

Add key on frame 300.

8 The geometry of the exploded mask should now be
   hidden.

9 Repeat steps 1–8 to hide the Helmet and
   Headphone (Sphere01) objects using visibility tracks.

10 Click the Unhide All button on Display to unhide
   the body. Now press the Play button to view the
   explosion.

Motion Blur

To make animation more realistic, add motion blur.

1 Select the three PArray emitters and right-click an
   emitter to access the Properties menu.

2 Select the Image option in the Motion Blur field and
   click OK to close the dialog box.

3 Move the time slide to frame 320 and click the
   Quick Render icon. On your screen, you should see
   something similar to the image on the right.

4 Go to Display, unhide the body object (Normal-face),
   hair, and hair01.

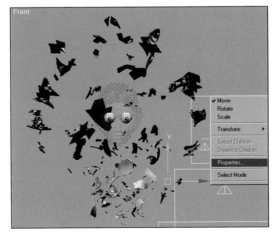

Apply motion blur in
Properties.

Right-click Front view and
select Quick Render.

GROWING HAIR ANIMATION

At this point, we need to put hair on the woman. (There was no need to have a mesh before because her hair would theoretically be under the helmet.) After the helmet has exploded, we will make the hair visible using visibility tracks, and make it grow using morphing techniques.

If you want to start from here, open 17mem04.max from the CD-ROM.

1   Click the smaller unit of hair in the front viewport. Click the Select and Move icon on the toolbar. Right-click the Select and Move icon. In the pop-up menu, type –30 as the Offset: Screen X value. The hair should position itself on the character's head.

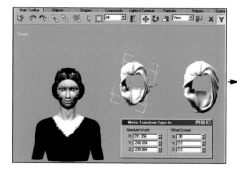

Use the Transform Type-In dialog box to enter precise positioning.

2   Move Time Slider to frame 0.

3   Click the Select and Link icon on the Main toolbar.

4   Click and drag the hair object to Normal-face to link them.

Use the Select and Link icon to link objects.

5   Go to Modify and click the More button. From this menu, select Morpher.

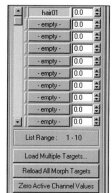

Use Morpher modifier to create a hair-growing animation.

6   Click the Pick Object from Scene button on the right menu and click the bigger hair, named hair01.

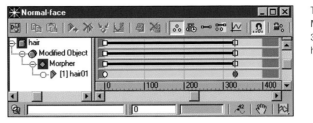

Turn on the Animate button. Move the time slide to frame 330. Type in 100 for the hair01 parameter.

7   Click the Animate button on the bottom of the screen. Move the time slide to frame 330.

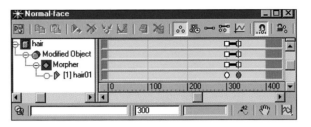

Move the key on frame 0 to frame 300.

8   Type in 100 for the hair01 parameter on the right in the Morpher channel list.

9   Open a TrackView. On the Morpher modifier's hair01 track, move the key on frame 0 to frame 300 by clicking and dragging.

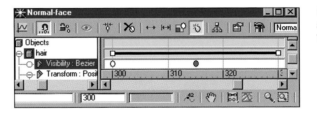

Insert the keys on frame 300 and frame 315 on the Visibility track.

10   In TrackView, click the hair in the directory on the left.

11   Click the Add Visibility track icon on the toolbar and insert keys on frame 300 and frame 315 on the Visibility track.

12   Click the Function Curves icon on the TrackView toolbar. The Graph Editor should appear.

13 Click the key on frame 300 and drag it down vertically from the 1 to 0 position.

You will see the hair animate when you click the
Play button.

14 Delete the hair01 object—we don't need it anymore.
Turn off the Animate button.

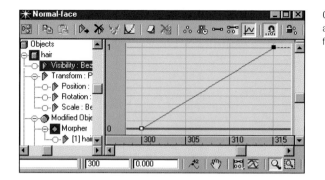

Click the key on frame 300
and drag it down vertically
from the 1 to 0 position.

THE CAMERA TECHNIQUE

Now we will learn how to set up the camera technique. First, you should hide all
unnecessary objects. If you want to start from here, open 17mem05.max from the
CD-ROM.

1 Go to Display and check the options to match the
image on the right.

Check the Display options.

2 Go to Create, Shapes. Click the Circle button and
make the radius 70 in the top viewport, centered on
the character.

The cameras will be placed along the circle's
circumference.

Create the circle.

3   Go to Create, Cameras. Click the Free button.
    Create a camera in the front viewport.

Make the camera.

4   Go to Motion. In the Assign Controller rollout,
    click Position to activate the Assign Controller
    button.

5   Click Assign Controller. The Assign Position
    Controller menu comes up. Select the Path option.

6   Click the Pick Path button in the menu and click
    Circle01 in the viewport. The camera should move
    onto the circle's path.

7   Check the Follow option under Path Options.

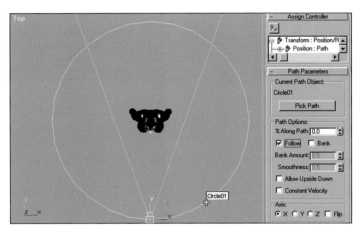

Use Path controller to
move the camera onto the
circle's path.

8   Click on Circle01 and rotate it −90 degrees as
    shown.

9   Click Camera01. Click the Snapshot button. (Hold
    down the Array icon and a flyout menu should
    appear with a few choices.)

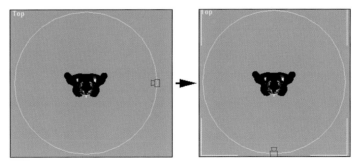

Rotate Circle01 −90 degrees.

10 From the Snapshot menu, select Range and type 90 for the Copies parameter.

You should have 90 more cameras, as shown on the right.

There will be two extraneous cameras overlapped on the same original camera.

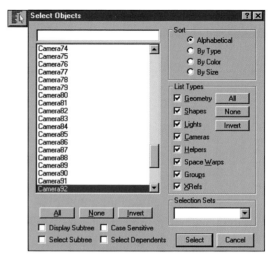

First, use Snapshot to copy a camera. Next, delete cameras overlapped on the same original camera.

11 Click the Select by Name icon on the toolbar. Select Camera01 and Camera92 and delete.

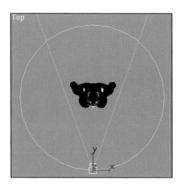

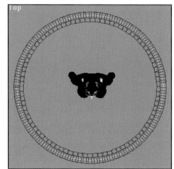

Before and after using Snapshot.

RENDERING SETUP

This portion of the tutorial teaches you how to render all 90 cameras automatically without having to render one camera at a time. When you add Event, make sure there is nothing highlighted in the left list on Video Post. Otherwise, Video Post will improperly create a hierarchy to execute the action.

If you want to start from here, open 17mem06.max from the CD-ROM.

1   Go to Display and uncheck all options in Hide by Category.

2   Go to the Main menu and select Rendering, Video Post. There should now be a Video Post window.

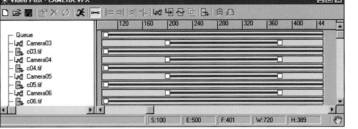

Open the Video Post window.

3   Click the Add Scene Event icon on the Video Post toolbar.

4   Select Camera03.

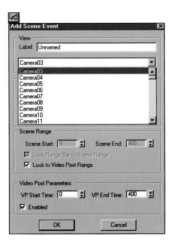

Click the Add Scene Event icon.

5   Click the Add Image Output Event icon. Click the Files button and name the file C03, selecting the .tif format. If the TIF Image Control dialog box is displayed, select the Color Image attribute.

6   Click the Add Scene Event icon on the Video Post toolbar.

7   Select Camera04.

Name the file C03, selecting the .tif format.

8   Click the Add Image Output Event icon and name
    the file C04, selecting the .tif format.

    One thing you should remember is that if you use
    this method, you will have to set up a total of 89
    cameras, which is extremely time-consuming. The
    previous steps illustrate the workflow of the camera
    setup, but the effect can be achieved much more
    efficiently: You can simply open the Video Post
    script file to set up all the cameras in the click of one
    button.

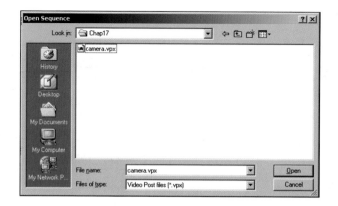

To save time adding all the cameras, open the
camera.vpx Video Post sequence.

9   Click the Open Sequence button on the Video Post
    toolbar and select the Scene folder on the CD-ROM.
    Open the camera.vpx file.

    You may have problems if your computer does not
    have a D: drive because the output location is set up
    on D: drive. Therefore, if you have no D: hard drive
    on your computer, all 89 Image Output events in
    the Video Post must be changed.

CAMERA ANIMATION

Next, adjust the camera animation to zoom toward the object and then rotate
around it.

1   Turn on the Animate button on the bottom of
    the screen.

2   Move the Time slider to frame 300.

3 In the top viewport, move Camera03 down as much as desired.

4 Turn off the Animate button.

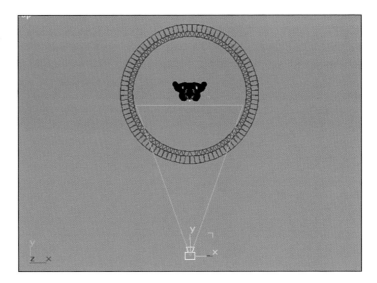

Animate Camera03.

5 There are two keys under the Time slider. Move the key from frame 300 to frame 200. Then move the key from frame 0 to frame 300.

6 Click the Play button. The camera should start zooming in at frame 200 and stop at frame 300.

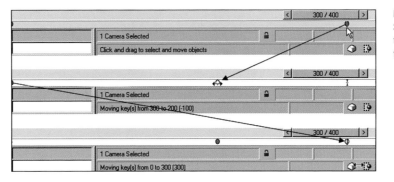

Move the key from frame 300 to frame 200. Then move the key from frame 0 to frame 300.

RENDERING

It is time to render.

If you want to start from here, open 17mem07.max from the CD-ROM.

1   Click the Render Scene icon on the toolbar and set up the resolution: 320×240. Set the image format as .tif.

2   Name the file exp.tif and set Range field 200 to 400.

3   After rendering the file, go to Video Post and click Execute Sequence. Render size should be set to 320×240.

4   Set the Single field to 315 and click Render.

5   The first rendered scene was the explosion itself. The second is the camera rotating around the explosion. It is now time to merge the two rendered sequences.

    Until now, you rendered a lot of the image files that you need to put together to make a movie file. Normally, we use Premier or Aftereffect to do this, but now you will learn how to do this in MAX.

6   Open Video Post and click the New Sequence icon to clean up the Video Post setup.

7   Click the Add Image Input Event icon. Next, click the Files button and select the image (exp0200.tif) rendered the first time. Check the Sequence option. Change the End Frame value to 115.

    When you add Add Image Input Event, make sure there is nothing highlighted on the left side in Video Post.

8   Click the Add Image Input Event icon. Then click the File button and select the second sequence (C03.tif) you rendered.

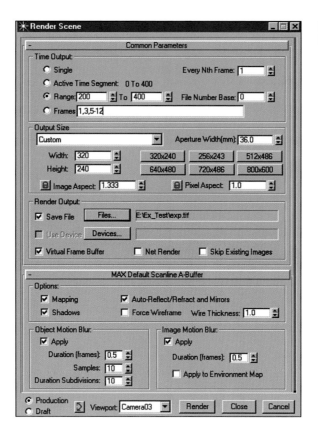

Click the Render Scene icon to open the menu.

9. Check the Sequence Option. Leave the End Frame value as it is. Click the OK button.

10. Change the VP Start Time value to 116 and the VP End Time value to 204.

11. Click the Add Image Input Event icon. Next, click the Files button and select the image rendered the first time (exp0200.tif).

12. Check the Sequence option. Change the Start Frame value to 116.

13. Change the VP Start Time value to 205 and the VP End Time value to 289.

    If the timeline doesn't look like the picture, change the timelines on the Video Post window by clicking and dragging the blue bars into the positions as shown in the figure on the right. The first sequence, exp0200, is the camera zoom to the character and the beginning of the explosion. The second sequence is the camera rotating animation, and the third sequence is the rest of the explosion.

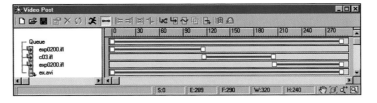

Make the timeline in the Video Post as shown.

14. Click the Add Image Output Event icon. Click the Files button, select the .avi file format, and name it ex.avi.

15. After saving, play the animation with Media Player and watch the results.

PLUG-INS

There aren't really any plug-ins that would augment this effect. However, there is some software that can help. From step 6 of rendering, when you use MAX to make an .avi file, you can use video editing software such as Aftereffect or Premier to do this instead.

VARIATIONS

Try using this technique for all sorts of animations. Instead of an explosion, for instance, you can use this camera technique for a fighting scene as in the movie *The Matrix*, or with a dancing sequence as in the popular Gap advertising campaign. The possibilities are endless.

HAIR

"I'm not only the Hair Club President, I'm also a client."

—SY SPERLING,
HAIR CLUB FOR MEN

USING PARTICLE HAIR TO CREATE REALISTIC CHARACTER HAIR

Particle Hair is a freeware particle system

plug-in that is capable of creating particle

strand effects ranging from waving grass to

thin trailing tentacles on a jellyfish. It also

happens to be good for making hair on a

character's head. When rendered with Glow,

it can simulate long flames trailing an object.

Particle Hair can use a large amount of RAM

when the number of hairs exceeds 3–4,000,

so it is not practical for creating an entire

lawn. However, it works well for creating

clumps of grass, caterpillars, or any strand-like

material such as fringe on cloth.

HAIR

BY SANFORD KENNEDY

GETTING STARTED

Particle Hair is a freeware plug-in written by Peter Watje. Particle Hair can be used to create long-hair wigs for any polygonal model. You can apply particle hair to a NURBS or a patch model, but only a polygonal model will let you select a small section of the skull and accurately generate a long-hair wig from selected faces on a one-piece model. Because Particle Hair is still considered an Alpha plug-in, meaning that it is still a work-in-progress, not all of the commands will work. Some of the commands may even crash MAX. I have found that by experimenting with the features that do work well and simply avoiding those that don't, I can make excellent long hair for characters. The main factor to keep in mind is that the hair-to-object collision does not work. That means that the hair will pass through or penetrate the surface of the model. Later in this tutorial, I explain how to get around this limitation by creating a Snapshot mesh copy of the Particle Hair system, deleting the particle hair, and using the Flex modifier to animate the resulting mesh–hair wig so it moves like real hair.

INSTALLING PARTICLE HAIR

The freeware Particle Hair plug-in is available on the CD or can be downloaded from Peter Watje's Web site at www.max3dstuff.com. At his site, click the New button and locate the MAX 3.0 plug-in updates called Hair. Click the Hair link to Download hair_V3.zip. (**Caution:** The Particle Hair plug-ins for MAX 2.0 and 2.5 will not work in MAX 3.0 or 3.1.) Actually, you should download all of Peter's plug-ins. They are great additions to your tool set.

1 Load the Hair_V3.zip file into a temporary directory. Unzip the file. You will notice that it unzips and creates a directory named Shiva. This is a MAX code name indicating that this plug-in is still un-finished Alpha software. Easier yet, just load it from the CD-ROM.

Note: 3D Studio MAX 3.1 was used for this tutorial, but these steps also apply to Particle Hair for MAX 2.0, 2.5, and 3.0, except for Flex, which is not available in MAX 2.0 or 2.5.

2 Next, step through the directories until you reach \Shiva\Maxsdk\Mystuff\Pw_hair3\Outv3. In this directory, you will find the plug-ins, the source code for the plug-in, and the help file. Print out the help file so you have access to the technical data and the spline cage tutorial that comes with the plug-in.

Note: To run Particle Hair, you must first place the mgraph.dlo and the pw_hair.dlo files in your MAX 3.0 or 3.1 plug-ins directory. When you open MAX, you will find Particle Hair in the Create, Particle Systems menu, represented by the Hair radio button. Click Hair to open the plug-in.

CREATING HAIR

In the following steps, you will create particle hair on a sphere.

1 Create a standard primitive geosphere with a radius of 50 units in the front viewport. Next, open the Create, Particle Systems rollout and click the Hair radio button. When the Particle Hair opens, you will see the menu as shown in the figure.

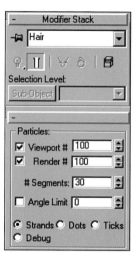

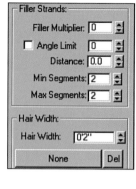

Create a geosphere with a radius of 50 units. Open Particle Systems and click the Hair radio button.

2 Click and drag the cursor in the viewport next to the sphere to create a particle system icon, and then scroll the rollout menu upward until you see the Emitter Shape menu. Click the button marked None and, in the selection dialog box, select geosphere01. If you find that the hair will not generate at frame 0, try moving the time slider above 0. You should see dotted orange lines projecting out from each face aligned with the face normals.

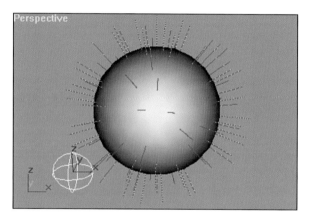

Click and drag the cursor to create a Particle Hair icon. Locate the Emitter Shape radio button, and then click it and select the geosphere.

3 A default hair strand is composed of particles along a path. The Three-Sided Strand hair looks like a tapered cylinder. Go to the Hair, Render Info menu and change Particle Type from Six Point to Three-Sided Strands, which, when adjusted correctly, makes the most realistic-looking hair. Render the view. The particle hairs will look like cones. Change your render background to a light color and change the sphere wire mesh color to a dark color so you can see the rendered hair more easily.

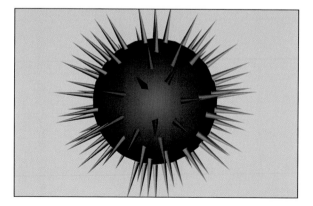

Render the sphere with the default thickness setting.

4 In order to make the three-sided strands look more like hair, reduce the hair-width setting. In the Hair Width entry box, type a width of 0.3 units and then rerender the sphere. The hair strands should now be thin.

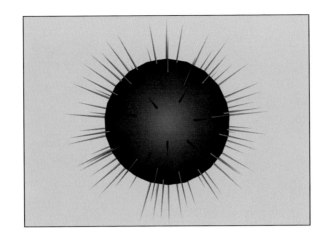

Set Hair Width to 0.3 units to obtain thinner hair strands.

Styling the Hair with a Spline Cage

Straight spiky hair has limited usefulness unless you are creating a hedgehog or a character with a crewcut, so you will need to create a spline to give the hair shape and curl. Particle Hair can be styled by drawing a spline known as a Spline Cage to shape the hair. A smooth spline is used as a pattern for shaping the hair and controlling its curl and length.

In the following steps, you will add a spline to curl the hair.

1 To create a spline that can be used as a spline cage to shape the hair, you will draw a smooth spline extending out from the emitter surface. Click Create, Shapes, Line.

2 In the Creation Method dialog box, set Initial Type and Drag Type to Smooth so the spline and the hair strand will be smoothly curved. Draw a curved spline consisting of four or five vertices in the front viewport starting at the top surface of the sphere, and then extending upward and to the left, as shown. The first vertex of the spline should touch the sphere.

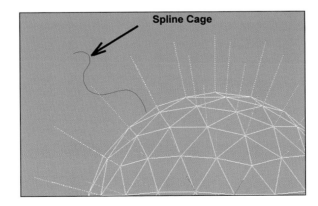

Spline Cage

Draw a smooth spline curve to create the Hair Spline Cage. Make sure the curve touches the emitter shape.

3 After you have drawn the spline, select the Hair01 icon, and then click Modify to reopen the Hair menu. Scroll the menu to Spline Cage and click the large button marked None. From the dialog box that opens, select Line01. Usually, no change will occur at frame 0. When you move the time slider, Particle Hair will redraw and change the hair strands to match the shape and length of the spline cage.

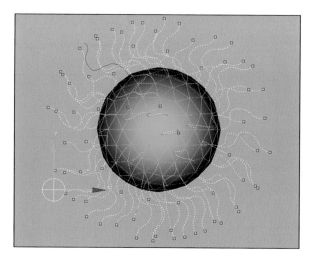

Click Modify, then in the Hair menu, click the Spline Cage selection button marked "none" and choose Line01. The hair will redraw to match the spline shape.

4 Notice that there is a button labeled Absolute Direction under Spline Cage. Turn on Absolute Direction so the hair conforms to the direction of the spline. You should now see curly hairs that all point in the same direction.

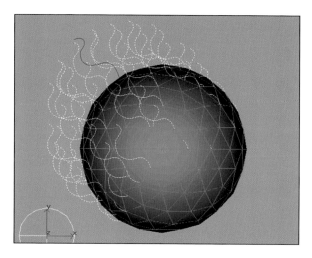

Click the Spline Cage button and select the curve. Turn on Absolute Direction to see the effect of the spline cage on the hair.

WHERE AND HOW THICK THE HAIR SHOULD GROW

Particle Hair lets you limit hair generation only to selected faces of an emitter shape, which could be the scalp area of a human head.

In the following steps, you will select only the top portion of the sphere using the Mesh Select Modifier to create a "scalp" to simulate the scalp of a human head.

1   Select the sphere and click Modify. Click the Mesh Select modifier and turn on SubObject, Face mode. In the Main toolbar, change Object Select Type from Rectangular Region to Fence Selection Region. This will let you select a group of faces on the sphere that will simulate selecting the scalp portion of a human head. In the front viewport, select only the upper-left faces of the sphere to create a scalp.

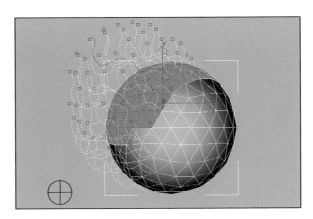

Apply the Mesh Select Modifier and use a fence selection region to select a group of faces at the top left side of the sphere. Click the Hair icon, then click Modify, and in the menu, click Selected Faces Only.

2   After the scalp is selected, leave SubObject turned on and click the Create tab to exit Modify. Next, click the Particle Hair icon in the viewport and then click Modify. The Particle Hair menu will open. Scroll to the Emitter shape menu and click Selected Faces Only. The Viewport should redraw and the hair should now only emit from the selected faces.

Note: You should read the release notes in the Particle Hair document to find out which features are finished and which do not work. Some features still do not work and will make MAX crash. To avoid any crashes in this tutorial, I have only used parameters here that work without trouble. This tutorial is not intended to be a demonstration of all of the plug-in's features and is limited to one purpose: making Flexible head hair for characters.

3   You will now increase the density of the hair in the rendering. Scroll to the top Hair menu called Particles. Notice that there are two entry fields: one for Viewport # (number) of strands and another for Render # of strands. In Render #, enter 500 and press Enter, and then render the sphere. It should now have a dense clump of fine hairs.

Load the 18mem02.max file from the CD to see a finished example. (This file is intended only for MAX 3 or 3.1.)

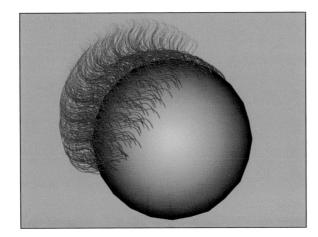

Increase the number of hair strands to 500. Render to see the fine hair.

HAIR REACTS TO MOVEMENT

Because Hair is a particle system, it reacts to the movement of the emitter object and tends to lag behind it. If you move the sphere 25 units to the right over 30 frames, the hair will lag behind the movement and straighten out like real hair. When the sphere movement stops, the hair then assumes its original shape. This is great for simulating dynamic movement of the hair and is one of the most interesting, and at the same time, most difficult problems of particle hair. As it currently functions, Hair does not have collision detection even though it is listed in the menu. As stated earlier, this is an Alpha plug-in and not all of its features work yet. Therefore, the Hair will pass through any object, whether or not it is a deflector. Later in this tutorial we will learn a "work around" designed to avoid this problem and create hair that does not penetrate the skin of the model while still remaining flexible.

PUTTING HAIR ON A CHARACTER

Creating good particle hair for a model takes practice. You can build your own character, or use a model from a model dataset service or one of the Web sites that offer free models on the Internet. I decided to use a model that is included with Character Studio because it is on the 3D Studio MAX installation CD. I have used the Character Studio Gremlin model in the following tutorial to demonstrate how to apply dynamic particle hair to any polygonal model. If you have Character Studio installed, the Gremlin model can be found in Cstudio\Charactr\Meshes directory. Otherwise, you can load 18mem01.max from this book's accompanying CD-ROM. If you wish to use a different model, substitute your model's file in place of the Gremlin file in the following steps.

Load the Gremlin model from Character Studio from the Cstudio/Charactr/Meshes directory.

USING PARTICLE HAIR WITH PHYSIQUE AND SKIN

Many 3D Studio MAX users employ Character Studio, Bones Pro, or the Skin Modifier with MAX's Bones to animate characters. Usually, I animate a one-piece mesh model with a Biped skeleton. However, the following steps will work just as well with either Skin or Bones Pro.

Particle hair has a few idiosyncrasies that make it unsuitable to apply directly to a mesh with Physique. I was hoping that I could just add Particle hair to the selected faces of a mesh that was bound to the biped skeleton with Physique, but, unfortunately, Particle Hair does not like Physique. I found that if I select faces that were already bound with Physique, and then apply Particle Hair to selected faces only, the system would go into long-term calculation mode (the computer equivalent of brain lock) and take a very long time to do anything except calculate. On the same mesh without Physique applied, Particle Hair works almost instantly. To get around this, I decided to create a separate scalp mesh and position it exactly where the original scalp was. That way, I could apply Particle Hair to a separate mesh object and avoid Physique. After I linked the scalp to the Biped's head bone, everything worked well because Physique does not distort the top of the head when it animates the figure. The scalp moved along with the mesh, without showing any seams or edges.

CREATING HAIR FOR THE GREMLIN

In the following steps, you will clone the Gremlin's scalp area to create a separate base for the Particle Hair wig.

1   Load the Gremlin model, (or your own model) and then zoom in on the head in all views.

Click Modify panel and examine the Stack. If you already have Physique applied to the mesh, you probably want to create the separate skull mesh without removing the skin deformation modifier. You do not need to remove it, only make it inactive for the moment. To make Physique (or any other modifier) inactive, click the Active/Inactive Modifier Toggle (the icon looks like a light bulb).

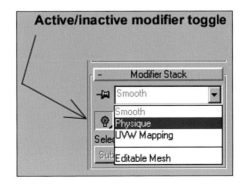

Click the Gremlin skin, then click Modify. In the Stack window, click the Active/Inactive Modifier Toggle (the lightbulb icon) to deactivate Physique.

2 With Physique inactive, apply an Edit Mesh modifier to the mesh and then set the Select Object type to Fence Selection Region. Turn on SubObject/Face mode and then, in the left view of the character's head, select the region of the head where you would like hair to grow. If you accidentally select the ears, use Alt+Select to deselect them.

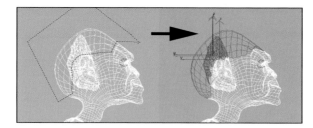

Apply an Edit Mesh modifier, then select the faces of the scalp area of the Gremlin's head using fence selection region.

3 When the scalp area is selected, scroll down into the Edit Mesh menu and click Detach. In the dialog box that opens, select Detach as Clone and click OK. This will create a clone of the scalp. Rename the new object Scalp.

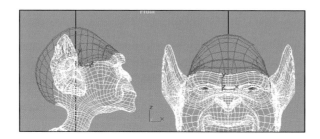

Make a scalp: Apply Edit Mesh and select the faces at the top of the head. Detach the faces as a separate object.

4 Delete the Edit Mesh modifier from the stack and toggle Physique back on. Then unhide the Biped (if it isn't unhidden already), select the new scalp, and link it to the Biped head (Bip01 Head). Don't move it: It must line up perfectly with the original mesh. You are now ready to apply Particle Hair to the scalp.

APPLY PARTICLE HAIR TO THE SCALP

In the following steps, you will apply Particle Hair to the scalp.

1 In the same way you created the hair in part 1 of this tutorial, you apply Hair to the scalp. (Review those steps if necessary.) Create a Particle Hair icon in the viewport, and then pick the scalp as the emitter object. The hair will stick out straight in the direction of the face normals of the scalp.

2 To control the shape, direction, and length of the hair, draw a spline. Click Create, Shape, Line with Smooth Initial and Drag Types turned on. Draw the spline by clicking the top of the scalp and setting points to create the spline shape.

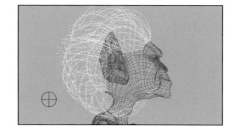

Open the Particle System menu, then click and drag the create a Hair icon. Select the new scalp object as the emitter. Hair will be generated as straight lines. Then draw a spline that represents the hair shape you want.

3 After the spline is finished, go to the Spline Cage menu and click the Spline Cage selection button (marked None). Turn on Absolute Direction. The hair will update and conform to the shape of the spline.

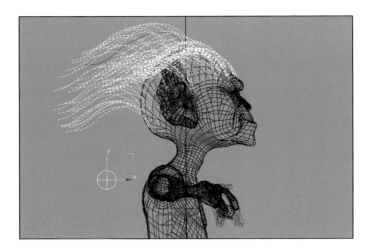

Create a Hair particle system icon. Draw a spline to make a spline cage to shape the hair, and then turn on absolute direction.

4 Notice that there is only one hair per face, and that they are all parallel to the Spline Cage. This is not very attractive. Before increasing the amount of hair, you should change the hair type to Three-Sided Strands by clicking that button in the Render Info menu and turning on Generate W Mapping. Next, go to the Particles menu and change Viewport # to 500 and Render # to 500. This will create a dense clump of hairs. Render the character to see the hair.

I tested the Filler Strands command that is supposed to increase the amount of hair per face, but I decided not to use it because it often crashed MAX. By increasing the Render number of hairs, I avoided using Filler Strands.

Set the number of hairs to 500. Render to see the hair.

CONTROLLING HAIR PENETRATION

When the character is animated, the hair lags behind the motion of the figure, giving it a dynamic quality. The problem is that the hair sinks right through the surface of the model even when Emitter Object Collision is turned on and the mesh is a deflector. To work around this problem and prevent the particle hair from sinking through the model's skin, I created a separate "snapshot mesh wig" clone of the hair strands using the Tools, Snapshot command. This makes a polygonal mesh copy of the hair strands that are stiff like a rigid wig. Then, by applying the Flex Modifier, the wig becomes partially soft and flexible, but still stiff in the hair root area so it does not sink into the skin.

In the following steps, you will create a snapshot mesh wig from the particle hair.

1   Make sure you set the time slider to frame 0 so the hair is not distorted by the motion of the Character. With the particle hair (Hair01) selected, go to the top menu bar in the MAX interface and click on Tools. Also be sure that you have at least 500 hairs displayed in the viewport. From the drop-down menu, select Snapshot. In the Snapshot dialog box, select OK to accept the default settings for a mesh clone, and then click OK. A mesh copy of the hair will be generated that I have called the "snapshot mesh wig."

2   Now you can delete the Particle Hair icon, which leaves only the snapshot mesh wig. Click the Link icon and link the wig to the scalp object.

3   You now have a mesh wig that is capable of being deformed and animated with a number of MAX's tools. Use the Editable Mesh modifier with Soft Selection applied to the hair (set falloff to 2.0) to further shape the wig. The color gradient indicates that the blue area will not be moved whereas the yellow will, so you can move the tip of the hair without disturbing the rest of the wig.

4   Before going on to the next step, you should run the Optimize Modifier on the mesh hair with a Face Threshold setting of approximately 11.0. That will reduce the number of faces by about one third and make the hair much easier to animate with Flex.

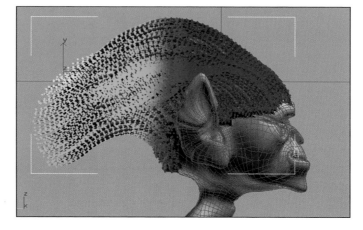

Because particle hair cannot be prevented from penetrating the model, create a mesh copy of the hair. Set viewport display of hair to 500 and Create a mesh copy of the particle hair using Snapshot. Optimize the hair mesh. Delete the particle hair.

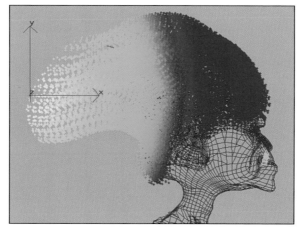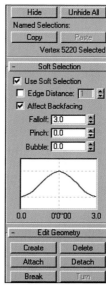

To shape the mesh hair wig, apply an Edit Mesh Modifier, turn on Soft Selection, and click the tips of the hair. Change the Falloff to about 3.0 so the yellow area only surrounds the hair tips, then use Move to adjust the position of the hair strands. Don't move the hair around the scalp.

DYNAMIC HAIR ANIMATION WITH FLEX

In the following steps, you will apply the Flex Modifier to make the hair react to the head's motion in a controllable way.

1   Select the snapshot mesh wig, and then click Modify. Click the More button and select Flex from the Modifier menu. A Flex Center of Influence will be created near the center of world space. Zoom out to locate it.

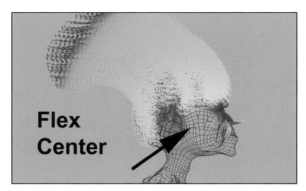

Apply the Flex Modifier, then click SubObject, select Center mode, the move the Center of Influence to the middle of the Gremlin's head. Then link the Center of Influence icon (a cross) to the Scalp object so that it moves with the model.

2   Click SubObject and select Center. Move the Center of Influence to the middle of the character's forehead. You *must* link the Center of Influence to the Scalp object. If you do not do this, the hair will be left behind when the character moves.

3   The falloff of the Flex effect is indicated by the color, ranging from yellow, which does not flex, to blue, which is fully flexible. The green area is semi-flexible.

    In this figure, the character is in motion and the hair is slightly elongated by its flexibility. Load the Grem.Avi animation from the CD to see how the hair acts with Flex applied.

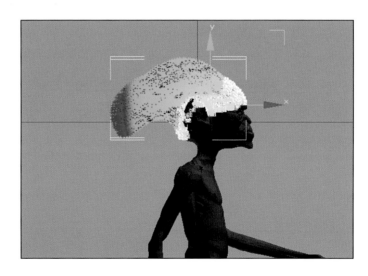

Link Scalp to the biped Head bone and link Mesh hair to the scalp. Apply Flex to the mesh hair and link the center icon to the scalp. Position flex center.

4   To make the hair on top of the head stiff enough to keep its shape, but still flexible enough at the ends of to whip around if the head is turned quickly, you must adjust the Flex vertex weights. The simplest method of controlling the way the hair moves is to leave the Flex parameters in their default settings and then concentrate on painting weights to control the hair's motion.

.5 To keep the hair from accidentally pulling away from the scalp on the gremlin's forehead, go to Sub Object, Weight. Select all the vertices around the front edge of the scalp and then, in the Vertex Weights menu, turn on Absolute Value. Enter the value 99 and press Enter. The vertices will all turn yellow, indicating they are rigid and will not be affected by flex. The rest of the hair remains flexible.

You should now have a wig that will move with the character and flex like real hair. It is up to you to experiment with painting weights to control exactly how the hair moves. This procedure can be applied to any model, even a simple segmented model, so you no longer need to have "hairless" models in your animations.

For many types of animated particle hair effects, the conversion into a mesh can be skipped. That procedure is needed only if you want stiff hairs. The natural dynamic property of the particle hair strands can then be used as demonstrated on the sphere above and an enhanced dynamic effect can be obtained by applying a Noise Modifier to the emitter to make the hair wave and clump. If you wish, the hair can be snapshot at any frame to preserve its shape. For example, I have started a library of various shaped clumps of grass that I can paste into any project.

Particle Space Warps do not work with this version of the Particle Hair plug-in.

Flex menu: Set absolute vertex weight to 99 next to the skull. Animate the character and adjust Flex parameters to control hair motion.

Note: For a complete explanation of how Flex works and how to paint vertex weights, consult the 3D Studio MAX help files or the MAX reference manual.

Plug-Ins

After the hair has been converted to a mesh using Snapshot, any plug-in that can affect a mesh object can be used to modify the results.

The particle hair emitter can be affected by other plug-ins such as Melt for an interesting effect.

Variations

Select the faces on the edge of a cloth object and add a spline cage to create soft fringe that moves with the cloth.

To create stiff toothbrush bristles, use it with selected faces and Snapshot.

Also, try applying a low level of animated Noise to the emitter mesh object to create waving grass.

Apply Particle Hair to a geosphere and set the render number of strands to 3,000 to make great Tribbles, the pesky creatures from *Star Trek*.

SEASCAPE

"I do not know what I may appear to the world; but to myself I seem to have been only like a boy playing on the sea shore and diverting himself and then finding a smoother pebble or a prettier shell than ordinary while the greater ocean of truth lay all undiscovered before me."

—ISAAC NEWTON

USING DISPLACEMENT MAPS AND SPACE WARPS TO CREATE A REALISTIC, NATURAL-LOOKING SEASHORE ENVIRONMENT

Using MAX to create a rocky seashore simply involves combining a few patches (or meshes) with a few Space Warps and complex materials. Creating white water and animating the wave rhythms takes more time and involves animating the Phase spinners in the Space Warps. The difficulties arise because waves usually contain secondary motions moving in different directions and that wave color results mainly from reflections. In this project, you'll create a realistic water and landscape environment.

SEASCAPE

BY JEFFREY ABOUAF

GETTING STARTED

The following exercise takes advantage of R3's Displacement Map channel and Displace Mesh World Space modifier (WSM) to create one set of water deformations as well as the Space Warps to create a second and third set of animated motions. R3's Shellac Material lets you blend raytraced reflections from the sky with the darker sea water color. The landscape comes from a QuadPatch deformed into the shape of a rocky island, texture-mapped with a complex terrain material. The sky is a spherical environment mapped with a procedural material; the mist and atmosphere come from a Volume Fog.

We proceed by first creating and texturing the shore, next the Environment map for the sky, and then the material for the water surface. Next, we'll add Space Warps to the water geometry and then blend the water and sky together with Volume Fog.

The first step in the process is to create the land and texture-map it. A Quad Patch has the advantage of sculpting well for gross features such as peaks and valleys, yet deforming nicely to a Noise modifier or material displacement, which provides a rugged, raw look. This scene uses a single Quad Patch with a single material.

1 In the top viewport, create a QuadPatch 400×400. Change Length Segs to 12 and Width Segs to 12. Apply an Edit Patch modifier. Go to the vertex Sub–Object level. Set Surface View Steps to 5 and Render Steps to 7. Select several vertices or sets of vertices and pull them along the Y-Axis above and below ground-level (use the grid in the figure for reference). The goal is to create a rocky Pacific North Coast quality; that is, waves crashing against rocks with no sand present. By creating extreme deformations cutting into or through the interior of the patch, you create the impression of an island with water washing through the caves. Pull the corners of the patch downward to avoid making the island look square. (If you'd like to skip this step, you can just load 19mem01.max from the Chapter 19 folder on the accompanying CD-ROM.)

2 Leave Sub-Object mode and apply a Noise modifier. Sample settings are:

Seed: 10,000
Scale: 5.0
Strength
X: 5.0
Y: 5.0
Z: 25.0

3 Apply a second Noise modifier with sample settings as follows:

Seed: 15,000
Scale: 1.0
Check Fractal
Roughness: 1.0
Iterations: 5.0
Strength
X: 10.0
Y: 10.0
Z: 10.0

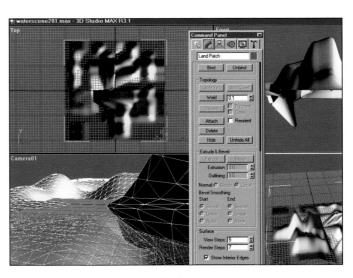

Pulling vertices is the easiest way to create gross deformations to the land. Use the grid as a reference to water-level...

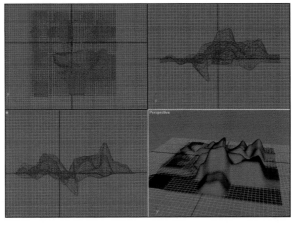

...or you can just load the 19mem01.max scene from the accompanying CD-ROM.

Note: If you get an error message at this point, it may be because you do not have Habware's Toy Train plug-in. The scene here contains a mobile camera linked to the Toy Train system, which is a string of dummy objects that move along a path. The Toy Train plug-in is freeware available at www.habware.at/duck3.htm, or in the Chapter 19 folder of the accompanying CD-ROM.

4 Apply a UVW Map modifier to the entire patch. The model should appear as shown.

5 Collapse the stack so only an editable mesh and UVW Map modifier remain (that is, use Collapse To).

You can collapse both land and water geometry to editable patches. However, the Displace Mesh WSM (to be applied later) requires significantly more time to process a stack with patches than an editable mesh.

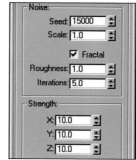

Add a UVW Map modifier to the entire patch. The top half of the terrain material is itself a Blend material consisting of sand and cracked mud bitmaps.

6 Create the first part of the land material: Select an empty slot in the Material Editor. Click the Type button (next to Standard) and select a Blend material (discard old material). Click Material 1 and go to the Maps level. Using the Asset Manager (Utilities, Asset Manager), select sandwave.jpg from the accompanying CD and drag it to the Diffuse Map channel. Drag the Diffuse Color channel as an instance to the Bump channel.

7 Open the Material/Map Navigator and move to Material 2. Move to the Maps rollout and, using the Asset Manager, drag crackmud.jpg to the Diffuse Color channel. Drag the Diffuse Color channel to the Specular Level and Bump channels using Instance as the method in both cases. Set the Bump Amount equal to 200.

8 Click the Diffuse Color Map channel to go down to the Bitmap level of crackmud.jpg. Set U and V Tiling each to 10.0.

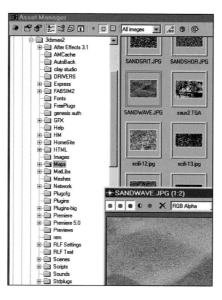

The Asset Manager is a useful tool for examining and loading bitmaps directly into a map channel in the Material Editor.

9   Go to the top level of the Blend Material. Drag SANDWAVE.JPG from the Material/Map Navigator to the Mask button. This completes the first of the two Blend materials.

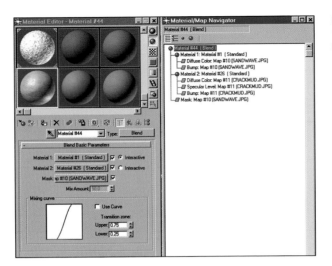

Blend the materials in the First Blend material using a bitmap as a mask.

10 Now we'll nest the First Blend material into a Second Blend material. Click an empty slot, click the Type button, and choose a Blend material (discard old material). Click the slot in the Material Editor containing the Blend material created in steps 6 through 9. Drag that window onto the Material 1 button for the second Blend material as an instance. The first Blend material is now nested inside the second and Material 2 is open.

11 Next, we'll make Material 2 for the second Blend material. Click the Material 2 button to go to the Standard Material level. Go to the Maps rollout and click the Diffuse Color channel. Pick the Gradient map type.

12 Set U and V Tiling each equal to 2.0. Set Blur Offset to 0.004. Open the Noise rollout and check On. Set Amount to 25.0, Levels to 3, and Size to 0.1.

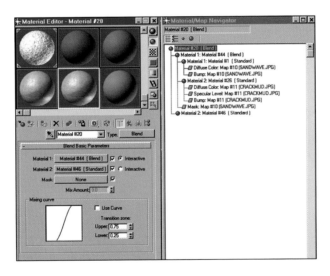

Drag-copy the Material Editor Slot containing the first Blend material to the Material 1 button for the Second Blend material.

13 Open the Gradient Parameters rollout. Confirm that Gradient type is Linear. Within this rollout is a second Noise section. Set the following values:

Amount: 1.0

Size: 25.0

Levels: 4.0

Noise Thresh

Low: 0.335

High: 0.3

Smooth: 0

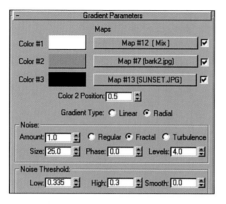

Open the Gradient Parameters rollout and make changes to the Noise parameter.

14 Use the Asset Manager to drag-copy sunset.jpg to Color #3 and bark2.jpg to Color #2 of the Gradient Parameters rollout.

15 Click the Color #1 button and choose a Mix map. Use the Asset Manager to drag-copy goldfoil.gif to Color #1 and foliage.tga to Color #2 of the Mix Parameters rollout. Set Mix Amount equal to 60. Check Use Curve and set Upper to 0.82 and Lower to 0.33.

16 Using the Material/Map Navigator, go to the Material 2 level of the second Blend material. Drag the Diffuse Color Channel button to the Specular level and Bump channels using the instance method. Set Bump Amount equal to 500.

17 Go to the top of the second Blend material. Drag-copy the crackmud.jpg bitmap from the Material/Map Navigator to the Mask channel.

18 Assign the Material to the land patch.

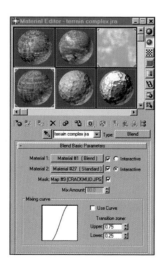
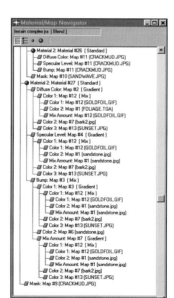

Instance-copy the complex gradient from the Diffuse Color channel to each of the Specular Level and Bump channels.

19 In the top viewport, create three target cameras, positioning them at different viewpoints around the "island." Keep them close to the water level; that is, at the viewer's eye level at different points on the shore. The enclosed final file includes a sample camera animated along a path using the Toy Train plug-in— free on the accompanying CD-ROM. Toy Train is a systems plug-in (located on the Creation/Systems tab) that strings several dummy objects together to follow a path as a group. By linking a target camera to one dummy and its target to another, you can gain precise control over the camera movement around and through the island.

20 Adjust the UVW mapping on the land: Select the UVW Map modifier in the stack. Check Spherical, click the Fit button, and set the following parameters:

Alignment: Y
U Tile: 5.0
V Tile: 5.0
W Tile: 1.0

21 Create the Sunlight system: Select the Systems button in the Create Command panel and then click the Sunlight button. Create a Sunlight system in the top viewport. Adjust the compass orientation using the North Direction spinner while you observe the direction of the sunlight through one of the camera viewports. If the lighting is not pleasing, fix it by reorienting the Compass in the top viewport. You can make further adjustments to the Sunlight system by selecting the Sun01 object and changing the parameters under the Motion panel.

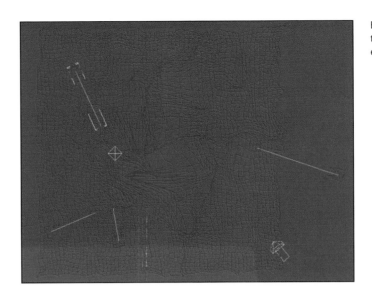

By assigning multiple cameras to the scene, you can observe entirely different seascapes.

Note: A Sunlight system is a light source that combines a free directional light with a Compass object. It allows you to accurately simulate and animate the geographically correct angle and movement of the sun over the earth at a given location, time, and date. When you create the Sunlight system, it derives its default values from your computer clock. In other words, if you add the Sunlight system to your scene at 11:00 P.M., the light will be created under the geometry shining up at it. You can adjust the angle of the "sun" by changing the values of the time, date, and North Direction spinners. The scene provided with this exercise does not animate this object. However, the scene variation, waterscene221.max (used to make seascape_extra.avi and included on the accompanying CD) uses an animated Sunlight system, making the sun appear to rise and set across 500 frames.

22 With Sun01 selected, go to the Modify panel. Set the following parameters:

Cast Shadows: On

Multiplier: 2.0

Contrast: 25

H: 34

S: 53

V: 241

Set these parameters in the General Parameters rollout.

23 Create an Omni light (for a fill light) centered on the island and elevated above the tallest peak; that is, X=−75, Y=0, and Z=150. Set Multiplier equal to 0.5.

24 Render one of the camera viewports. The result should resemble the figure shown.

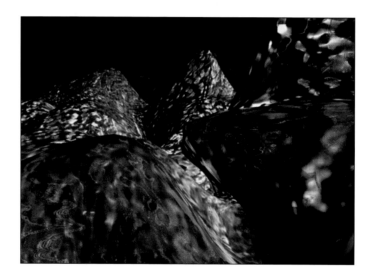

Render one of the camera viewports. You'll see the land mass, texture-mapped and lit by the Sunlight system. With a complex material tree, you can vary the scale of the material as mapped on the terrain surface (or any part of it) by adjusting the Tiling settings at different map levels in the material tree and the additional settings in the UVW Map modifier.

CREATING THE SKY MAP

There are two ways to create an environment. One way is to create a very large squashed hemisphere with a camera placed on the inside, invert the face normals, and map this with a non-repeating material. This is the approach used by the Environment Generator that ships with R3. The alternative is to apply a non-repeating map to the Environment, using Spherical Environment mapping. This exercise uses the latter approach in order to get the optimum reflection of the sky onto the water.

1   Pick an empty slot in the Material Editor. Click the Get Material button and choose the Noise map. (The Environment accepts *maps* only [for example, green parallelograms], not *materials* [for example, blue ball].) Under Noise Parameters, swap Color #1 for Color #2 (Color #2 is black). Change the black color to sky blue. Complete the other settings as follows:

Source:	Object XYZ	
X Tiling:	6.0; Angle:	90.0
Y Tiling:	2.0; Angle:	0.0
Z Tiling:	2.0; Angle:	90.0
Noise Type:	Fractal	
Size:	50.0	
High:	0.56	
Low:	0.345	
Levels:	6.0	

2   Add a second layer Noise map to Color #1 (white). In this second layer, leave Color #1 white and click Color #2 to a second Noise map. Set the other values as follows:

Noise Type:	Fractal	Low:	0.25
Size:	25.0	Levels:	6.0
High:	1.00		

3   Set the third layer Noise map as follows:

Tiling		**Colors #1:**	
X:	1.0	H:	221.0
Y:	6.0	S:	116.0
Z:	0.0	V:	11.0
Noise Type:	Regular	**Colors #2:**	
Size:	10.0	H:	7.0
High:	0.675	S:	157.0
Low:	0.25	V:	198.0
Levels:	6.0		

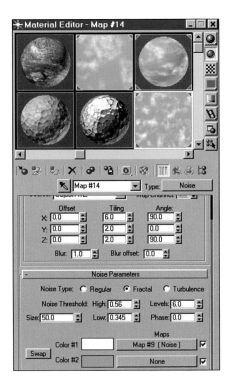

Make the Sky map from a multilayered Noise map in which the blue sky is maximized while white clouds take on additional detail with a second layer of noise.

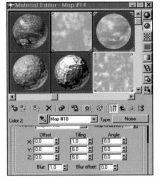
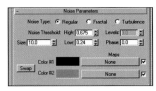

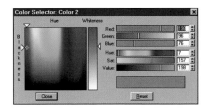

Create the third layer of noise in the Sky map.

4 Open the Environment dialog box (Rendering/ Environment). Assign the Sky map to the environment by dragging it from the slot in the editor to the Environment map button as an instance.

SETTING UP THE WATER

Three approaches can be used to create waves. The first method is to use a nonanimated material with the Displace Mesh, Wave, and Ripple Space Warps. The second is to map the water surface with a more complex, animated material and use the Displace Mesh WSM to let the material deform the surface. The third method combines the first and second. The first choice offers more motion variables (and therefore, better control); the second offers more complex reflections, which lend to realism. Depending on your taste, a combined approach may be just right or overkill.

The interaction of the Quad Patch with the Displace Mesh WSM makes working with a large mesh (or converting the Quad Patch to a mesh) highly advisable. On the machines used to prepare this exercise (an Intergraph dual 333 PII and a clone dual 550 PIII with an Elsa Synergy II), the texture-mapped patch file took 20 minutes or more to load, whereas the mesh version took about one-fourth of that.

1 Create a second Quad patch in the top viewport 1600×1600 with 48 segments each direction, with the land patch at center. Collapse to an editable mesh. Label it Water. Go to the vertex Sub-Object Level. Turn on Use Soft Selection and set Falloff to 100. Use the circular selection tool to create a large circular selection with the island at center.

2 The first alternative uses a simpler material. Create a Shellac material in an empty slot in the Material Editor (discard old material). Label it water_alt1. Click the base material.

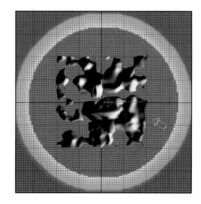

Create a large circular selection with the island at center.

3   Set the Specular Level and Glossiness each at 0. Under the Extended Parameters rollout/Reflection Dimming section, check Apply. Set Dim Level=1.0 and Refl. Level=3.0.

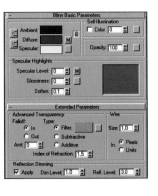

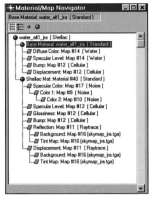

Set these parameters in the Material Editor.

4   Go to the Maps rollout. Click the Diffuse Color Channel button and choose a Water map. (The Water map will animate the wave motion, but only in a single direction over a positive integer.) Set parameters to:

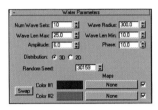

Set these parameters in the Water Parameters rollout.

Numb. Wave Sets: 10.0   Amplitude: 6.0

Wave Len Max: 25.0   Wave Radius: 300

Wave Len Min: 10

Right-click the Play button and set the number of frames to 500.

Phase: Animate 0–10 over 500 frames

Colors #1:		Colors #2:	
H:	160.0	H:	145.0
S:	123.0	S:	74.0
V:	60.0	V:	104.0

5   Go to the parent level. Drag the Diffuse Color Map channel as an instance to the Specular Level channel.

6 Click the Bump Map channel and choose a Cellular map. Set the parameters as follows:

Coordinates

Source: Object XYZ

Tiling

X: 2.0

Y: 2.0

Z: 2.0

Cellular Parameters

Cell Characteristics: Circular

Size: 25.0

Spread: 0.5

Fractal: Checked

Roughness: 0.2

Thresholds

Low: 0.0

Mid: 0.42

High: 0.81

Output Rollout

Invert: checked

7 Go to the parent level. Drag the Bump channel as an instance to the Displacement channel. Set Bump Amount to 100. Set Displacement Amount to 1.

8 Go to the top level and choose the Shellac material. Go to the Maps rollout. Drag the Sky map to the Specular Color channel. Do this as a copy. Because the sky works in the scene, and we may want to modify how it behaves in the specular channel, a copy is safer and easier.

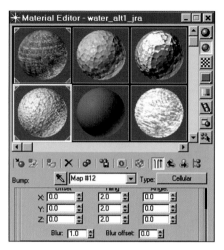

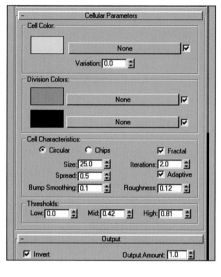

Set these parameters in the Material Editor.

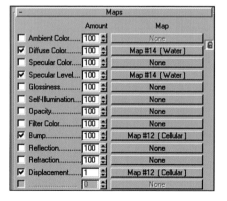

Set Bump to 100. Set Displacement to 1.

9   From the Material/Map Navigator, drag the Cellular map (from the Base Material Bump Map channel) as an instance to the Specular Level Map channel. From within the Shellac Material maps rollout, drag the Cellular map (in the Specular Level Channel) to the Glossiness Map and Bump Map channels as an instance in both cases. Set Bump Amount equal to 100.

10 Click the Reflection Map Channel button and choose a Raytrace map. Set:

    Raytrace Parameters

    Trace Mode: Auto Detect

    Options: Check All

    Background: Use Environment Settings

    Global Parameters: Check Fast Adaptive Antialiaser

    Basic Material Extensions

    Basic Tinting: Enabled

    Use a copy of the Sky Environment map

    Refractive Material Extensions

    Fog: Enabled

11 Go to parent level. Drag-copy the Raytrace map (in the Reflect Map channel) as an instance to the Displacement Map channel. Assign the water material to the water mesh.

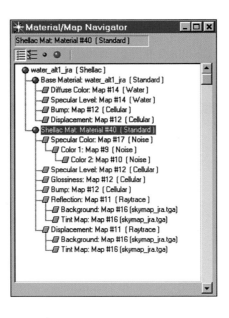

Drag the Cellular map to the Glossiness map and Bump map channels as an instance.

Assign the water material to the water mesh.

12 Apply Space Warps to the water mesh: Leave the
water mesh Sub-Object level (if you haven't already).
Create a Ripple Space Warp centered on the island.
Set as follows:

Amplitude 1:   1.5

Amplitude 2:   0.5

Wave Length: 67

Phase: Animate −5.0 to 0.0 over 500 frames

Circles: 30

Segments: 16

Divisions: 4

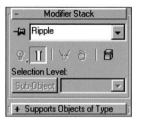
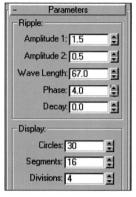

Create a Ripple Space Warp
centered on the island.

13 Apply a Wave Space Warp (angled at 10:00 from
the island):

Amplitude 1:   1.0

Amplitude 2:   1.0

Wave Length: 20

Phase: Animate 0.0 to 5.0 over 500 frames

Sides: 63

Segments: 74

Divisions: 10

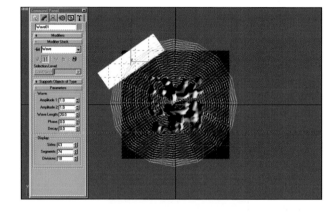

Set up the Ripple and Wave
Space Warps.

14 Select the water mesh and go to the vertex Sub-
Object level. Choose Bind to Space Warp and bind
first to the Wave and second to the Ripple Space
Warp. Play the animation and view it through the
cameras in place. Adjust the Space Warp settings if
necessary to reflect the desired motion of the water.

Here's the final water material.

15 The last step for the water is applying the Displace Mesh WSM. This makes the Displacement Map channel active in deforming the water mesh. **Caution:** When you do this, your system will grind to a halt. Keep the Displace WSM turned off (that is, the light bulb icon in the Modifier Stack rollout) or not present while you perform other tasks.

Apply the Displace Mesh WSM.

BUILDING THE MORE COMPLEX WATER MATERIAL

This material is designed to create the entire water motion and texture by itself. It consequently contains several multilayered and Mix maps. Also, you control wave direction solely by rotating the UVW Map modifier gizmo, whereas in the first material you control wave directions with Space Warps. Otherwise, the principle is the same: The material has an underlying base color layer and a top reflective Shellac layer. The deformation takes place via the Displace Mesh WSM.

1 In an empty slot, create a new Shellac Material. Click the base material. Under Extended Parameters, check Apply Reflection Dimming and set the Dim. Level to 0.5 and Refl. Level to 3.0

2 Click the Diffuse Color channel and choose a Water map. Use the Get Material button to bring up the Material Map browser. Check Browse from Mtl Editor. Find the first water material you made. Drag the Water map from that material *as a copy* to the Diffuse Color Map channel. Alternatively, get a new Water map and use the recipe from step 4.

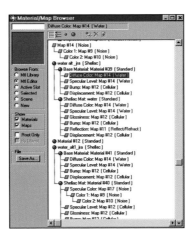

Use the Material/Map Browser set to Browse from Editor to drag-copy maps or map trees from one material to another.

3 In the new material, drag the Water map to the Specular Level Map channel as an instance.

4 Click the Bump Map channel and get a Mix map. Using the previous techniques, drag the Water map to Color 1 as a copy and the Cellular map (from the other water material) to Color 2 also as a copy. Within the new Mix Map, drag-copy as an instance the Water map from Color 1 to the Mix Amount button.

5 Go to the parent level (of the new base material). Drag the Mix map from the Bump channel to the Displacement channel as an instance. Set Bump Amount equal to 100 and Displacement Amount equal to 10.

6 Using the Material/Map Browser, drag the Shellac Material/Reflection map from the other water material to the new Base Material Reflection map as a copy. Set Reflection Amount equal to 100.

Go to the top of the new water material, set Shellac Color Blend to 50,0 and click the Shellac material.

H: 145.0
S: 73.0
V: 137.0

7 Copy the Water map from the Base Material to the Diffuse Color and Specular Level Map channels. Copy the Mix map to the Bump and Displacement map channels. Another option is to go into these maps and vary them from the settings for the base materials.

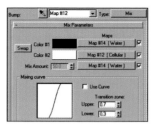

Drag the Water map to Color 1 as a copy and the Cellular map to Color 2 as a copy.

Note: When dragging a material or map from one material slot or tree to a new one (that is, from material A to material B), drag the map or material *as a copy* so changes to the new material do not affect your prior version. However, when dragging *between* map channels within the new material (that is, Diffuse to Specular), copy as an instance *unless* you plan to be using the map differently in the new channel.

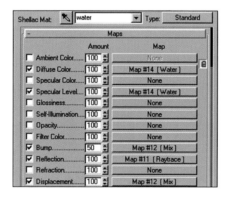
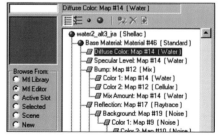

Copy the Water map from the Base Material to the Diffuse Color and Specular Level Map channels.

8   Click the Reflection Map channel and get a
Raytrace map. Use the prior settings for this map,
except copy the Sky (Environment) map to the
Background/Environment channel and to the Tint
Map channel. Enable Fog under the Refractive
Material Extensions rollout and copy the same map
to the Fog map channel. The final material tree
appears in the figure to the right.

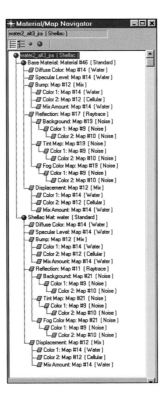

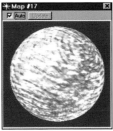

The alternative water material
is more complex, but easily
built using drag-and-drop
from the first version. The
complex tree gives the
advantage of being able to
change the mood and feel of
the scene simply by changing
values, instead of building
new materials from scratch.

ADDING VOLUME FOG

In most landscapes, haze obscures the horizon line. This is especially true for
seascapes. This scene must have fog that is subtle and must blend the water with the
sky. If the scene has only one camera, R3's Standard or Layered Fog will suffice. It has
the advantage of taking both Color and Opacity maps, simplifying the blending process.

However, the fog placement and ranges are measured from the camera lens. Because this scene contemplates many cameras, it uses the Volume Fog, which does not accept Color or Opacity maps.

1   Create a Box gizmo in the top viewport (Create, Helpers, Atmospheric Apparatus, Box Gizmo). Set Length and Width each to 1200.0 and Height=20.0 In the front viewport, adjust the gizmo downward so the fog reaches the ground layer.

2   In the Modify panel, Atmospheres rollout, click Add to add the Volume Fog. Highlight Volume Fog and click Setup. This brings up the Volume Fog parameters. (You can also get to this via Rendering, Environment, Atmosphere.) If you haven't done so already, click Pick Gizmo and choose the Box gizmo.

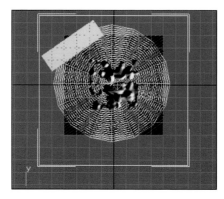

Create a BoxGizmo in the top viewport.

3   Set the Volume Fog parameters:

Soften Gismo Edges:	1.0
Fog Color	
H:	146
S:	18
V:	199
Exponential:	Checked
Density:	10.0
Fog Background:	Checked
Noise	
Type:	Turbulence
High:	0.9
Low:	0.0
Uniformity:	0.4
Levels:	3.0
Size:	20.0
Wind Strength:	20.0 from the left

Setting up Volume Fog to blend with the sky and water.

Putting It All Together

The last step is to apply the Displace Mesh WSM to the water mesh. Render the scene. The accompanying CD contains two versions of the final MAX file. They differ in the water setup. Waterscene207.max uses the simpler water material with wave and ripple Space Warps; waterscene113.max uses the complex water material and only the Displace Mesh WSM. Sample AVI files are included to show the different results from the two techniques.

You now have a versatile environment. The materials lend themselves to an extensive customization. You can have several cameras in place without duplicating the viewpoint. Your only other limitation is that the cameras cannot be elevated very high before revealing the edge of the water mesh.

This effect will not work if you substitute a giant squashed dome for the mapped environment. The reflection detail vanishes.

You can Customize the land further by adding selected rock and foliage objects on the land or at the water line. Try using an Attachment Controller to add objects such as floating kelp or boats moving with the waves. Consider adding one or more particle systems to simulate spray where waves crash into the rocks.

Plug-Ins

Three free plug-ins can enhance this effect and the variations on it: Toy Train by Sam Gueydan of Moose Enterprises and Watercell and Waterwash by Blur Studios, all of which are included on the enclosed CD.

■ Toy Train is a system of dummies, strung together much like the cars on a toy train. Because you can control the number of dummies and the distances between them, and can place the toy train on a path, it works well for animating a target camera.

■ The Watercell and Waterwash plug-ins are used to build variations on this effect. The former creates a foam pattern on the waves, whereas the latter works well to create the water color beneath the waves.

Variations

The water appears more reflective with less foam if you use Blur Studio's Waterwash and Watercell plug-ins. This material is "water variation 1" included in waterscene221.max on the accompanying CD. The animation seascape_extra.avi was created from this file. The transparencies caused by the use of these maps slow the Raytracing map operations, thereby increasing the render times. Save this for use on a fast machine or render farm.

In the animation, the water changes directions—this is caused by animating the Phase spinner of the Water map from 0 to 5 over 500 frames (jump to this level using the Navigator) and instancing it in the Displacement Map channel. The file included on the CD has been changed to animate only the Space Warps and not the displacement maps, resulting in one direction of wave animation.

You can vary detail in the landscape by adding vegetation or additional rocks. This can be done by hand, or by using MAX's compound object Scatter. Here, one rock or tree can be multiplied across a face selection with varied scale, position, and rotation. If you apply an Edit Mesh modifier on top of Scatter and go to Sub-Object, Element, you can reposition any scatter object.

"A friend of mine once sent me a post card with a picture of the entire planet Earth taken from space. On the back it said, 'Wish you were here.'"

—STEPHEN WRIGHT

ASTEROID
IMPACT

Using Motion Blur, Noise, and Particle Systems to Create a Realistic Asteroid Impact Effect

Because of recent advances in science and

astronomy, the general public is much more

aware of the possibility of asteroids impacting

on Earth. This was illustrated in the movies

"Armageddon" and "Deep Impact." In this

effect, you will use MAX to create a similar

effect of an asteroid crashing into Earth and

creating a fairly large explosion. This effect

will be viewed from a considerable distance

in this exercise.

ASTEROID IMPACT

BY MICHAEL TODD PETERSON

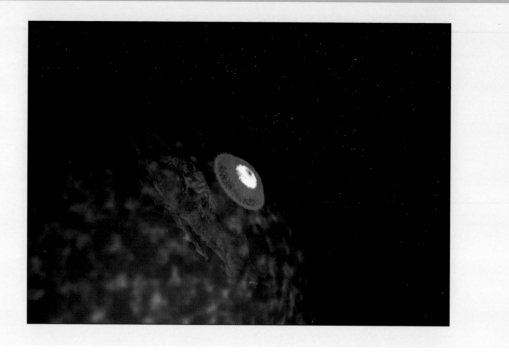

CREATING THE EARTH

To make this effect work, you must combine several different techniques including motion blur, noise, and particle systems. After these are combined, you can create a scene that will both fascinate and frighten viewers.

To start the project, you will first create a digital version of Earth and the environment where you will create the impact. This consists of simple geometry with some good materials.

1   Start a new scene in MAX.

2   In the top viewport, create a sphere with the
    following settings:
    Radius: 22000
    Segments: 64
    Name: Earth

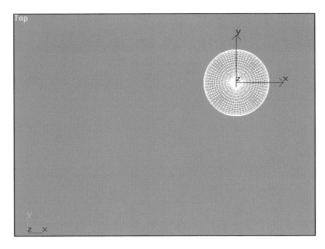

Create a sphere in the top
viewport.

3   Use the Transform Type-In to place the sphere at
    −333, 733, −22025. These numbers are large, but
    necessary after the camera is placed.

Use the Transform Type-In to
place the sphere.

4   Open the Material Editor and select the first open
    Material slot. Name the material Earth. Set the
    following properties:
    Shading: Blinn
    Ambient: 23, 16, 46
    Specular: 229, 229, 229

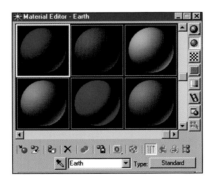

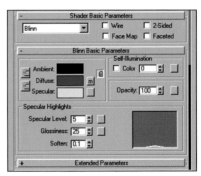

Set the properties in the
Material Editor.

5   Expand the Maps rollout and add a bitmap to the
    diffuse color of the material. Select the file
    EarthMap.jpg to use as the map. This is a standard
    map that ships with MAX 3.

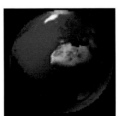

Apply the EarthMap material
in the Material Editor.

6 Turn on Show Texture in Viewport and apply the
material to the sphere in the scene.

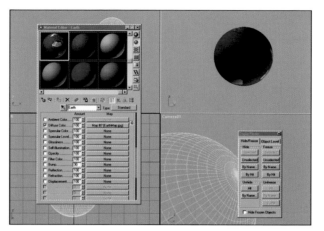

Apply the material to the
sphere.

7 Apply a UVW Map modifier to the Sphere. Set the
following UVW map property:
Mapping: Spherical

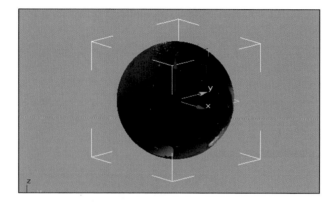

Apply the UVW Map modifier
to the sphere.

8 Return to the Create Command panel. In the top
viewport, create a target camera. Place the camera at
−27530, −24788, 21316.

Place the camera.

9 Place the target of the camera at −1305, 1202, 0.

10 Switch the Perspective view to the Camera View
and turn on Smooth and Highlights shading.

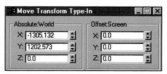

Place the target.

11 With the Camera View active, click the Roll Camera button and roll the view approximately 45 degrees until it looks like you are not looking at the top of the planet, but more at an angle. Check the figure for reference.

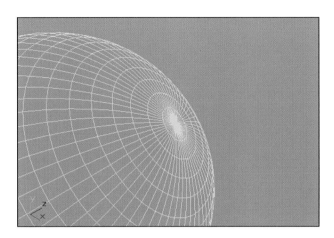

Roll the view 45 degrees.

12 Select the sphere and return to the Modify command panel. Turn on Sub-Object mode and rotate the Sub-Object gizmo until the map of Earth displays the North American continent in the viewport, similar to the figure.

13 Save the file at this point. Now, you have a view of Earth, so let's add the lighting and stars to the scene.

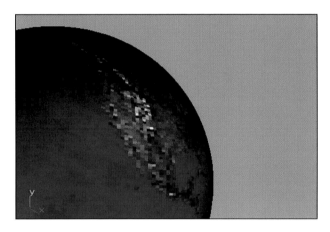

Rotate the Earth map until North America is displayed.

ADDING LIGHTING AND STARS

Now that you have the sphere and the camera, you will add the proper lighting to view Earth from space, and then add stars as a background using Video Post.

1 Create a target spotlight. Place the light at −10311.072, −36021.98, 30858.629. Place the target at −464, 1802, 0.

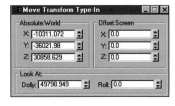

Create and place a target spotlight.

2   Set the following Spotlight parameters:

Multiplier: 1.2

Hotspot: 118

Falloff: 120

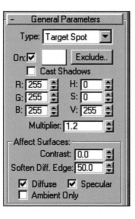

Set the Spotlight parameters.

3   Choose Rendering/Video Post from the pull-down menus. Add the camera view to the queue.

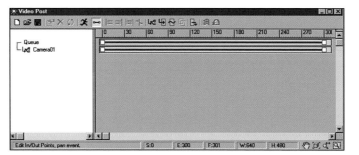

Add the camera event to the Video Post.

4   Select the camera and then add a Starfield filter to the camera. Choose OK and then double-click the Starfield entry to bring up the Edit Filter Event dialog box. Click Setup and set the following parameters:

Dimmest Star: 25

Count: 30000

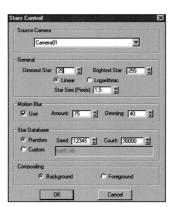

Set up the Starfield background in the Star Control dialog box.

5   Render the scene from Video Post to see the results. From this point on, if you want to see the stars, render out of Video Post; otherwise, render as normal.

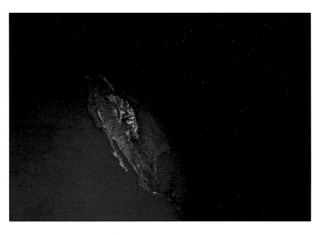

Render of the scene to see the results.

6   Now that we have a nice-looking Earth situated in a bed of stars, let's add a little detail to Earth; in this case, some clouds. These clouds will be generated procedurally in MAX. Select the Earth. Make a copy of it and scale it to 106% of its original size. Name the new object Clouds.

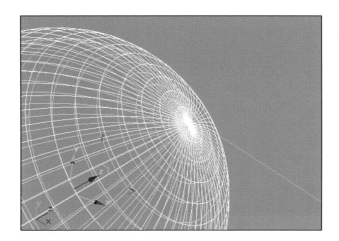

To make the clouds, first make a copy of the Earth.

7   Open the Material Editor and select an open material slot. Name the material Clouds. Apply a Noise map to the Diffuse Color channel and drag it to the Opacity channel as an instance.

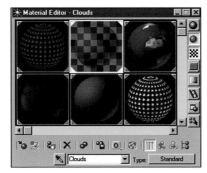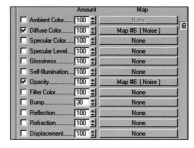

The Material Editor with the Cloud material.

8   Set the following Noise parameters:

Size: 1000

Noise Type: Fractal

Levels: 2

Set the Noise parameters for the clouds.

9   Apply the material to the second sphere. The scene should look similar to the following figure.

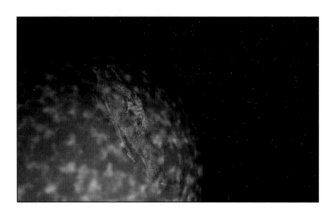

Apply the material. Your scene should look something like this.

CREATING THE ASTEROID

Now that you have a good view of the Earth as seen from space, it's time to create the asteroid. This is actually quite easy. Because of the distance that the camera is away from the Earth, the asteroid will be fairly small, so you won't need a lot of detail. But you will want to see the streak of smoke behind the asteroid, so you will have to create that. Both the asteroid and its streak will be created out of spheres, as shown in the following steps.

1   Activate the top view and create a GeoSphere in the center of the Earth. Create the GeoSphere with a radius of 210 and a segment count of 4. Name the object Asteroid.

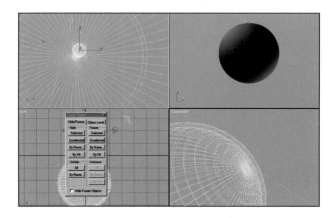

Create the first sphere, representing the asteroid.

2 Open the Material Editor and select an unused material slot. Name the Material Asteroid.

3 Set the Diffuse Color of the material to 147, 116, 49. Apply the material to the Asteroid.

4 Create a clone of the GeoSphere. Scale the clone 114% and name the object Streak. Set the number of segments to 8.

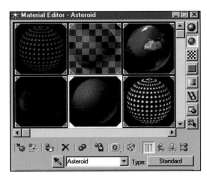
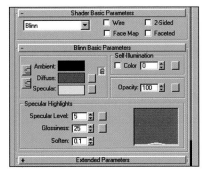

Open the Material Editor and name the material Asteroid.

5 Convert the Streak object to an editable mesh. Go to Vertex Sub-Object and turn on Use Soft Selection and set the Falloff to 400. Select a vertex at the center top of the sphere.

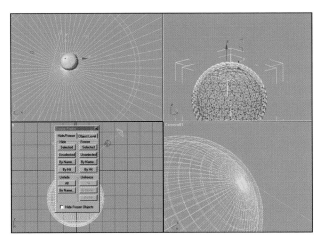

The proper soft selections to create the asteroid tail.

6 Rotate the view to the side and move that vertex up approximately 300 units. Stop and release the mouse button. This resets the soft selection.

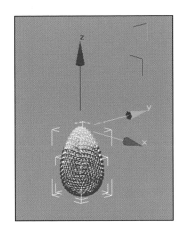

The tail after the first soft selection adjustment.

7   Move the vertex another 1000 units along the Z-Axis
    and let go again to reset the soft selection.

The tail after the second soft
selection adjustment.

8   Move the vertex another 2500 units along the Z-Axis.
    Turn off soft selection and you have created the tail
    of the asteroid.

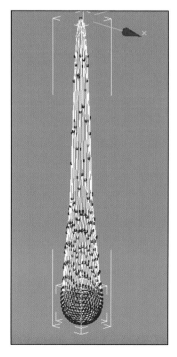

The final soft selection
adjustment for the tail of
the comet.

9   Open the Material Editor and select an empty material slot. Name the material Asteroid Tail. Apply a Noise map to the diffuse color. Then, drag the noise map from the Diffuse Color channel to the Opacity Map channel as an instance.

 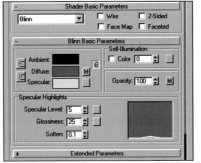

Open the Material Editor. Name the material Asteroid Tail.

10   Set the following Noise parameters:

Noise Type:	Turbulence
Size:	300
Levels:	3
Colors #1 and #2:	Swap

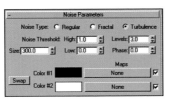

Set the Noise parameters for the Asteroid Tail.

11   Apply the material to Asteroid Tail and save the file.

12   Set the length of the animation to 400 frames.

13   Select Asteroid Tail and link it to Asteroid. This way, if you move the asteroid, the tail moves as well.

14   Select the Asteroid object. Use the Transform Type-In dialog box to place the sphere at –222, 930, 19882.

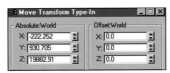

Place the Asteroid object.

15   Move the Animation time slider to frame 100. Turn on Animate.

16   With the Transform Type-In, move the Asteroid object to –222, 930, –4860. This places the asteroid inside of the Earth and places the asteroid impact right at around frame 80. Turn Animate Off.

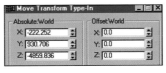

Set the Transform Type-In with the animated set of coordinates.

17 Now, because our asteroid is moving quickly, you need to apply some motion blur to both the Asteroid and the Tail objects. Select both, right-click them, choose Properties, and enable Image Motion Blur.

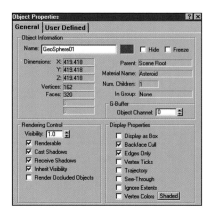

Turn on Motion Blur in the Object Properties dialog box.

CREATING THE EXPLOSION PARTICLES

When the Asteroid hits the Earth, it releases a large amount of energy in the form of a huge explosion. You will simulate this explosion by using two particle systems. One will wrap around parts of the planet. The other will shoot particles out into space. You will make use of both materials and Space Warps to control the look and motion of the particles. The first particle system will represent the outward shock wave of the explosion. You will create this using a Particle Cloud and a Torus to control the shape and motion. The second particle system is simply a SuperSpray.

1 Activate the top viewport. Create a Torus with the following parameters:

Radius 1:   166
Radius 2:   35
Segments: 24
Sides: 12

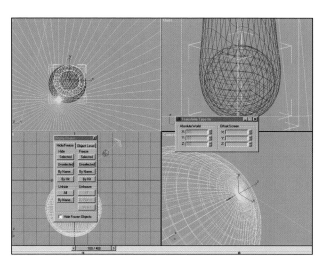

The location and size of the Torus that will act as a particle emitter.

2　Use the Transform Type-In dialog box to place the Torus at −197, 973, −1071.

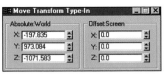

Place the Torus with the Transform Type-In.

3　Turn on the Animate button and go to frame 300 in the animation.

4　Use the Transform Type-In to scale the Torus at 1200% in the X- and Y-Axes and 400% in the Z-Axis. This creates a Torus that grows wider, but not substantially taller. Turn off Animate.

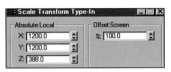

Use the Transform Type-In to scale the Torus.

5　Because the Torus is just an emitter, it does not need to render. Right-click the Torus and select Properties. Turn off Renderable, Cast Shadows, and Receive Shadows. Choose OK to return to the scene.

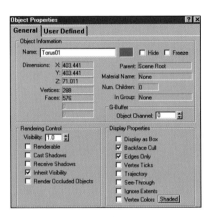

Use the Object Properties dialog box to control the visibility of objects in the scene.

6　Create a Particle Cloud particle system. Set the Particle Formation to Object-Based Emitter. Choose Pick Object and select the Torus you just animated.

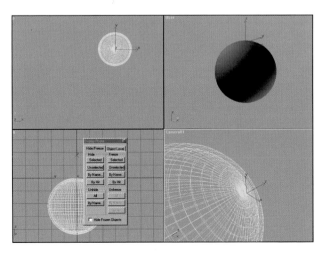

Create a Particle Cloud emitter in the scene.

7 In the Particle Generation rollout, set the following parameters:

Use Rate: 15 (You will change this later to 100)

Speed: 8.0

Direction Vector: On

X: 0

Y: 0

Z: 1.0

Emit Start: 80

Emit Stop: 400

Display Until: 400

Life: 320

Size: 80.0

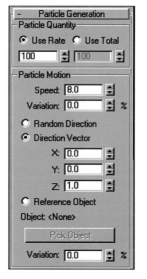

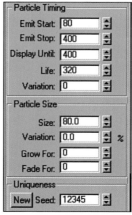

Set how the particles are created in the Particle Generation rollout.

8 In the Particle Type rollout, set the following parameters:

Standard Particles: On

Type: Facing

9 Save the file at this point. Now, you are ready to create some materials for the explosion. In this case, a slightly red material will work well to simulate molten rock. To begin, open the Material Editor and select an unused Material Slot.

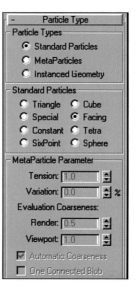

Define how the particles look in the scene in the Particle Type rollout.

10 Name the Material Main Explosion and set the
diffuse color to 108, 10, 10. Set the following
parameters:

Self-Illumination: On
Self-Illumination Color: 149, 149, 149
Face Map: On

11 Apply a Gradient Ramp map to the Opacity slot of
the material.

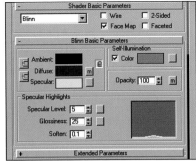

Name the material Main
Explosion.

12 Set the following Gradient Ramp parameters:
Flag 1:   Color 255, 255, 255 Position 0
Flag 2:   Color 0,0,0 Position 100
Delete all other gradient Flags
Gradient Type: Radial
Noise Amount: 1.0
Type: Turbulence
Size: 10.0
Levels: 4

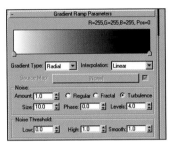

Set the parameters in the
Gradient Map Parameters
rollout.

13 Apply the material to the particle system and save
the file. Now, let's create the second particle system.

14 In the top viewport, create a SuperSpray particle
system. Use the TTI to place the particle system at
−225, 941, −1193.

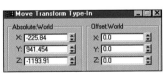

Place the particle system
with the Transform Type-In
dialog box.

15 Go to the Modify command panel. Set the following
Basic parameters:
Off Axis: 0.0
Spread: 12.0
Off Plane: 0.0
Spread: 161.0

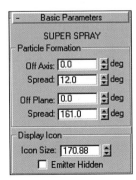

Set the Basic parameters.

16 In the Particle Generation rollout, set the following parameters:

Use Rate:	15 (You will increase this to 100 later)
Speed:	20.0
Emit Start:	80
Emit Stop:	400
Display Until:	400
Life:	200
Size:	80.0

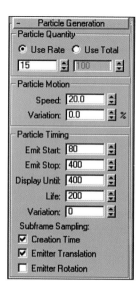

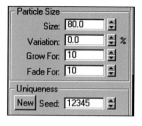

Define how the particles are created in the Particle Generation rollout.

17 In the Particle Type rollout, set the following parameters:

Standard Particles:	On
Type:	Facing

18 Open the Material Editor. Make a copy of the Main Explosion Material and name it White Particles.

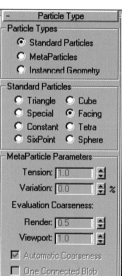

Define the type and nature of the particles in the system in the Particle Type rollout.

19 Set the Diffuse Color and Self-Illumination Colors
    to 255, 255, 255. Apply the material to the particle
    system.

20 Save the file.

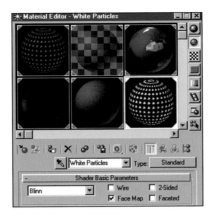

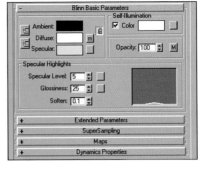

The White Particles
material in the Material
Editor.

ADDING THE SPACE WARPS

Now that you have the basic particle systems, it's time to add the Space Warps to
control the particles. You will make use of gravity, wind, and Udeflector Space Warps.

1 Create a Wind Space Warp. Use the Transform
   Type-In dialog box to place the Space Warp at −182,
   980, −1330.

2 Set the following properties on the Wind Space
   Warp:
   Strength: 0.25
   Spherical: On

3 Bind the Space Warp to the Particle Cloud particle
   system.

4 In the top viewport, create a Gravity Space Warp.

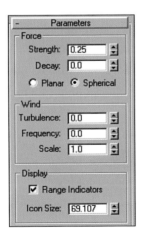

Set the Wind Space Warp
properties.

5 Set the following Gravity parameters:

Strength: 0.3

6 Bind the Space Warp to the Particle Cloud particle system.

7 In the top viewport, create a Udeflector Space Warp. Click Pick Object and select the Earth as the deflector.

Set the Gravity Space Warp parameters.

8 Set the following Udeflector parameter:

Bounce: 0.5.

Set the Udeflector parameter for the system.

9 Bind the Space Warp to the Particle Cloud particle system. If you play back the animation, you should see a result similar to the one shown here.

10 In the top viewport, create a Wind Space Warp. Set the following parameter:

Strength: 0.3

11 Bind the Space Warp to the SuperSpray particle system.

12 Render the animation from frame 0 to 400 from Video Post to see the final results. Note that due to the number of particles, the rendering may take some time.

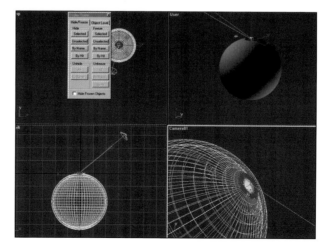

Play back the animation. The scene here shows you the particle systems in action.

Final Touches

After you are satisfied with the motion of the particles, it's time to set up the final settings.

1 Select the Particle Cloud particle system. Set the Use Rate variable to 100.

2 Select the SuperSpray particle system. Set the Use Rate variable to 100.

3 Rerender the animation.

Plug-Ins

This particular effect, creating an asteroid impact scene, can make use of many different plug-ins to significantly enhance the resulting animation. Here's a list of a few with some brief descriptions:

■ Particle Studio. This plug-in, which is available from Digimation, is a very powerful, highly configurable particle system. Because of its ability to control the particles over time, this system would make creating the particle system much easier and better-looking. For example, by using Particle Studio, you can define the speed of the particles at any time in the animation. This means you can have them speed up and slow down as the particles move through the explosion.

■ Essential Textures: This plug-in, also available from Digimation, provides you with literally hundreds of procedural material controls. These can be used to create more realistic-looking asteroid surfaces.

■ UltraShock or Afterburn. Most of the time, when an asteroid hits a planet, there's going to be lots of explosions and smoke. Either of these plug-ins can create true volumetric clouds and explosions. They could also be used when the Asteroid passes through the cloud layer. If you built the layer out of particles and used Afterburn or UltraShock, you could create realistic movement in the clouds as the asteroid passes. You can also use this to make much more realistic-looking smoke trails for the asteroid itself.

■ Phoenix. This plug-in can be used to create very realistic fire. You can use this to make the asteroid burn as it passes through the atmosphere.

Variations

The techniques shown in this exercise can easily be adapted for other types of effects. Some of these effects include:

■ Water Fountains. Using the particle system effects, you could easily adapt these particles to function like a water fountain simply by changing the material.

■ Smoke and Fog. By changing the opacity of the particles in the materials, you can create smoke and fog just as easily as exploding particles.

■ Space Capsules and Others. You can use the same techniques to create the passage of objects through various medium such as space capsules through air or rockets through water. Simply create a surrounding object and apply an opacity-mapped material to create the effect.

APPENDIX A

WHAT'S ON THE CD-ROM

This appendix is a brief rundown of what you'll find on the CD-ROM accompanying this book.

BROWSING THE CD-ROM

If you browse to the CD in Windows Explorer, you will see three directories called "CDBonus," "Examples," and "3rdParty." The "CDBonus" directory contains four bonus projects in PDF format. In the "Examples" directory you will find the installer for the examples and a directory for each chapter in the book. In the "3rdParty" directory you will find multiple directories, one for each software vendor that contributed to this CD.

If you have "AutoPlay" turned on and you right-click on the CD-ROM drive, you will see our extended Autorun options. In addition to the standard CD-ROM options, you will see "View ReadMe," "Browse Software," "View Examples," and more. "View ReadMe" will bring up an HTML version of the ReadMe. "Browse Software" will open up the 3rdParty directory. "View Examples" will open up the Examples directory.

Bonus CD Projects

There are four extra chapters included on the CD. We have included them (in PDF format) as a bonus to you.

To view these chapters, you will have to install Adobe's Acrobat Reader (if you don't already have it). You can find it in 3rdParty\Adobe\Acrobat\ on the CD.

Author Example Files

On this CD you will find Example files provided by the authors. You can install these to your system from the CD-ROM interface. If you are not using the CD-ROM interface, you can find the Examples in: /EXAMPLES. To install them, just click SOURCE.EXE. The Example files will use 178MB of space.

THIRD-PARTY SOFTWARE, DEMOS, AND PLUG-INS

If you are not using the CD-ROM interface, you can find these products in: /3rdParty.

Although we have tried our best, it is possible that newer versions have been released between the time this book was finished and the date you purchased it. Please check with each manufacturer to ensure that your products are up to date.

Here is a list of the things you will find in the 3rdParty folder on the CD-ROM:

- **Ultimate MAX Internet Guide (by Applied-Ideas)** A database search containing over 500 Internet sites related to MAX! The full product is included. For more information, visit http://www.applied-ideas.com.

  To install Ultimate MAX Internet Guide, go to: 3rdParty\Applied Ideas\UltimateMAX\.

- **Communicator 4.7 (by Netscape)** The latest and greatest! Just as the Web is constantly evolving, so too is Netscape Communicator. To meet the needs of its customers, Netscape Communicator provides next-generation browsing, email, calendar, and information management features. The full product is included. For more information, visit http://www.netscape.com.

  To install Communicator 4.7, go to: 3rdParty\Netscape\Communicator47\.

- **Internet Explorer 5 (by Microsoft)** Internet Explorer 5 delivers the most rewarding Web experience ever by bringing you the best browser, complete communication and collaboration, True Web Integration, and webcasting including Active Channels. Find what you want quickly with Explorer Bars. View the coolest, most entertaining Active Channels and surf safely, thanks to Internet Explorer's Security Zones. Browse the Web and your PC with a Single Explorer. The full product is included. For more information, visit http://www.microsoft.com.

  To install Internet Explorer 5, go to: 3rdParty\Microsoft\IE5\EN\.

- **WinZip 7.0 (by Nico Mak)** WinZip brings the convenience of Windows to the use of Zip files and other archive and compression formats. The optional wizard interface makes unzipping easier than ever. WinZip features built-in support for popular Internet file formats, including TAR, gzip, Unix compress, UUencode, BinHex, and MIME. ARJ, LZH, and ARC files are supported via external programs. WinZip interfaces to most virus scanners. A 30-day trial version is included. For more information, visit http://www.winzip.com.

  To install WinZip 7.0, go to: 3rdParty\Nicomak\Winzip\.

- **Acrobat Reader 4 (by Adobe)** The free Adobe Acrobat Reader allows you to view, navigate, and print PDF files across all major computing platforms. Acrobat Reader is the free viewing companion to Adobe Acrobat and to Acrobat Capture software. The full product is included. For more information, visit http://www.adobe.com.

  To install Acrobat Reader 4, go to: 3rdParty\Adobe\Acrobat\.

- **Texporter 3.2 (by Cuneyt Ozdas)** A 3D Studio MAX plug-in that unfolds the texture coordinates of a given mesh object as a bitmap image which can be used to position precisely the features of the texture to be painted by hand. Needed for Chapter 4. The full product is included. For more information, visit http://www.cuneytozdas.com.

  To install Texporter 3.2, go to: 3rdParty\Cuneyt\Texporter\Plugins

- **Particle Studio 1.09 (by Digimation Inc.)** Get ready to experience the future of particle systems! Particle Studio is the most advanced particle generation system available for the 3D Studio MAX platform. Completely event-based, Particle Studio gives you unprecedented control over everything a particle does; it's birth, death, spawning, following an object, its material and much more are independently controllable within our unique interface called the Event Map. Create entire sequences of events for a particle to follow or use Particle Studio's Quick Setups to efficiently generate complex particle motions with just a few mouseclicks. And similar to its predecessor, Sand Blaster, Particle Studio can take ordinary 3D Studio MAX geometry and break it into thousands of particles in no time, and then reassemble them into a completely different object! For those of you who need the extra interactivity, you can even have the Event Map floating window open while adjusting other objects in the Modify or Create command panels–making Particle Studio invaluable when timing is critical. Needed for Project A. A limited demo version is included. For more information, visit http://www.digimation.com.

  To install Particle Studio 1.09, go to: 3rdParty\Digimation\Particle\.

- **Particle Paint 1.0 (by Peter Wajte)** A blend material based on a particle system. Needed for Chapter 7. A shareware version is included. For more information, visit http://www.max3dstuff.com.

  To install Particle Paint 1.0, go to: 3rdParty\PWajte\Ppaint\.

- **Particle Displace 1.1 (by Peter Wajte)** A displacement modifier controlled by a particle system. Needed for Chapter 7. A shareware version is included. For more information, visit http://www.max3dstuff.com.

  To install Particle Displace 1.1, go to: 3rdParty\PWajte\Pdisplace\.

- **Solidify 2.0 (by Terralux)** Solidify is a modifier plug-in that makes surfaces solid. An easier way to describe it would be to say that it does extrusion along vertex normals. No more wrestling with extrusion or double sided materials. Solidify makes it a snap to give your surfaces thickness, with as many segments as you need. Needed for Chapter 7. The full product is included. For more information, visit http://www.max3d.com/~terralux.

  To install Solidify 2.0, go to: 3rdParty\Terralux\Solidify\.

- **HighLightOnly 1.02 (by Blur Studios)** Material only generates the highlight part of the shade equation–for use with shellac. Needed for Chapter 9. The full product is included. For more information, visit http://www.blur.com/blurbeta.

  To install HighLightOnly 1.02, go to: 3rdParty\Blur\Highlight\.

- **Blurlib 1.11 (by Blur Studios)** Utility Library required for several of Blur's plug-ins. Needed for Chapter 9. The full product is included. For more information, visit http://www.blur.com/blurbeta.

  To install Blurlib 1.11, go to: 3rdParty\Blur\Blurlibrary\.

- **Shellac 2.03 (by Blur Studios)** Material additively combines two materials together to "shellac" on a second highlight. Needed for Chapter 9. The full product is included. For more information, visit http://www.blur.com/blurbeta.

  To install Shellac 2.03, go to: 3rdParty\Blur\Shellac\.

- **Hair 3.0 (by Peter Wajte)** An advanced hair particle system. Needed for Chapter 17. A shareware version is included. For more information, visit http://www.max3dstuff.com.

  To install Hair 3.0, go to: 3rdParty\PWajtel\Hair\.

- **Toy Train 3.2 (by Habware)** Toy Train is a system plug-in that allows you to define trailors, following an engine at a given distance. Needed for Chapter 19. The full product is included. For more information, visit http://www.habware.at/duck3.htm.

  To install Toy Train 3.2, go to: 3rdParty\Habware\Toytrain\.

- **Watercell 1.04 (by Blur Studios)** Cellular-based water color splatter. Needed for Chapter 19. The full product is included. For more information, visit http://www.blur.com/blurbeta.

  To install Watercell 1.04, go to: 3rdParty\Blur\Watercell\.

- **Waterwash 1.02 (by Blur Studios)** Water color washes. Needed for Chapter 19. The full product is included. For more information, visit http://www.blur.com/blurbeta.

  To install Waterwash 1.02, go to: 3rdParty\Blur\Waterwash.

READ THIS BEFORE OPENING THE SOFTWARE

By opening the CD package, you are agreeing to be bound by the following agreement:

You may not copy or redistribute the entire CD-ROM as a whole. Copying and redistribution of individual software programs on the CD-ROM is governed by terms set by individual copyright holders.

The installer and code from the author(s) are copyrighted by the publisher and the author(s).

WINDOWS 98/95/NT INSTALLATION INSTRUCTIONS

1. Insert the CD-ROM disc into your CD-ROM drive.

2. From the Windows 98/95/NT desktop, double-click on the My Computer icon.

3. Double-click on the icon representing your CD-ROM drive.

4. Double-click on the icon titled START.EXE to run the CD-ROM interface.

Note: If Windows 98/95/NT is installed on your computer and you have the AutoPlay feature enabled, the START.EXE program starts automatically whenever you insert the disc into your CD-ROM drive.

INDEX

Page numbers for topics included in the chapters on the CD-ROM are designated as *xx*[CD].

D

Darkling Simulations
  DarkTree, 63
  DarkTree Textures, 231

DarkTree (Darkling Simulations), 63

DarkTree Textures
  Darkling Simulations, 231
  Digimation, 200

debris from explosions, 100-102
  colliding, 110-112

deflecting fire (streams of), 169-170

Deflector + (Peter Watje/Spectral Imaging), 121,
  252, 274

deflectors, crowds
  activating, 244-246
  creating, 240-244

Deform Paint (Peter Watje/Spectral Imaging), 200

details, adding to characters with Mix maps, 58-62

detonation, anticipating explosions, 96-98

diffuse glow, 83-84
  variations of, 88

Digimation
  Atomizer, 120, A19[CD]
  Clay Studio Pro, A19[CD]
  DarkTree Textures, 200
  Digimation Gradient, 200
  Digipeople, 252, 273
  DNT, A18[CD]
  Essential Textures, 351, A18[CD], C12[CD]
  Four Elements, 200
  Fractal Flow MAX, 120
  Glider, 200, 252, 273
  Instant UV, 63

Lightning, 120

Multires, 252, 273

Pandora, 120, 252, 274

Particle Studio, 120, 174, 252, 274, 351,
  A4[CD], D13[CD]

Seascape, A18[CD]

Splash, A19[CD]

Spray Master, 120, 200, 252, 274

Texture Lab, 231

Tree Factory, 200

Tree Still, 200

Tree Storm, 200

UltraShock, 120, 174

Digimation Gradient (Digimation), 200

Digipeople (Digimation), 252, 273

Digital Fusion (rim lighting), 88

Digital Nature Tools, 31

direction of fragments from explosions, 281, 283

directional light, suns, 226-227

Dirt (Blur Studios), 201

Displace Mesh World Space modifier, 314

Displacement Map channel, 314

Displacement modifier, 186

Distance Blender (Blur Studios), 201

DNT (Digital Nature Tools), Digimation, A18[CD]

Driftwood Thinktank, Seascape, 31

duplicating texture art, 214

dust material, creating, 132-133

dust trails, 126-127
  dust material, creating, 132-133
  emitters, aligning, 127-128
  expressions, setting, 130-132
  SuperSpray particles, setting parameters, 129

E

earth
  adding lighting and stars, 337-340
  creating for asteroid impact, 334-337

emitters
  dust trails, aligning, 127-128
  explosions, 279-281

energy (explosions), fading, 116-117

Environment Generator, 320

Essential Textures
  Digimation, 351, A18[CD], C12[CD]
  Worely Labs, 63, 231

expanding lights, explosions, 107-108

exploding stars (supernovas), 3-4
  glow, 10, 12-16
  lighting, 9
  materials, creating, 8-9
  particle systems, 6-7
  RingWave objects, 5-6
  scenes, setting up, 5-6
  variations of, 17
  Video Post, 10, 12-16

explosion particles, variations of, 351

explosions, 92, 278-279
  aftereffects, 112-114
  animation, hiding, 283-285
  camera techniques, 288-289
  cameras
    rendering, 290-291
    shaking, 119-120
  debris, colliding, 110-112
  destroying only part of the object, 93-96

NEW RIDERS
PROFESSIONAL LIBRARY

3D Studio MAX 3 Fundamentals
Michael Todd Peterson
0-7357-0049-4

3D Studio MAX 3 Magic
New Riders Development
0-7357-0867-3

3D Studio MAX 3 Media Animation
John Chismar
0-7357-0050-8

3D Studio MAX 3 Professional Animation
Angela Jones, et al.
0-7357-0945-9

Adobe Photoshop 5.5 Fundamentals with ImageReady 2
Gary Bouton
0-7357-0928-9

Bert Monroy: Photorealistic Techniques with Photoshop & Illustrator
Bert Monroy
0-7357-0969-6

CG 101: A Computer Graphics Industry Reference
Terrence Masson
0-7357-0046-X

Click Here
Raymond Pirouz and Lynda Weinman
1-56205-792-8

<coloring web graphics.2>
Lynda Weinman and Bruce Heavin
1-56205-818-5

Creating Killer Web Sites, Second Edition
David Siegel
1-56830-433-1

<creative html design>
Lynda Weinman and William Weinman
1-56205-704-9

<designing web graphics.3>
Lynda Weinman
1-56205-949-1

Designing Web Usability
Jakob Nielsen
1-56205-810-X

[digital] Character Animation 2
Volume 1: Essential Techniques
George Maestri
1-56205-930-0

Essentials of Digital Photography
Akari Kasai and Russell Sparkman
1-56205-762-6

Fine Art Photoshop
Michael J. Nolan and Renee LeWinter
1-56205-829-0

Flash 4 Magic
David Emberton and J. Scott Hamlin
0-7357-0949-1

Flash Web Design
Hillman Curtis
0-7357-0896-7

HTML Artistry: More than Code
Ardith Ibañez and Natalie Zee
1-56830-454-4

HTML Web Magic
Raymond Pirouz
1-56830-475-7

Illustrator 8 Magic
Raymond Pirouz
1-56205-952-1

Inside 3D Studio MAX 3
Phil Miller, et al.
0-7357-0905-X

Inside 3D Studio MAX 3:
Modeling, Materials, and Rendering
Ted Boardman and Jeremy Hubbell
0-7357-0085-0

Inside Adobe Photoshop 5.5
Gary David Bouton and Barbara Bouton
0-7357-1000-7

Inside Adobe Photoshop 5, Limited Edition
Gary David Bouton and Barbara Bouton
1-56205-951-3

Inside AutoCAD 2000
David Pitzer and Bill Burchard
0-7357-0851-7

Inside LightWave 3D
Dan Ablan
1-56205-799-5

Inside LightWave 6
Dan Ablan
0-7357-0919-X

Inside trueSpace 4
Frank Rivera
1-56205-957-2

Inside SoftImage 3D
Anthony Rossano
1-56205-885-1

Maya 2 Character Animation
Nathan Vogel, Sherri Sheridan, and Tim Coleman
0-7357-0866-5

Net Results: Web Marketing that Works
USWeb and Rick E. Bruner
1-56830-414-5

Photoshop 5 & 5.5 Artistry
Barry Haynes and Wendy Crumpler
0-7457-0994-7

Photoshop 5 Type Magic
Greg Simsic
1-56830-465-X

Photoshop 5 Web Magic
Michael Ninness
1-56205-913-0

Photoshop Channel Chops
David Biedny, Bert Monroy, and Nathan Moody
1-56205-723-5

<preparing web graphics>
Lynda Weinman
1-56205-686-7

Rhino NURBS 3D Modeling
Margaret Becker
0-7357-0925-4

Secrets of Successful Web Sites
David Siegel
1-56830-382-3

Web Concept & Design
Crystal Waters
1-56205-648-4

Web Design Templates Sourcebook
Lisa Schmeiser
1-56205-754-5

The CD that accompanies this book contains valuable resources for anyone using 3D Studio MAX 3, not the least of which are:

- **Bonus chapters:** Four bonus projects ("Tidal Wave," "Dr. Freeze," "Ship Flying Through Fog," and "The Burning Bush") are included on the CD.

- **Project files:** All the example files provided by the authors are here, to help you with the step-by-step projects.

- **MAX-related third-party software:** This includes Particle Studio 1.09 (demo version), Particle Paint 1.0, and Texporter 3.2. (For a full list of the included third-party software, please see Appendix A.)

ACCESSING THE PROJECT FILES FROM THE CD

Many projects in this book use pre-built MAX files that contain pre-set parameters and other important information you will need to build the final project. In many cases, several MAX files are available to show the project at various stages of completion. The MAX files have a .max extension. Several of the projects also come with additional files, such as ready-made images and textures.

All the files for a project are conveniently located in the CD's Examples directory. To access the project file for the Asteroid Impact project (Chapter 20), for example, locate the following directory on the book's CD: Examples\Chap20.

We recommend you copy the project files to your hard drive, but that is not absolutely necessary if you don't intend to save the project files.

For more information about the contents of the CD-ROM, please see Appendix A.

Colophon: 3D Studio MAX 3 Magic was layed out and produced with the help of Microsoft Word, Adobe Acrobat, Adobe Photoshop, Collage Complete, and QuarkXPress on a variety of systems, including a Macintosh G3. With the exception of the pages that were printed out for proofreading, all files—both text and images—were transferred via email or ftp and edited on-screen.

All the body text was set in the Bergamo family. All headings, figure captions, and cover text were set in the Imago family. The Symbol and Sean's Symbols typefaces were used throughout for special symbols and bullets.

3D Studio MAX 3 Magic was printed on 60# Influence Soft Gloss at GAC (Graphic Arts Center) in Indianapolis, IN. Prepress consisted of PostScript computer-to-plate technology (filmless process). The cover was printed on 12-pt. Carolina, coated on one side.

Learning Resources
Centre